Marie Curie

MARIE CURIE
A Life

♣ ♣ ♣

by Françoise Giroud
translated by Lydia Davis

1986 **HM**
HOLMES & MEIER

New York   London

First published in the United States of America 1986
by Holmes & Meier Publishers, Inc.
30 Irving Place
New York, N.Y. 10003

Great Britain:
Holmes & Meier Ltd.
Hillview House
Pindar Road
Hoddesdon, Hertfordshire, EN11 0HF

Book design by Gloria Tso

Library of Congress Cataloging-in-Publication Data

Giroud, Françoise.
  Marie Curie, a life.

  Translation of: Une femme honorable.
  1. Curie, Marie, 1867–1934. 2. Chemists—Poland—
Biography. I. Title.
QD22.C8G4813 1986   540'.92'4 [B]   85-27241
ISBN 0-8419-0977-6

My warm thanks to Francis Perrin and Bertrand Goldschmid for their extremely valuable information and comments

The value of men's minds can be
measured by what they demand. I am
worth what I *want*.

—*Paul Valéry*

E INSTEIN said she was "the only person to be uncorrupted by
fame." What was it that made the most famous woman in our
century incorruptible? The fact that she was a woman, of course—
though the explanation might have been brief, it seemed right.

I came across that sentence of Einstein's, and I held onto it the way
you hold onto a pebble that you've picked up on the beach and put in
your pocket, rolling it between your fingers now and then. It doesn't
really matter how other pebbles came to join the first. One day, they
merged to form the faint image of a woman's face—and this woman
was irritating, captivating, intriguing, not at all like the woman I
had learned about in school.

When you try to understand the traces left by a person's life, you
can arrive at several different interpretations. This book is my inter-
pretation of Marie Curie's life, how her life has appeared to me ever
since I stumbled on her—this gray-eyed sorceress—and couldn't
shake her off.

It is not an academic book. It doesn't have an imposing apparatus
of footnotes testifying to the researcher's qualifications. From time
to time, though, some explanation has seemed necessary for readers
who are unfamiliar with the scientific or political history of the
period in which Marie Curie-Sklodowska lived, the years between
1867 and 1934.

She was a proud, passionate, and hard-working woman who
played an important role in her time because she had the ambition
and the means to do so, and who has played an important role in our
own time too, since there is a direct relationship between Marie
Curie-Sklodowska and atomic energy. It was also atomic energy that
caused her death.

1

HUMILIATION

one

A FEW people in Warsaw today still remember the old man who used to come sit in the square where the statue of Marie Curie stood and stay there for a long time gazing at it. If Casimir Zorawski, professor of mathematics at the Ecole Polytechnique, had been a little more courageous when he was twenty years old, if he had defied his parents' opposition, Marie and he would have married, and the history of science would have been different.

The episode is not important in itself—it was only a youthful love, not enough to fill a whole chapter in such a rich life—but it gives such a good picture of the sort of woman Marie was that it is worth describing in some detail.

She might be suffering a thousand deaths, but she would continue to think clearly. This handsome young man, who rode, skated, and waltzed so well, who was such a good match and was coveted by all the mothers for miles around, might actually be quite ordinary after all.

Her heart was broken, but what did her heart matter, compared to her pride? "There were some very difficult days, and I will certainly count them among the cruelest in my life. The only thing that makes the memory of them easier to bear is that in spite of everything, I came out of it all honorably, with my head held high."

She was horrified by the violence of her impulses and the ardor of her feelings, and already determined to wall them up in ice. "I have a difficult nature, a nature that has to be conquered."

And she was also fully conscious, at the age of eighteen, of what she was worth. Who am I and what am I here to do? She

5

would ask herself this question—the only one that really matters—and her answer was that she would be "someone."

When, at the age of twenty-three, she thought she would have to give up that notion, she wrote to her sister Bronia: "My heart breaks when I think of my squandered talents, which I'm sure were worth something."

And to her brother Jozef: "Now that I have lost the hope of ever becoming someone, all my ambition is focused on Bronia and you."[1]

How would she turn out, then? Would she suffer the "usual fate of women"? She never imagined accepting that. Her gifts, her education, her philosophy of life, the kind of ambition she had—everything made it impossible. But in September 1891, when she was staying alone in a chalet in Zakopane, taking melancholy walks under the tall, black pine trees of the Carpathians and suffering from a persistent cold, a man named Casimir Zorawski seemed likely to impose that fate on her. And in some sense she wanted it.

In two months she would be twenty-four. She was poor. She wasn't as beautiful as she would be in later years. The highest degree she had was the equivalent of a French *baccalauréat*. How could she ever become "someone"? And the fact was that she loved Casimir. She was waiting for him.

Where had she sprung from, this nervous young woman with her odd mixture of shyness and confidence? She had an almost mystical relationship with the earth, an almost sensual relationship with nature. She needed to be around trees, in the open air. Plants blossomed under her fingers. The flowers she took care of thrived. Horses were docile under her hands.

As far back as anyone could remember, the numerous Sklodowskis had been sharecroppers or farmers on the estate of the lord of Sklody, whose coat of arms they bore. At the

---

[1]Quoted by Eve Curie in *Madame Curie* (Gallimard). See page 287 for sources of letters quoted.

beginning of the nineteenth century, they fell from a relatively comfortable situation to a poor one, from which Marie's grandfather Jozef succeeded in escaping. He managed to get an education and ended by becoming the headmaster of a school.

Like all the patriots of his generation, in 1830 he took up arms against Nicholas I, Czar of all the Russias and King of Poland. Nicholas, excited by the revolution in Paris, had prepared the Polish army for war with the intention of mounting an expedition against France, and the officers had revolted. This was only one of the many insurrections that had punctuated the history of Poland, which was regularly torn apart by its neighbors. This time, a Russian army of a hundred thousand men was ordered to crush them. Lafayette asked for help to be given immediately to the Poles, who were fighting to free their country and who had so many ties with France.

"Sedition is always a crime," answered the president of the Council, Casimir Périer. And so it was with the active complicity of the French government that the rebellious troops were defeated, as Louis-Philippe boasted that "We are the ones the cabinet of Saint Petersburg should thank for crushing Poland."

This was the sinister fate of a people whom so many other nations, either one by one or working together, kept trying to wipe off the map.

The repression was brutal. Entire families were deported, soldiers forcibly drafted into the Russian army, poor children removed from their parents and taken to Russia, huge numbers arrested. But whether Poland found itself under Russian, Prussian, or Austrian rule, or under all three combined, it went on producing insurgents as abundantly as it produced rye. Two of Jozef Sklodowski's seven children, one boy and one girl, were to take part in all the struggles of their generation.

The oldest of the Sklodowski children, who would later become Marie's father, did not have the same fierce strength as the rest of his family. He was a scholar, fond of music, literature, and science. In order to continue his education, he made his peace with the system and attended the Russian University, the only one whose degree would allow him to teach in a State school. Then he married a pretty young woman with brown hair and gray eyes, the daughter of landowners who had been ruined by Poland's troubles.

A teacher, like him, she had been appointed headmistress of the same boarding school for well-born young ladies that she herself had attended. There, in Freta Street, the couple lived in the small apartment that went with the job, and this was where Mme Sklodowska gave birth to her five children within a period of eight years.

During the night of January 15–16, 1863, four years before the birth of Marie, who was the last child, the police rounded up all the young men in the city who were suspected of subversive tendencies and inducted them into the Russian army. Once again there was an uprising, eighteen months of desperate fighting that ended in five gallows being raised on the ramparts of Warsaw and five bodies—the bodies of the rebel leaders—swinging at the end of five ropes.

"Strike down the Polish people until they despair for their lives!" Bismarck recommended. "I have some sympathy for their situation, but if we want to survive, our only recourse is to exterminate them."

He himself did everything he could to accomplish this. Almost five million Poles were then living under his rule, and eighty thousand men were forcibly enrolled in the Prussian army when war broke out in 1870 against France. More than eighteen million learned that they could expect no indulgence from Alexander II, Nicholas's successor. "Don't have any illusions," he said. "What my father did was the right thing to do." The year Marie was born, in Warsaw, the Russian part of Poland lost even its name. It was now known as "the Vistula territory." Even the catechism had to be taught in Russian. Poles were gradually replaced by Russians in all public offices. This time the cover had been screwed on tight.

These episodes in Poland's history had a crucially deter-

8

mining effect on the moral, social, and family environment in which the children of Wladyslaw and Bronislawa Sklodowski grew up.

From birth, Marie possessed three natural aptitudes that make for brilliant pupils, pupils whom teachers love: she had a good memory, good concentration, and an appetite for knowledge.

Three small scenes remain part of the family folklore.

In the first, Marie is four years old. She is in the country with her parents, staying with some of the Sklodowski relatives who had remained on the land and who enjoyed having their Warsaw cousins come visit them during the vacations.

The five children gallop through the fields, climb trees, paddle in the streams, take care of the horses, hide under the hay in the barns. It is heaven. But the parents are very serious about their children's education. Bronia, who is seven, must learn to read before she goes back to school. She applies herself to it, using letters cut out of cardboard that Marie shuffles for her.

One morning, she is struggling to decipher the text of a picture book her father is holding. Marie becomes impatient, grabs it, and reads the first sentence, hardly stumbling at all. Everyone is dumbstruck, silent. Delighted with the effect she has produced, she goes on. And then she dissolves in tears, suddenly aware that her behavior has been indecent, even unforgivable. She stammers out her apologies: "I didn't do it on purpose. It was because it was so easy."

The second scene takes place one morning at the private school where the Sklodowska girls, their hair in braids, wearing navy blue uniforms with starched white collars, are having a history class. Marie is ten years old. Without having to make any perceptible effort, she is taking the same class as her sister Hela, who is two years older.

Questioned about Stanislas-Auguste, she answers:

"Stanislas-Auguste Poniatowski was elected king of Poland

in 1764. He was an intelligent man. He understood the problems that were weakening the kingdom and he tried to find solutions for them. Unfortunately, he was a man without courage."

The teacher is pleased, encourages Marie to go on. Against the rules, she is teaching the history of Poland, in Polish, to the twenty-five captivated girls. Before them on their desks are notebooks and Polish textbooks.

Suddenly, a bell rings.

When the classroom door opens for M. Hornberg, the inspector of private schools in Warsaw, and the rather pale headmistress, the little girls look up innocently. Each of them is holding a square of cloth on which she is embroidering flowers. On each desk is a pair of scissors, some thread, and lying open conspicuously in front of the teacher, a Russian book.

"This is a sewing class, Inspector," says the headmistress. "These children study sewing for two hours a week."

Hornberg opens the top of a desk. Nothing. It is empty.

Between the ringing of the bell, which is a signal given by the porter, and the moment when the inspector reaches the door of the classroom, books and notebooks have evaporated. They are stowed away in the boarders' dormitory.

Hornberg has settled himself in a chair. Question time. The teacher will pick out a student. Of course it is Marie. She is always at the top of the class in every subject—arithmetic, history, literature, German, French—and she speaks Russian perfectly, with a Saint Petersburg accent.

The Polish child will feel ashamed as she is put through an ordeal which so many schoolchildren have experienced with a mixture of trepidation and pride. For the inspector is testing very specific areas of knowledge:

"Name the czars who have reigned over our blessed Russia since Catherine II."

"Give the names and titles of the members of the Imperial Family."

"What is the title of the czar in the hierarchy of dignitaries?"

10

"What is my title?"

Marie performs faultlessly.

What else can the inspector ask in order to make sure the Sikorska School is offering an irreproachable education? This is what he thinks of:

"Tell me who governs us."

The teacher and the headmistress freeze. Twenty-four petrified young girls hang on Marie's words, while Marie herself hesitates, tense and rigid.

"Come now! Who governs us?" Hornberg repeats.

"His Majesty Alexander II, Czar of all the Russias."

Hornberg stands up and leaves the classroom, followed by the headmistress, to continue his inspection in the next room.

"Marya, come here," says the teacher.

The child leaves her row and goes forward. The teacher gives her a kiss. Marya bursts into sobs. Thoroughly humiliated by her forced servility before the Russian inspector, she will never forget this moment. But then she never forgets anything.

The third scene takes place during the same period, in the dining room where the children repeat their lessons at the tops of their voices after tea. Marie is engrossed in a book, her elbows on the table and her thumbs in her ears to block out the noise. The other children are always amused by the way she becomes so absorbed, the way she isolates herself.

That day, their mischievous cousin Henriette is plotting with Hela and Bronia. The three girls build a pyramid of chairs around Marie and wait, smothering their laughter, for the edifice to collapse.

The minutes pass. Marie has seen nothing, heard nothing, felt nothing. Suddenly she moves and the chairs fall with a great racket. The girls howl with joy. Marie stands up rubbing her shoulder, which has been bruised by a chair. She picks up her book, says, "That was stupid," and leaves the room with dignity.

Young Mlle Sklodowska wasn't very accommodating when her dignity was threatened by a practical joke. Children always hate that. As an adult, she didn't like it any better. She had no sense of humor, she had no distance from herself. She took everything seriously, and herself most of all. This was not her most attractive quality, but it often stood her in good stead.

Bronia finished her secondary education at the gymnasium, winning a gold medal for being one of the best students. It would have been strange if Marie hadn't won the medal too, and she did win it when she was fifteen.

Under the strain of this success, she broke down. "Nervous troubles," the doctor said vaguely. There were to be more of these breakdowns in later years, and the fact was that they showed a more appealing aspect of Marie than her succession of triumphs. They showed that some part of her was fragile.

Or were the Sklodowski children being pushed too hard by their father, who was proud of them and, remarkably enough, made no distinction between the girls and the boy when it came to enriching their minds, developing their knowledge in all areas, stimulating their intellectual ambitions?

No, apparently Jozef, Bronia, and Hela were none the worse for it, and Marie did not need to be pushed. In fact, she had to be held back. This was what her alarmed father did after her breakdown. He sent her to the country to stay with an uncle who was a notary. She spent the winter there, and after that a former pupil of Mme Sklodowska's invited her and Hela to stay with her for the summer.

Early in the visit, Marie wrote to a friend:

"I'm doing nothing, nothing at all! . . . I'm not reading any serious books, only some anodine and stupid novels. . . . I'm feeling incredibly dumb. Sometimes I start laughing all by myself and I think with real satisfaction about my state of total stupidity!"

The years that she had just lived through had been filled with disasters for this highly emotional little girl who always "took things to heart." Her oldest sister, Sophia, had died of typhus when she was fourteen. Her mother had died of tuberculosis. The presence of the disease had been discovered just after Marie was born. The child had never been allowed to kiss her mother, and she was not told why—which was a typical attitude for that time. The Sklodowskis, in their own way, were profoundly conformist.

Marie's mother had been a pious woman, and her premature death undermined Marie's religious faith. She was first revolted by, and then completely indifferent to, what she would later call "a lost happiness."

Promoted to the position of assistant inspector at the gymnasium, where he continued to teach physics and mathematics, M. Sklodowski left Freta Street and moved with his family to the apartment attached to his new post. He was a scrupulous and meticulous official. And yet, one day in 1873 he returned from vacation to find on his desk a notice informing him that he was in disgrace. The Russian director of the gymnasium had decided he was not zealous enough in his duties.

How was he to make ends meet now?

He chose to do what so many other bourgeois families did when they fell on hard times—he took in boarders. The family moved to a new apartment, bringing with them the imitation leather couch, the Restoration armchairs, the malachite clock, the Sèvres cup, the painting "attributed" to Titian, the professor's large desk around which the children sat in the afternoon to do their homework, and now they made room for two, three, five, ten of M. Sklodowski's gymnasium pupils, who were lodged, fed, and given private lessons here.

Depressed, overworked, the unfortunate man now did the only thoughtless thing he was ever to do in his life: he handed all his savings over to a brother-in-law to be invested in what seemed like a marvelous speculation. His thirty thousand rubles evaporated and he was consumed with guilt.

The picture was not all black, however, for the Sklodowskis loved life and loved each other. They were a loyal tribe and they would remain loyal. And money, necessary though it was, was not part of their system of values.

13

In the eyes of his children, M. Sklodowski possessed the only riches they had learned to covet: culture, knowledge, scholarship. And it was true that this modest Polish professor did more than just keep up with the latest developments in physics, which was his specialty. He had the wide-ranging interests of most intellectuals of his time—a time when, particularly in Eastern Europe, it was not unusual for an intellectual to speak four languages, to know Greek and Latin, to have memorized a thousand lines of verse, and sometimes to write verse as well. It was a time when, the farther away or the more isolated one was from the bright lights of culture and creativity, the more avid one was to seize this fire and warm oneself by it.

On Saturday evenings, the family would gather around the samovar and the father would read aloud from English, French, German, or Polish literature and comment on what he read, sometimes pontificating a little, no doubt, while four pairs of clear eyes watched him and listened, fascinated. With the mother gone and the household in financial trouble, the tablecloths were probably frayed, the mahogany dull, the pinafores unstarched, the meals less than ample, but there was a spiritual richness in the family.

During the period of more than a year when she was away from home, Marie wrote often. She was an avid correspondent, and to judge from her letters, now that she had recovered from her breakdown, this serious adolescent was finding out what fun it was to be alive.

"I can't believe that geometry and algebra exist. . . . I have completely forgotten them."

"Oh, how gay life is in Awola! There are always lots of people here and there is a freedom, an equality, and an independence here that you can't imagine."

"I tasted the delights of the carnival last Saturday and I think I will never again have so much fun."

"This *kulig* was a delight from beginning to end. My escort was a boy from Cracow, very handsome and very elegant. We

14

danced a mazurka at eight o'clock in the morning in broad daylight. . . . I danced so much that during the waltzes I had several partners reserved in advance."

"Our life is wonderful. . . . I'm learning to row—I'm already making progress—and the swimming is perfect."

She and her sister were the leaders of a happy gang of boys and girls who were freely indulged and spoiled by the master and mistress of the house. And what with gallops on horseback and fun fairs, dances, and raids on the kitchen, the weeks flew by.

"We're doing everything we can think of, sometimes we sleep at night, sometimes in the day, we dance, we do such crazy things that sometimes we deserve to be locked up in an insane asylum."

Coming home one morning, at dawn, she had to throw away her bronze-colored dancing shoes—the soles had given out because she had danced so much that night.

"All I can say is that maybe never again, never in my whole life, will I have such fun."

The delightful parenthesis closed. Marie was sixteen now.

The Sklodowski children were no longer children. Jozef, a tall athletic boy, was studying medicine, and Bronia had taken over the management of the household with a firm hand. She cooked, she polished, she mended. And she fumed, because the university was not open to women. Hela, the beauty of the family, the heartbreaker, was studying singing. Marie was giving private lessons. "Lessons in arithmetic, geometry, and French available from young woman with degree. Moderate prices." On she went, her eyes fixed on her star.

One day, she read the following words in a book: "As he was crossing the courtyard of the Sorbonne, Claude Bernard . . ." The courtyard of the Sorbonne was the gate to Olympus. How could she get there? Warsaw was teeming with young men and women hoping to earn enough by giving private lessons to pay for an education abroad. M. Sklodowski fretted. If it hadn't been for that disastrous speculation . . . Soon, with his meager civil servant's pension, he would not even be able to provide for his brood—he who had dreamed of seeing them spread their wings in the skies of science.

By now, Marie was a robust, rather pretty girl with fresh skin and unruly blond hair. Later, she would be beautiful, very beautiful, but she would never pay much attention to her appearance, not because she was modest but because she was proud.

At an age when most girls would stand in front of the mirror daydreaming and tying different colored ribbons in their hair, she disfigured herself, with the help of her cousin Henriette, by cutting off her curls. This was an odd gesture. It can't simply be seen as a desire to deny her femininity. There are no signs, either in her intimate journal, or in her correspondence, or in the direction her life took, that she ever rejected the feminine side of herself. What she was showing— and this was different—was a scorn for frivolous things.

She did, however, reject the animal side of her nature, the part of herself that became hungry, cold, sleepy, the part that often caught cold because, as her father put it, she "never deigned to adapt her clothing to the atmospheric conditions." These were her only signs of weakness. Just as her lightning fits of anger betrayed the storms she was suppressing.

Being accomplished young people of their time, the Sklodowska girls spoke five languages and could embroider, play the piano a little, draw, skate, swim, and dance. They had also learned to be thrifty. They had seen their mother putting new soles on their shoes with her own hands.

What bothered them was not the fact that a certain dress would have to be dyed and transformed yet again by the dressmaker ("It will be just right and very pretty!" wrote Marie). It was that they could see no way out of the impasse they were in.

Marriage? That wasn't part of their plans. Not that they were systematically avoiding it. But it wasn't a goal, even less a way of satisfying their thirst for education, and education was inseparable in their eyes from the emanicipation of women, which they considered a major element of social progress.

The rebellious women of Marie's generation still believed that if the means were given to them to prove they were the intellectual equals of men, they would prove it. But they needed higher education to prove it. Where and how could they get it?

Bronia had just turned twenty, Marie seventeen. Together, they dreamed up wild plans, swearing to help each other succeed in getting what they wanted.

The relationship between the two sisters was a strong one and would remain so right up to Marie's death. Bronia was exuberant, warm, maternal, sensitive to the needs of others. She had a boundless love for her little sister. Marie, who was reserved and uncompromising, never opened herself to anyone but Bronia, but when she did, she opened herself completely.

Bronia would be the only one to see Marie become depressed, weep, call for help. Bronia would always protect and comfort the child in Marie, and Marie could be always certain that wherever Bronia was, she would come running. And perhaps this confidence in the dependable Bronia helped foster the attitude Marie later had toward other women, who consistently played an important role in her life. Clearly, in any case, she felt that strength was to be found in women and not in men.

At the moment, though, she wasn't crying. She was very busy.

A woman named Mlle Piasecka, a schoolteacher considerably older than she was and engaged to a student who had been expelled from the university for subversive activity, introduced her to the "Flying University."

The Flying University was an ambitious group consisting

mainly of young women and a few young men. The members of the group were intensely patriotic and cultivated a clandestine positivism.

Polish resistance had not been broken. But so much blood had been spilled, so many uprisings subdued and illusions crushed, so much useless suffering endured, that it had lost its romanticism.

Europe, moreover, had seen a decline in the great wave of sentiment and religion by which people had tried to compensate for the implacable materialism of the machine age. A new message had gone out from Paris, found its way across the border of France, reached Poland despite its isolation, entered the libraries, and engaged the minds of young people who were ripe to receive it—the new message was Auguste Comte's "Course in Positivist Philosophy." And from England came Spencer's evolutionist philosophy, bringing with it an astounding notion, the survival of the fittest.

The intellectuals in Warsaw got into heated arguments, rejected "vain chimeras," and sought to fit the new scientific disciplines to Polish society and to the new kind of struggle that had to be waged to liberate it. Subversion would no longer take the form of physical battle but of the proliferation of knowledge. People would be taught, not how to assemble bombs and throw them, but how to set fire to other people's minds: here lay the secret of social progress.

The Flying University undertook to educate the masses. Everyone who had some learning was to transmit it to others, who in turn would become teachers themselves. They met at each other's homes in the evenings. Professors from the university risked being put in jail to come and give courses in history, anatomy, sociology.

At first distrustful, Marie soon became wildly enthusiastic, and brought Bronia in with her. At the age of seventeen, she had turned her back on religion. Positivism provided a framework for her rationality and her faith in progress, and the application of positivism to the case of Poland gave her a way to take action.

18

A photograph shows her standing next to Bronia, and she has inscribed it to a friend in the following words: "For an ideal positivist, two positive idealists." A different influence might have thrown her in with another group of students who had discovered Marx and viewed positivism as a compromise solution, a form of subservience to the bourgeoisie. But in retrospect, judging by the position Marie consistently adopted, this rebel does not really seem to have been cut out to be a revolutionary.

At the end of her life, describing the time when, under the very noses of the czar's police, she carried the flame of knowledge into a garment workshop and created a library for the employees there, she was to write: "The means by which we took action were paltry, and the results could not be very great: however, I still believe that the ideas that guided us then are the only ideas that can bring about real social progress. We can't hope to build a better world without improving individual people."

No doubt the teachers and student teachers in the Flying University would have been disappointed to learn that their secret activities didn't really worry the Russian authorities. The socialist students, on the other hand, were dealt with harshly. Two hundred were arrested, and several were shot. Their leader died in prison, reportedly of starvation.

This was a brief but intense period in Marie's life. She was accumulating a heterogeneous fund of knowledge in which, to judge from her private notebook, Sully Prud'homme rubbed shoulders with Louis Blanc, Dostoevsky with Musset, Renan with Paul Bert.

In September 1885, when she presented herself at an employment agency looking for steady work, she was seventeen years old and full of ambition and idealism.

People are touched by the image of the great scientist Marie Curie "seeking employment in a good household." Or they look on it as evidence of her independent spirit, exceptional in a young woman of her century. But the fact was that for young tutors and undowried young ladies to take charge of the education of the children of the rich was a common practice in the society of that time, and not only in Poland. French literature is full of them.

Besides, Marie had no choice. What was remarkable was the way she would use her salary.

By giving private lessons for two years, Bronia had saved enough money to pay for her ticket to Paris and the expenses of one year at a university—"At the Sorbonne," said Marie, who couldn't conceive of studying anywhere else. She had not forgotten the magical sentence she had read—"As he was crossing the courtyard of the Sorbonne, Claude Bernard . . ."

So Bronia would be able to go to the Sorbonne. But what about the next few years? The study of medicine was interminable. Would Bronia be able to go to Paris now? Or would she have to wait longer?

Apparently the family talked it over and Marie got what she wanted. Bronia would go now, and Marie, who would have room and board where she worked, would send her everything she earned. "And when you become a doctor," she said, "you can pay for my education."

Did Bronia hesitate at the thought of the sacrifice her little sister was going to make? Marie would have to mark time for five years. And why shouldn't Marie be the first to leave?

"You're twenty, I'm seventeen. Let's be practical," said Marie. And Bronia went.

two

TRAVELING alone, living alone in Paris, London, or Berlin—
this was unthinkable for French women of their age and
their station at the end of the century, but it wasn't at all
unusual for Eastern Europeans like the Sklodowska girls.
During this same period, Sonia Delaunay came to Paris from
Moscow at the age of twenty and set herself up in Montparnasse to learn to paint. It is important to keep this freedom of
behavior in mind because in some sense it gave Marie a head
start.

During one of her worst periods, she wrote to her brother,
"I'm sure you will manage all right: I firmly believe it. For
'good women' there are always more problems—but even so, I
still have the hope that I won't disappear completely into
obscurity."

Certainly "good women" have problems. But she would be
spared some of them, at least—those they create for themselves. She did not have to restrain her independent spirit
either in relation to herself or to anyone else. She believed this
independence went without saying. And she did not have to
train herself out of coy, timid, or impudent mannerisms.

The agency Marie went to in September quickly placed her
with a family of lawyers in Warsaw.

A letter she sent in December to one of her favorite correspondents, her cousin Henriette, is wonderful. It has everything—form, elevation, a gift for observation.

> I wouldn't wish it upon my worst enemy to live in such a
> hell! [she wrote] By the end, my relations with Mme B. had
> become so icy that I couldn't take it any more and I told her so.

Since she was just as enthusiastic about me as I was about her, we understood each other marvelously.

This was one of those rich houses where people spoke French when company came—gutter French, that is—and where they didn't pay the bills for six months, but threw money out the window while stingily economizing on gas for the lamps. They had five servants, they pretended to be liberals and really there was nothing there but the worst stupidity. They slandered everyone in the sweetest possible voices, there was so much slander that no one was left unscathed.

I had the good fortune to get to know the human species a little better there. I learned that the characters described in novels actually exist and that one shouldn't have anything to do with people who have been demoralized by wealth.

Another position became available and she took it. She would receive a higher salary, but this time she was going into exile—to get to the place from Warsaw she would have to travel three hours by train and four hours by sleigh. If it was difficult for her to leave, however, to go into isolation like this, far away from her family and friends, Marie didn't show it. And on January 1, 1886, "Mademoiselle Marya" began working in the home of the Zorawskis.

There was M. Zorawski, his wife, a daughter of eighteen, another girl of ten, and two small children. The household also included three boys who were away studying in Warsaw, and a host of servants. The family owned forty horses and sixty cows.

Reading Marie's letters and imagining this large, low house in the heart of the country, with its verandas and pergolas, its great ovens of glazed earthenware, and its croquet lawn, as well as the red-roofed barns, stables, and cattle sheds, the constant coming and going of guests, the chattering and the silence around the samovar, it is hard not to think of Chekhov.

But M. Zorawski was not about to sell his cherry orchard. His crop was beets, and he was doing well. Marie's windows looked out over two hundred hectares of clay beet fields and a factory with a smoking chimney—the refinery where sugar was extracted from the beets sown and harvested by the peasants of the Sluski estate. M. Zorawski, an agronomist, was in charge of farming part of the lands of the Czartoryski princes, and a principal shareholder in the factory.

He was a competent and pleasant man, "old-fashioned, but full of good sense, likable and reasonable," wrote Marie. His wife, a former teacher, had "risen" rather rapidly, but "when you know how to deal with her, she is nice. I think she rather likes me."

The oldest daughter was delightful, "a rare gem," Marie noted,

> whereas the young people of this area are not really at all interesting: the girls are geese who don't open their mouths except to be as provocative as possible. They all dance perfectly. They're actually not bad, some of them are even intelligent, but their education has not developed their minds, and the festivals around here, which are insane and incessant, have ended up making them scatter-brained. As for the young men, almost none of them are very nice or in the least intelligent. . . . Words like "positivism," "Swietochowski," "the question of the working class," are truly mystifying to all of them—assuming they've ever heard them, which is rarely the case. The Zorawski family is very cultivated by comparison.

In short, Marie—who was being a bit of a blue-stocking there—had been lucky.

So had the Zorawskis.

"If you could only see," she wrote to Henriette, "how exemplary my behavior is! I go to church every Sunday and every holy day, without ever claiming I have a headache or a cold in order to stay home. I almost never talk about higher education for women. In general, I maintain a discretion in my speech that is suitable to my position."

"Mademoiselle Marya," as she was called in the household, was in turn treated with consideration and even affection.

M. Zorawski agreed to look the other way when his older daughter, Bronka, told him about the bold plan dreamed up

23

by Marie. Simply put, it involved applying the theories of the Flying University to the illiterate, poor, filthy young peasants of Sluski. The positivist idealist had not fallen asleep.

With the active complicity of Bronka and the tacit permission of M. Zorawski, she brought together a dozen children, who would slip furtively up the stairway that led directly from the courtyard to Marie's room, and for two hours every day the two girls would teach them to read, write, and recite their country's history.

There was always the danger that someone would stumble on this subversive activity, and so at the least sound of a step on the stairway, the blackboard would fold back and all that would show was a surface covered with Russian characters. But there was never any serious alarm. And sometimes the parents would crowd into the room, too, and watch with fascination as their little boys and girls proudly entered the paradise of knowledge.

She had been with the Zorawskis for a year when the boys came back from Warsaw for Christmas vacation, and the inevitable happened. Casimir, the oldest, fell in love with Marie. He had never met a girl like her before.

Marie told no one about her own feelings. Perhaps she hadn't even been able to untangle them and admit that the confusion into which Casimir plunged her was not exactly an intellectual confusion. Her feelings were clear enough, in any case, after a long summer vacation filled with walks, dancing, horseback rides, and interminable conversations, so that she was ready to marry him. Of course M. and Mme Zorawski were opposed. One didn't marry a governess. Especially not when five young women with good dowries were available.

Casimir, who had been sure his parents would agree, returned to Warsaw distraught. He went on with his studies in agronomy, but he hadn't given up. Marie, on the other hand, had to swallow her outrage. She couldn't leave the Zorawski house, where she was so well paid, as long as the future of Bronia, who was alone in Paris struggling through her exams, depended on this precious salary.

24

After Casimir left, Marie was so serene, so rigorously reserved, that the Zorawskis, quite content to keep their excellent governess, said no more about it either.

The days went by as though nothing had ever disturbed them. What Marie was going through can be seen in some of her letters, as when she wrote to her brother about marriage plans of Hela's that didn't come off:

> I can imagine how Hela's self-esteem must have suffered. . . . Really, it gives one a fine opinion of people! If they don't want to marry a poor girl, let them go to the devil! No one is asking them to. But why heap insults on her, why disturb the peace of an innocent creature?
>
> My plans for the future? I haven't any, or rather they are so ordinary and so simple that it isn't worth the trouble of talking about them. To manage as best I can and, when I can no longer manage, to say goodbye to this world we live in: the damage will be slight, people won't miss me for long, no longer than they miss many others.
>
> These are my only plans at the moment. Certain people say that in spite of everything I will have to experience that species of fever called love. This absolutely doesn't enter into my plans. If in the past I had other plans, they went up in smoke. I have buried them, locked them up, sealed them up, and forgotten them because you know very well that walls are always stronger than the heads that try to knock them down.

And in the same vein, the following year: "I would give half my life to be independent again, to have my own home."

But for three more long years, sometimes without even enough to pay for the stamps she needed for her abundant correspondence, she would remain entombed in Sluski.

In March 1880, she wrote to her brother:

> Dear little Jozio,
> I am sticking the last stamp I own on this letter, and since I literally haven't a penny—not one!—no doubt I won't be writing to you before the holidays, unless by chance a stamp should fall into my hands.

The real purpose of my letter was to wish you a happy birthday, but believe me, if I'm late, it's only because of the lack of money and stamps which has plagued me frightfully—and I haven't yet learned how to ask for them.

. . . My dear Jozio, if you only knew how much I miss Warsaw, how much I would like to go there for a few days! I'm not even talking about my clothes, which are worn out. Oh! To get away for a few days from this chilly, chilling atmosphere, from these criticisms, from the perpetual watch I have to keep over my own words, the expression on my face, my actions: I need this change as much as a cool bath on a hot day. And I have many other reasons to wish for it.

. . . It has been a long time since Bronia last wrote me. No doubt she hasn't any stamps either. . . . But if you can sacrifice one, write to me, I beg you. Write me carefully and at length about everything that is happening in the house, because in Father's and Hela's letters there are always complaints; and I wonder if everything is really going that badly, and I torment myself. And on top of these worries there are the heaps of troubles I have here, which I could tell you about—but I don't want to. If I didn't have to think of Bronia, I would give notice this instant, and I would look for another position, even if it wasn't as well paid.

The Zorawskis were not treating her with much consideration. But she stuck it out. Clearly she was willing to sacrifice herself, as long as the cause was a worthy one, worthy of her. She had obviously transferred to the secular life the sort of transcendence that the sacred could no longer give her. Later, science would take the place of the sacred for her, but at the age of twenty-two, the cause that justified the life she inflicted on herself was Bronia, and also Jozef, who didn't have the means to set himself up in Warsaw. To him she wrote:

Practicing in a small town will prevent you from continuing your education and doing research. You will bury yourself in a hole, and you won't have a career. And if that happened to you, my dear, I would suffer enormously because now that I have lost the hope of ever becoming someone, all my ambition is focused on Bronia and you. The two of you, at least, have to plan your lives to suit your talents. These talents, which without any doubt exist in our family, must not disappear and must shine through one of us. The more regrets I have for myself, the more hope I have for you.

When she saw her contract coming to an end after four years with the Zorawskis, whose children were now grown, she looked for another position while still in Sluski and found one in the home of rich manufacturers in Warsaw.

Her penance was over.

three

Leaving that "provincial hole," Marie already breathed more freely. But she had given up most of her ambitious plans. All she aspired to now was to live with her father and find a position as a teacher in a boarding school. At least this was what she said, and what she wrote. It might have been what she believed, too.

But M. Sklodowski had retired from teaching and found an unpleasant but well-paid job: he was the warden of a penitentiary near Warsaw. Now he could send Bronia her stipend, and Marie could therefore begin saving her own nest egg. Her new position was also a good one.

She had been hired for a year, again as a governess, by a glamorous, elegant, wealthy young woman who bought her clothes in Paris, surrounded herself with artistic types who paid homage to her beauty, and received the cream of Warsaw society in her home.

This woman was enchanted by Marie, found her delightful and unusual, and displayed her in her salon. This was a rather pleasant interlude for Marie, who was able to prove to herself, if she needed to, that she was indifferent to luxury. She did not see the sense of it, felt no need for it, and had no taste for it.

In the middle of the school year, in March 1890, a letter arrived from Bronia announcing that she was engaged to another student whose first name was also Casimir. She wrote:

> Next year you can come to Paris and live with us, and you'll have a place to eat and sleep. You absolutely must have a few hundred rubles to pay the entry fees at the Sorbonne.

. . . I guarantee that you'll have your degree in two years. Think it over, save your money, put it in a safe place, *don't lend it*. Maybe it would be better to change it into francs right away, because the exchange rate is good now and later it might fall.

Bronia had thought of everything.

Marie's answer was strange. Melancholy, confused, resigned to what she called "my spoiled future," she wrote: "I've been stupid, I am stupid, and I will be stupid all the rest of my life, or rather, to put it another way, I've never been lucky, I'm not lucky and I never will be lucky. I had dreamed of Paris as of redemption, but for a long time now I haven't had any hope of going there. And now that the possibility presents itself, I don't know what to do."

She went on to talk at length about the family, a matter of getting a loan to establish Jozef, a promise made to Hela: "My heart is so black, so sad, because I know how wrong it is for me to talk about all this and poison your happiness. You're the only one of us who is what they call lucky. Please forgive me, but you see, so many things are hurting me that it is hard for me to end this letter cheerfully."

We know that Marie easily became depressed. But what was hurting her?

There is no way to say exactly what role Casimir Zorawski played during these long months while she hesitated, swearing she wouldn't leave her father, swearing other things, too.

What we can be sure of is that she saw him again. And that M. Sklodowski wrote to Bronia, "How original it would be if each of you had her own Casimir!" And that he became worried when he saw her growing depressed, fearing that "Marya may be in danger of suffering the same grief as before, because of the same people."

Casimir's feelings had not changed during the four years that had gone by. On the contrary, the obstacle they had encountered had probably only intensified them. And he had lost none of his charm either.

What he didn't know, however, when he spoke of their future together, was that he now had a rival. And what a rival—a laboratory!

In Warsaw, a cousin of Marie's named Jozef Boguski had created what he called "The Museum of Industry and Agriculture." This was actually a front for one of the clandestine centers of teaching that flourished in the city. Here, teachers from the Flying University introduced young Poles to the sciences.

Boguski had been the assistant of the famous chemist Mendeleev in Saint Petersburg. Another of his teachers had studied with the German chemist Robert Willhelm Bunsen, the inventor of spectrum analysis. These were magical names. What was most exciting was that the so-called museum contained a small laboratory where the students were taught elementary laboratory work.

"Believe it or not," Marie had written to her brother during her exile in Sluski, "I'm learning chemistry from books!"

What Marie discovered here was something no book could communicate—what it feels like to try to reproduce a concrete experiment that either fails or succeeds.

"I didn't have much time to work in this laboratory," she wrote later. "Usually I could only go there during the evenings after dinner or on Sundays, and I was left to myself. . . . The results were sometimes unexpected. . . . On the whole, though, while I learned to my expense that progress in these things was neither rapid nor easy, I did acquire my taste for experimental research during these first tests."

Eighteen months had elapsed since Bronia's invitation when, at the end of the summer, 1891, Casimir joined Marie in the mountain chalet where they were to spend two days together. It seems that he had once again tried to sway his parents, that Marie had demanded this, and that even as she did so, she knew in her heart of hearts what their answer would be and that this would give her the strength to break with him, by virtue of her very humiliation. And no doubt she felt some gloomy satisfaction in announcing, "I'm leaving."

"Proud and haughty," M. Sklodowski would later say, as he described his daughter's behavior toward Casimir.

Yet she was shaken, as we can see from the letter she immediately wrote to Bronia in the dramatic style she tended to adopt so easily: "Now, Bronia, I'm asking you to give me a final answer. Decide if you really can take me into your home, because now I can come. So if you can feed me without depriving yourself too much, write to me and tell me. It would make me very happy, because it would put me back on my feet, in a spiritual sense, after the cruel trials I've been through this summer, trials that will affect the whole rest of my life."

It seemed that the weak and charming Casimir did, then, deserve more than a passing mention.

The other Casimir, Bronia's Casimir, was more interesting.

He was thirty-five years old, he had character and a sense of humor, and he was handsome. There was also a card on file at the Ministry of the Interior containing information about him that would prevent him, even though he came from a rich Polish family, from ever obtaining his French naturalization papers.

When he was a student in Saint Petersburg, he had been suspected of complicity in the assassination of Czar Alexander II. He had fled Poland, taking refuge first in Geneva, where he published a revolutionary newspaper, and then in Paris where, after getting his degree in political science, he began studying medicine.

In short, everything about Casimir Dluski was pleasing to a young Sklodowska lady, and in the Polish emigrants' circle in Paris, he was particularly popular.

The only problem was that he couldn't enter Russian Poland.

Once he and Bronia had their doctorates, therefore, they both practiced in Paris. Their first patients were the families of the butchers in the Villette quarter, where they had chosen to live. Bronia delivered the babies.

As soon as she received Marie's supplicating letter ("You could put me anywhere, I won't get in your way, I promise I won't be any trouble, I won't cause any disorder. . . . I beg you to answer me, but answer me very frankly!") Bronia told her, "Come!" Marie had never doubted that she would say that, of course, but she had to inflict some feeling of guilt on herself. The enormous pleasure she would feel at leaving for the Sorbonne had to be tainted by the concern that she would be in the way in Bronia's home. Bronia was expecting a child.

The Sklodowskis traveled between Warsaw and Paris with disconcerting ease. If it hadn't been for the price of the train ticket, they would have been going back and forth constantly, even though it took more than thirty hours to get from one city to the other.

This was not an unusual thing to do for people of the "best society" of that time. That society was cosmopolitan, and the borders between European countries were much more open than they are now.

But Marie prepared for her departure as though she were moving an entire household. On Bronia's advice, she had sent ahead her mattress, sheets, blankets, and towels on the slow freight train. And, in a large wooden trunk, everything she might need for two years, perhaps three. There was no question of buying anything in Paris. Not even tea—and the two sisters drank a great deal of tea.

Every ruble Marie had saved, as well as whatever her father would be able to send her, had to be put to judicious use. She crossed Germany sitting on a folding chair, because the fourth-class compartments had no seats.

Other young people did exactly the same sort of thing in those days, just as they do today—only the style has changed.

As for the scrupulously pondered and recorded expenses, the thrift and parsimony, they were the rule in those days too, when people spent lavishly only for the sake of "appearances," which had never worried the Sklodowskis much.

But just to get along in life, one needs something, however minimal. That minimum was sometimes more than Marie had.

At least the franc was wonderfully stable in France in the fall of 1891 when the twenty-four-year-old Polish woman arrived there.

four

THE DAY the transcontinental steam-driven railway train deposited Marie in the Gare du Nord, loaded down with packages, a young deputy named Maurice Barrès commented on the front page of the *Figaro* about the latest debate taking place in the Chamber of Deputies: should schoolchildren be required to translate from Greek and Latin, or from English and German?

"The speakers raised the level of the debate so that it became truly patriotic. They asserted that the Greek and Latin and French civilizations had educative properties completely lacking to the English, German, and Scandinavian civilizations."

France, the world's guiding light.

A few columns over from this article, readers learned that "the Duke of Tremoille and the Duke of Noailles left for London yesterday morning," while the Duchess of Montpensier was "suffering from a serious inflammation of the lungs." That "more than a hundred pheasant, three hundred hares, and fifty deer were bagged during the presidential hunt that took place yesterday in the Rambouillet shooting preserve in honor of the Grand Dukes of Russia." And on page 2, that "a general strike will be announced tomorrow in the Pas-de-Calais coal fields." Unrest in the mines was a chronic problem.

At the Opéra Comique, Verdi was rehearsing *Falstaff*. Zola, at the height of his fame, had just published *L'Argent*, the eighteenth volume of his Rougon-Macquart series. Debussy had written *The Afternoon of a Faun*. Gauguin was painting Mallarmé's portrait before leaving for Tahiti. Rodin had been commissioned to do a statue of Balzac. Living alone in Provence, Cézanne was involved in a secret exploration of ways of perceiving things. Along the larger boulevards, which were lit by the first electric streetlights, one could see posters for the Moulin Rouge designed by Toulouse-Lautrec.

Two years had passed since the tower built by a genial engineer named Gustave Eiffel had made its appearance on the Paris skyline. Though it was a superb technical feat, it was also "a disaster that even America, commercial as it is, would not have wanted."

France, mother of the arts, had no great liking for her engineers and even less for her industry. Very few people believed in technological progress. No one imagined it would be capable of transforming the condition of society as it eventually did.

The bourgeois and liberal Third Republic, twenty years old, had been presided over by Sadi Carnot ever since the scandal that had obliged Grévy—whose son-in-law was a dubious character—to leave the Elysée Palace.

The shock waves propagated by the 1870 defeat and the Commune were still being felt. In the working-class neighborhoods of Paris, boulangism was still alive even though the handsome general, who had fled to Brussels, had recently killed himself there on the tomb of his mistress.

With its middle-of-the-road government, the Republic was challenged by the monarchist, right-wing nobility and disparaged by the Nationalists and the Socialists, who banded together to fight its policies.

In the Chamber of Deputies, Boulangists and Socialists joined forces to demand that workers be given a share in the profits of businesses, that there be a "close alliance between capital and labor," and that French workers be protected from foreign workers. There was serious unemployment. In high society as well as among the working class, anti-Semitism was rife. Protestants were out of favor.

Although they stood on different sides of the question of colonial expansion, the national right wing and the Socialists shared a fear of the effects of "machinism" and a hatred of the "financial barons" who were committed to the industrial adventure and profiting from it. Maurice Barrès called them the "fat men." Wealth was respectable only when it was inherited wealth.

There were many Frenchmen who might have said what the head of a religious college said about the trains that ran through his town on Sundays: "This is just as displeasing to God as it is to me."

May 1, 1891, was a tragic day.

Five years earlier, 300,000 workers in the United States had walked off their jobs in order to obtain an eight-hour day. Since then, the Second International had adopted the principle of holding a one-day strike on May 1 to make the same demand. In 1891, the demonstrations were more widespread. In Bordeaux, Roanne, Lyon, Saint-Quentin, and Charleville, the strikes were broken by force.

In Fourmies, a town in the department Le Nord, where the entire population worked in the spinning mills, a group of workers whose salaries had been reduced because of a slump in the textile industry decided to demonstrate for a higher salary, an eight-hour day, and a union. The employers, alerted to this plan, asked the prefect of Le Nord for help from the army. On April 30, two infantry companies were sent out. On May 1, after the mounted police had failed to disperse the demonstrators, the army arrived, opened fire, and killed nine people. Five of them were under twenty. A child of two was wounded.

The man who was brought to trial and indicted, however, was the organizer of the strike, a worker. He was sentenced to six years in prison by the Douai Court of Assizes. Fourmies was to remain the bloodiest episode in the history of France's May 1 demonstrations.

Parliament was shaken by it. But the misery of the workers in France was an aspect of France which no one but Zola reported—it was absent from literature, theater, painting, and from the consciousness of Paris society.

The provinces seemed very remote. And apart from the spinning mills, the mines, and the metalworking plants, there weren't any industrial enterprises that employed more than five workers.

The capital, which had just been redesigned by Haussmann, was beautiful. The luxury trade flourished. And though costly buildings were springing up along the new arteries, the population of artisans, white-collar workers, "little people" who made Paris what it was, who gave it its reputation as the capital of taste, of creativity, of wit, and sometimes of insurrection, were not pushed back toward the suburbs.

The Latin Quarter, that motley, vivacious, exuberant territory of the students, who had their own customs and fashions, their own cafés, their own whimsical notions, was the heart of intellectual Europe. Twelve thousand young men and a tiny handful of women attended the university.

The Boulevard, "the only one that incontestably deserves a capital letter," as *Le Petit Parisien* wrote, was lined with cafés frequented by, according to this popular newspaper, "the French elite. . . . Coming in crowds or singly, the glamorous and the famous congregate in the Boulevard, a meeting place for Paris and the whole world. . . . The last word in fashion emanates from here and becomes law for the rest of the world."

The author of the article laments the appearance on the Boulevard of a brasserie "such as exist only in savage countries full of savage men and savage girls and savage beer."

The tone of this small piece of patriotism was very common in those times. For instance, a newspaper advertisement for Virginie's Elixir was headed "Science and Patriotism" and began with the following words: "A foreigner might take advantage of our internal difficulties to throw stones at us and maintain that we are a degenerate people. And this in a country illuminated by the most famous scholars and where the greatest discoveries are made. One relatively recent one is . . ." And what was Virginie's Elixir? A cure for "hemorrhoids, phlebitis, all the ailments that occur during the critical age for ladies and other cruel afflictions."

Fortunately for Marie Sklodowska, who had come all this way looking for it, there was more to French science than this, and France had at least one great scientist, Pasteur, who was reaching the end of his life.

The quantity of work Pasteur had done was at once spectacular and lucrative. The vaccine against rabies guaranteed his fame, but he had many other discoveries to his credit, and several had been used in industry. The beer industry, for example, owed to him its ability to compete with German brewers. The country had profited enormously from this. In those days, Germany was the only country to research the applications of science to industry and exploit them systematically.

Pasteur had brought about considerable advances in medicine, chemistry, and also work methods. In other respects, French science, which had been brilliant and fertile at the beginning of the century, had slowed down. The teaching of science was the weakest, most neglected area of French education.

There existed in France only one single professorship in theoretical physics. There was no laboratory comparable to Cavendish's, created in 1870 by the English to train Cambridge University students in the scientific disciplines and to try to catch up with Germany.

Only the Ecole Française de Mathématiques, with Henri Poincaré at its head, was competing successfully in the domain of mathematical physics.

If she had been better informed, would Marie have chosen to study physics in Great Britain or Germany? It isn't very likely. Besides the fact that at her level of scholarship it didn't matter, as a proper Polish girl she was completely oriented toward France. And so it was to Paris that she came—to the rue d'Allemagne (today known as the avenue Jean Jaurès), in the peaceful, outlying, working-class neighborhood where the Dluskis had chosen to live and where Bronia had re-created a Warsaw-style home.

On November 3, 1891, she "crossed the courtyard of the Sorbonne," where she had registered, using the French form of her first name, for a bachelor's degree in science. On November 7, she would turn twenty-four.

Almost exactly fifteen years later, on November 5, 1906, Marie would become the first woman ever hired to teach in this same school. In the meantime, the buildings would be resurfaced and enlarged. The bust of Auguste Comte, father of positivism, would still stand facing the entrance.

These fifteen years were extraordinary in every respect— European science became very exciting, France was torn apart by the Dreyfus affair, and Marie's own life went through many changes.

But as far as she was concerned, those fifteen years were not bad at all.

five

THE FIRST stage of Marie's life in Paris was like a stay in a convent, except for a brief interlude in the beginning.

Bronia and Casimir worked hard, but they liked to amuse themselves too. They weren't rolling in money, but they were hospitable people, and they kept open house for the young people in Paris's small Polish colony.

These Poles engaged in endless arguments around the samovar and the piano; they made the world and Poland over as they ate cakes that Bronia had baked between consultations. On special occasions they went off to the theater and to concerts.

In a hall that was three-quarters empty, they acted as claques for a friend of theirs, a red-haired pianist who was trying to make a reputation for himself. His name was Ignace Paderewski.

They held midnight feasts, mounted amateur shows, staged *tableaux vivants*. Marie was the young woman draped in a garnet-red tunic, her blond hair loose and falling over her shoulders, who played the part of "Poland Breaking Her Bonds" during a patriotic festival while Paderewski played Chopin in the wings. She was proud of having been chosen.

But when she wrote to her father about the evening's activities, he gave her a stern lecture.

I'm sure you know [he wrote to her] that there are people in Paris who are watching your behavior very carefully. . . . This can cause a lot of trouble. . . .

People who want to earn a living in Warsaw later on without finding themselves exposed to various dangers should take care to keep very quiet and retiring so that they will be ignored.

It is hardly likely that Marie suddenly became prudent. But by the time four months had gone by, she had discovered her weaknesses in physics and mathematics compared to her fellow students. Though she knew French well, she had some trouble following the professors, who talked fast. She didn't know the scientific vocabulary. She would not be able to overcome these handicaps if she didn't devote herself entirely to her studies.

In March, she moved into a small rooming house in the rue Flatters, within walking distance of the Sorbonne. She was saving both time and money by walking to school, because from the rue d'Allemagne, she had had to take two horse-drawn buses each way. But now she had to pay for her room. She wrote to her brother: "Naturally, without Dluski's help I would never have been able to set myself up this way. I am working a thousand times harder than at the beginning of my stay in the rue d'Allemagne. My little brother-in-law was in the habit of disturbing me incessantly. He absolutely couldn't bear it that I was in the house and doing anything else than chatting agreeably with him. I had to get into a fight with him about this."

Chatting agreeably would never be her specialty. The affectionate "little brother-in-law," who was twelve years older than she and who had been asked by M. Sklodowski to look after her, had already laughingly noted that she showed him "no respect and no obedience." He was gently making fun of her tendency to dramatize things.

That was what she was particularly good at. After all, Bronia had pursued her studies in similar circumstances. But she didn't win the Nobel Prize for medicine and no one has written her biography, whereas the years that Marie spent first in the rue Flatters, then in a garret in the Boulevard du Port-Royal, and finally in the rue des Feuillantines, have become part of a legend.

Fifty years ago, there wasn't a schoolchild who didn't know the story of the evening when "Madame Curie" was so cold in her little room with no fireplace that she piled everything from her trunk onto her bed and then added a chair, while the water froze in her wash basin.

Actually, there was a coal stove in the room, but that day she had no doubt forgotten to go fill her bucket at the coalman's. Or had felt reluctant to ask him for credit. The living conditions she imposed on herself, when she lived alone, were certainly harsh, but her austerity sometimes bordered on masochism.

There was always a meal waiting for her at Bronia's house. However small her resources, which her father supplemented as best he could, she could have avoided fainting dead away as a result of eating nothing but radishes and tea. One day Dluski must have been told about this by someone who had witnessed it, because he came and took her by force back to the rue d'Allemagne, where she recovered her strength with the help of a good thick beefsteak.

Her waist constricted in a corset, one of her two hats always on her head, as decency demanded, worn shoes on her feet, and a carefully mended Polish dress on her back, she would walk with dignity from the lecture halls of the Sorbonne to the laboratories in the rue Saint-Jacques, from the laboratories to the Bibliothèque Sainte-Geneviève, and from the library home. Her contacts with the young people in the Polish community became more and more infrequent, to the point of stopping altogether.

Some of her fellow students found her pretty—this small blonde woman with ash-gray eyes who had lost some weight because of her meager diet—and would have said as much to her, but her distaste for all familiarity kept them at a distance. To call her by her first name was offensive to her, and she would find it loathsome all her life. No one dreamed of addressing her by the familiar *tu*.

The only person she formed any sort of friendship with at all was a young Polish woman named Mlle Dydynska, who one day took it upon herself to shake her umbrella at an overly zealous young man. But Marie did not need to be protected. She took care of that herself.

When the school year ended, she hadn't yet acquired the indispensable rudiments that she had lacked when she came from Warsaw, and so she spent the summer in Paris taking mathematics courses and perfecting her French.

By the time school started again, she had eliminated all "Polishisms" from her vocabulary. Only her slightly rolled r's would remain until her death, betraying her Slavic background and adding a certain charm to her already delightful voice. And, like everyone else, she always did her calculations in her native language.

She was making progress in the subjects she was studying, as one can see from her notebooks. These were a schoolchild's notebooks, carefully annotated in her sloping, clear, neat, and regular handwriting, with the new scientific terms emphasized.

Twenty years later, a handwriting analyst looked at this writing, not knowing whose it was, and saw the following traits:

> Reflective, prudent mind; capacity for enthusiasm, perseverance in endeavors. The brain is exercised regularly in a methodical way. Decisions arrived at through reasoning and manifested almost always in their final form. Keen sensitivity rarely betrayed by expansiveness. Habit of withdrawing into an inner life inaccessible to familiars. Less spontaneity than moderation; appearances sober and correct; little coquetry or none at all. Detachment from practical concerns, but a great ambition to bring out the personality, to assert it, to put it in the limelight.
>
> Taste for introspection, solitude. Scrupulous and somewhat mystical conscience. Loyal and dependable nature whose nervousness is constantly subdued by an ardent will to conquer all weakness.

It wasn't only her "ambition to bring out her personality" and to put it in the limelight that sustained her and removed

43

her from everything that might distract her. It was also her passion. She had encountered science. Through the courses of Lippmann, Paul Appell, Painlevé, she was beginning to understand it and also to master its vocabulary.

Naturally, when the time came to take the exams, she wrote to her father that she was afraid she wasn't ready, that she needed a few more months. As she entered the lecture hall where the tests were held she felt sick with apprehension. To fail—which meant to be perceived by others as incapable of showing what she could do—was something she would never be able to accept, and fear of failure put her on tenterhooks.

Not only did she pass, but when the results were announced before all the candidates in order of merit, her name was first. Marie Sklodowska had a bachelor's degree in physical sciences from the Université de Paris. And that was wonderful.

Writing about them thirty years later, she described these two years of intense effort, isolation, and privation as "one of the best memories of my life." It isn't hard to believe her.

This feat accomplished, she gave notice to her landlady, stored her bed, table, chair, and portable stove in Bronia's house, and took the train for Warsaw. She was going back home. To stay? Not yet. As soon as you begin to learn things you discover that you don't know anything. In the laboratories she had seen that in order to go further with physics and chemistry, she would have to pursue her training in mathematics.

However, to get another degree, she would have to surmount the same obstacle as before—her lack of money. She was down to her last pennies. This time it was Mlle Dydynska who made it possible for her to go on. During the vacation this woman, who was the first of her many admirers, went to some trouble on her behalf and succeeded in getting her the Alexandrowitch Grant, awarded by the Polish government to particularly brilliant students who wanted to continue their studies abroad.

The spies M. Sklodowski had been so afraid of must not

44

have noticed Marie's patriotic Polish activities in Paris. Anyway, she hardly indulged in this sort of thing anymore.

Six hundred rubles was a fortune! Until now Marie had been getting by on the equivalent of forty rubles a month, which would be about two hundred dollars today. Hers was a unique case, because she later deducted enough from her first earnings to pay back the foundation the sum of her grant. Clearly, Marie's relations to money were not simple.

No one knew better than she did how necessary and how valuable money was. Throughout her life she would write every last expenditure down in an account book. For years and years she was hard up, and sometimes her money troubles obsessed her. Yet she would never compromise her strict ethical standards. "Disinterested" would always be the highest praise she could give anyone.

With her grant in hand, in September 1893, she moved to a new room that had a parquet floor—her previous room had been paved with flagstones—and a window "that closes tightly," for a rent of 180 francs a year, and retrieved her bed, table, chair, portable stove, and kerosene lamp. She went back to work with a feeling of pleasure, a little less tense than she had been during the previous two years. She took a course in calculus with Paul Painlevé, a course in theoretical mechanics with Paul Appell.

In July, she received her degree in mathematics. She was second on the list of successful candidates. What her impertinent brother-in-law, teasing her, called "the heroic era" of her life was over. Now she could return to her beloved Poland and use her knowledge to free her people.

She was probably not even aware that the day before her exam the President of the Republic had been assassinated. On Sunday, June 24, while he was making an official trip to Lyon, Sadi Carnot had been stabbed in his carriage by a militant Italian anarchist named Vesario San Ieronimo.

Nearly every week there were assassination attempts, almost always reported in the newspapers under the heading, "The Anarchists." The result of all this was that when in December a bomb was thrown from the gallery of the Chamber of Deputies in the middle of a session, the Parliament passed the well-known "nefarious laws."[1] In February, a bomb thrown into the Gare Saint-Lazare had wounded twenty people. One person was killed. A week later, another bomb killed another person in the rue Saint-Jacques. In April, the famous restaurant Foyot was destroyed by an explosion.

The news of the assassination of the President of the Republic, kept back for several hours, didn't reach Paris until the next day. Published in the newspapers the day after, it must have caused some excitement at the Sorbonne.

But Marie certainly didn't dance on her chair the way she had twelve years earlier when Alexander II was killed by Casimir's friends. She no longer believed that violence accomplished anything, and President Sadi Carnot had not only been a decent man, but the son of a physicist and grandson of a mathematician as well!

A positivist, no doubt, he had refused to pardon Ravachol, who had been condemned to death after throwing a bomb in the Boulevard Saint-Germain, despite an appeal for clemency from Jaurès and the socialist leaders. But would Marie have pardoned him?

Perhaps she didn't even discuss it, or if she did, then only for a moment, with the physicist she had been seeing for a few weeks now. He would come to talk to her in her room, and where others would have brought a box of chocolates, he would come with a copy of an article with a title like "On Symmetry in Physical Phenomena, Symmetry in an Electrical Field and in a Magnetic Field." This particular booklet

---

[1] Thenceforth the government could seize and ban newspapers for "indirect provocation," suppress associations, and forbid meetings. It was later learned that the bomb had been thrown by an agent provocateur under instructions from the Minister of the Interior.

was inscribed "To Mlle Sklodowska with the respect and friendship of the author P. Curie."

When they were together, they talked endlessly, either about physics or about themselves. But as everyone knows, you can't tolerate hearing someone tell you all about his childhood unless you are in love with him.

six

PIERRE CURIE entered Marie's life at just the right time. The year 1894 was nearly half over. Marie was sure of receiving her degree in July. She was beginning to look ahead, she had more time on her hands, and the spring was beautiful.

Preoccupying her at the moment was a study she had been commissioned to carry out for the Société d'Encouragement pour l'Industrie Nationale—a study of the magnetic properties of certain steels. She was working on this in the laboratory of one of her teachers, the physicist Gabriel Lippmann, but the metal samples she needed were too cumbersome for the cramped laboratory.

A Polish physicist who had emigrated to Switzerland, where he was teaching, was passing through Paris on his honeymoon and got in touch with Marie. She told him about the study she was doing, and the practical problem she was encountering. He knew of someone, he said, who might be able to find a place for her and who could in any case give her some advice. He was a man of great ability who worked at the Ecole de Physique et de Chimie Industrielles. His name was Pierre Curie. If Marie would come for a glass of tea the next day, he would introduce him to her.

Marie herself wrote an account of this meeting:

When I entered the room, Pierre Curie was standing in the recess of a pair of French windows that opened onto a balcony. He seemed very young to me even though he was thirty-five years old at that time. I was struck by the expression in his clear eyes and by the slight appearance of neglect in his tall figure. His rather slow and thoughtful way of speaking, his simplicity, his smile which was at once serious and youthful, inspired confidence in me. We started talking and soon became friendly; our conversation revolved around scientific questions about which I was happy to ask his advice, and then social or humanitarian questions in which we were both interested. There was a surprising affinity between his conception of things and mine, despite the fact that we came from different countries, and this was no doubt attributable in part to a certain similarity in the moral attitudes of the families in which each of us grew up.

Marie Curie was over fifty when she wrote this and she had never been a woman to express herself emotionally. But beneath the conventional style and the ever-present constraint, we can see some signs of what was evidently love at first sight for both of them.

The story goes that at the end of this long conversation, Pierre Curie and Marie went to have dinner together in a little student restaurant, and that it was so late by the time he walked her home that he missed the last train for Sceaux, where he lived, and had to walk all the way back.

Whether this is true or not, it is certainly quite possible. Pierre Curie was already captivated by the unusual little blonde woman. And he was an absentminded man. Marie was always very direct. Why shouldn't they have dinner together if she wanted to?

In her three years in Paris, Marie, who was twenty-six years old and soon to be twenty-seven, had certainly met men in the Dluski home, at school, and in the laboratory who were drawn to her. During the time she lived with Bronia, a Polish student had fallen in love with her and had eventually swallowed some laudanum to attract her attention. Marie's reaction was: "The young man has no sense of priorities." Their priorities weren't the same, in any case.

By 1894 she certainly looked older. Her cheeks were hollow, her figure was slim, her earlier, rather rustic bloom had faded under the hardships of the way she had been living, and had been replaced by a certain transparency to her skin; her ash-gray eyes with their intense look seemed larger under the line of her eyebrows, which emphasized her beautiful rounded forehead. She didn't yet have the air of fragility that would later be so moving to people who came into contact with her, but something about this inflexible young woman, strangely enough, made people want to protect her.

A certain M. Lamotte—we don't know exactly who he was—paid court to her that year in a ceremonious and persistent way. He has left his faint mark on the story of Marie Curie only because she saved his letters. She must not have despised him, then, even if he didn't arouse very strong feelings in her.

But this obstinate person, who lived in the hope of "winning her by his patient friendship," was to come up against a rival he couldn't compete with—if he had ever had a chance anyway, which is something we can't know.

Marie was not like other women of her time. Whereas they found their self-affirmation in marriage, motherhood, or, for the licentious, in adultery—either enjoying their situation or resigning themselves to it—Marie found hers in her work.

This did not mean that she didn't need to be loved too, just as a man does, or that she didn't need to have children too, just as a man does. But at the same time, like a man, she needed to prove what she was capable of. And this need was all the more imperious because she had to prove herself as a woman in a society that denied women except in the functions they were intended to fill. "Housewife or prostitute," as the founder of French trade-unionism put it.

In the climate of this time, when young girls were not supposed to know they had bodies, or that their bodies could feel other pleasures than the pleasure of carrying a child—not even knowing how the child had come to be there—we can be sure that Marie would not have allowed her suitors to take many liberties with her.

She may have been better informed—at least technically, so to speak—than other women of her generation. She was also

50

free enough, or liberated enough, to go have dinner or—according to another version—to give Pierre Curie her address the same day she met him, and to find it normal to receive him in her room. This sort of behavior would have been unimaginable on the part of a young Frenchwoman of her social circle, even at the age of twenty-six.

Her mind was, finally, too important to her to imagine forming permanent ties, even of friendship, with an intellectually mediocre man. Even young Casimir Zorawski was not an ordinary man in this respect. As for Pierre Curie, however, he was exceptional in every way.

During this time of growing love in which it seemed as though two halves of a single being were coming together, in which the two lovers marveled to find they were "made for each other," in which each gauged how much of himself to reveal to the other, Marie experienced more than anything else the pleasure of allowing herself to be loved. Through Pierre she saw herself in the way that was most likely to please her: as a woman whose attraction came just as much from the vigor of her intelligence as from her grace, in the eyes of a man of science whose knowledge was infinitely superior to her own.

When she went back to Poland at the beginning of August 1894, to spend her vacation with her father, she had not committed herself to anything, not even to returning.

We can pretty much reconstruct what she knew about Pierre Curie at that time using what we know and the letters he wrote to her during the summer. She had told him about her family and he had told her about his. His father was a doctor and the son of a doctor, and they came from Alsace. Dr. Curie practiced in Sceaux, which was a small town just outside Paris. At the age of thirty-five, Pierre still lived with his parents.

She told him about the adventures she had had getting an education. He told her he had never been to school. His father had decided to spare his child this ordeal, because he was too dreamy, too distracted, too sensitive, with a "slow" intelligence, as he said, unadapted and unadaptable to conventional teaching methods. His mother had taught him to read and write. His father had taught him to observe nature and had let him feed on the vast family library before turning him over, at the age of fourteen, to a tutor. At that point he had discovered the beauty of mathematics. He swam in abstraction like a fish in water. At sixteen, he had his *baccalauréat* and at eighteen his *licence*. He probably didn't add that he had a special gift which Marie later described as "an unmistakably geometric mind and a great facility of vision in space."

On Sundays they would go for walks together in the country. This was Pierre's world, and had been since his childhood, his youth. He had disappeared hundreds of times in the morning or the evening, losing all sense of time, walking along the Bièvre, plunging into the Minière woods. "I would come back at dawn," he wrote, "with a dozen new ideas."

He would pick a periwinkle or catch a frog, and show Marie what was obsessing him—the symmetry of forms in nature.

She talked about Bronia. He talked about Jacques, his older brother, another erratic scholar but of a completely different temperament—extroverted, active. Jacques had been his well-loved companion in games, in adventures, in work, until the day he got married and left Sceaux to become a lecturer in the Montpellier Faculté des Sciences.

Marie talked about the progress she was making in her study of steels, and Pierre talked about his work with piezoelectricity. He and Jacques had discovered this phenomenon—the production of electrical charges upon the compression or expansion of asymmetrical crystals. The two brothers had then demonstrated the inverse phenomenon predicted by Lippmann—that an electrical charge applied to such crystals would deform them.[1]

As soon as they were published, the results of this work

----

[1] The supersonic microphone and the quartz watch were both developed as a result of this research.

aroused the strong interest of the reigning British physicist of that time, Lord Kelvin.

In order to carry out their experiments in the mineralogy laboratory where Jacques worked as Friedel's assistant, the Curie brothers conceived and built two instruments: a piezoelectric quartz electrometer capable of measuring weak electrical charges, and a magnetic scale capable of balancing forces on the order of $\frac{1}{100}$ milligram. Great skill in carrying out experiments was needed to use these instruments. Marie eventually acquired this skill, but Pierre's hands had always had "the gift."

Marie asked Pierre about the research he was doing now. She was certainly the only woman of that time who could understand what he was talking about, and he explained that he was trying to find out if there existed transitions, as far as magnetic properties were concerned, between the three states of matter—diamagnetic bodies, weakly magnetic bodies, and ferromagnetic bodies—and if it was possible to cause one single body to pass through these three states in succession.

This was to be the subject of his doctoral thesis. But his progress was slow. He had at his disposal neither the facilities nor the laboratory equipment for his own research, and he had been working in a hallway ever since, at the age of twenty-five, he had been appointed head of works at the Ecole de Physique et de Chimie Industrielles de Paris, where he was also overburdened with duties. He had been occupying this obscure position for ten years now.

Perhaps Marie was discreetly surprised that he had never thought of sitting for the entrance exam to a "large school," the Polytechnique or the Ecole Normale Supérieure.

He had told her that he couldn't tolerate competition; it was foreign to his way of doing things, to his attitudes, to his philosophy. Marie, who was born with a will to conquer, may have admired him all the more for this, seeing it as one more feature of that "disinterest" she valued so highly.

In fact, Pierre Curie was to protect himself from others all his life. He assiduously avoided conflicts, and when he was driven into a fight, he engaged in it with such repugnance that he lost more often than he won.

After his death, the mathematician Henri Poincaré said of him: "Pierre Curie received the highest honors with the attitude of a whipped dog."

If Marie agreed with this statement, she never gave any indication of it. But there is no evidence that she would have been able to live with a fighter for very long. That would have made one too many.

Dr. Curie, a Protestant but also an avowed freethinker, had never given his two boys the least religious education—which, in those days, went beyond indifference and bordered on the assertion of an independent belief. We don't know what his wife, the daughter of a small manufacturer from the Savoie, thought of this, but the fact remains that Pierre sided with his father.

One of the first times he climbed the six flights of stairs to Marie's attic room, he took her Zola's *Lourdes*, which had just come out. He was pleased to see that she shared his attitude toward religion.

Marie and Pierre were well acquainted with mysticism. But the object of their mysticism—science—was opposed by religion. As though a researcher automatically had to deny the existence of a reality to which physics could not have access. Research—looking through the keyhole, finding the key, opening a door behind which was another locked door, then another and another and another—was a driving force, not a philosophy.

Pierre Curie belonged to a generation that had rejected the Church, viewing it as a tool for social domination. And he was better acquainted than some with how tragic life could be.

The girl who had been his constant companion during his childhood had died when he was twenty. After her death, he had turned to his brother and had experienced the sweetness of perfect communion between two people. "We had the same thoughts; it was no longer necessary for us to speak in order to understand each other," he told Marie, describing their relationship. Ever since their separation, which had been difficult for him, Pierre Curie had been lonely.

What he writes in his journal is enlightening about the nature of his relations with women. He says:

> Women of genius are rare. Therefore, when we are driven by some mystical love to go in a direction that is contrary to nature, when we devote all our thoughts to some work that distances us from the humanity surrounding us, we must fight against women.
>
> More than anything else, a mother wants her child's love, even if thereby he should remain an idiot. A mistress also wants to possess her lover and would find it quite natural to sacrifice the greatest genius in the world for one hour of love. Almost always, the fight is unequal, because women are fighting for a good cause: it is in the name of life and nature that they try to bring us back.

If he was often engaged in this struggle, we don't know whom he was struggling with, or against, and it hardly matters. What we can see is that at the age of thirty-five he was still alone as he proceeded on his way through the realm of the sublime and through the realm of theoretical physics, and that Marie Sklodowska very soon appeared to him the only one capable of accompanying him on this journey.

Clearly it took Marie longer to convince herself that she should give up her independence, even for such a man as Pierre Curie. She always anguished over her decisions, and she always kept to them once they were made. But first she had to make them.

During the beautiful summer of 1894, diplomas in hand, she had to choose between Poland, to which she was tied by birth and by her commitment to patriotism, and her other country, what we might call her true country—science. Pierre Curie had said to her, "You are destined for science." And science meant pure research.

At that time, the French scientific world generally had nothing but contempt for "inventors." The electric telegraph and the telephone, the phonograph and the incandescent lamp, the typewriter and the microphone, all of which originated in the United States, were dismissed as mere conveniences. The ball bearing, invented by a Frenchman named Surtray, and the dynamo, invented by a German, Siemens, were considered merely ingenious. Clément Ader and his airplane were daring. Louis Lumière and his projector were amusing.

In a speech which caused some stir, Marcelin Berthelot, the great chemist of the day, who owed his popularity to his synthesis of alcohol and who was head of an industrial laboratory, drew a picture of the year 2000:

> By this time, there will no longer be any such thing as agriculture in the world, no pastures, no farmers: the problem of living by cultivating the soil will have been eliminated by chemistry. There will no longer be any coal mines nor other mining industries, and as a result no more miners' strikes. The fuel problem will have been eliminated by the cooperative efforts of chemistry and physics.
>
> There will be no more customs offices, no more protectionism, no more wars, no more frontiers drenched in men's blood. Aerial navigation, with engines fueled by chemical energy, will have relegated those outmoded institutions to the past. We will, therefore, be very close to realizing the dreams of socialism . . . provided someone manages to discover a spiritual chemistry to change man's moral nature as profoundly as our chemistry transforms material nature!

He announced that chemistry would enable food to be produced in the form of tablets so that its abundance would no longer depend on the weather, on good or bad harvests. He

56

added: "The basic problem is to discover inexhaustible sources of energy capable of renewing themselves with almost no work." Though he did not foresee that during the twentieth century this source of energy would be gas, he was clearly predicting that in the twenty-first century it would be the sun.

But Berthelot was an exception. He was one of the very few men of his generation to make an intellectual connection between scientific progress and the transformation of society. Most scientists of his age gave no consideratioin to what we call technology today, which was supposed to be the concern of engineers. In their eyes research had only one object: to push back the frontiers of knowledge. At its extreme, this attitude became a kind of esthetics, and it was certainly an aristocratic attitude that was to continue into the twentieth century and that prevailed in Great Britain too.

C. P. Snow reports that "the young researchers of Cambridge prided themselves on the fact that the kind of science to which they were devoting themselves could not in any instance have the slightest practical usefulness. The more certain one was that one was good for nothing, the more superior one felt."

It wasn't until the First World War, when toxic gases came into use and scientists were mobilized, that this attitude changed. Before then, medical research was the only kind of research respected in its practical as well as its theoretical application. But in this field too, Pasteur made the golden rule: "Encourage scientific disinterest, because it is one of the fertile sources of progress in theory, from which comes all progress in application."

Marie believed wholeheartedly in disinterest. Clearly, disinterested action would always be indispensable to the balance of her inner economy. Once she had succeeded in her first enterprise, to learn as much as a man might learn—an enterprise undertaken with the disinterested aim of transmitting this knowledge—she could, without betraying herself, at-

57

tempt to put her abilities in the service of an equally stimulating aim—theoretical research. Now pure research would be extending pure knowledge.

Although Marie's exalted patriotism might have served unconsciously to cloak her ambition, it remained ardent, as did the patriotism of Bronia, who would be ready to go back home once an amnesty allowed her unruly husband to return to his country. And so, at the end of July, Marie went to Poland, leaving M. Lamotte dismayed and Pierre Curie determined to join her.

Like many rather introverted people, Pierre found it much easier to write about his feelings than to talk about them. In the exchange of letters between him and Marie there was a communication of a completely different kind than in their talks. In the stilted book she dedicated to him, Marie speaks of the "bond of affection that was beginning to form" between them—she never wrote the word "love." "During the summer of 1894," she says, "Pierre Curie wrote me letters that by and large seem wonderful to me."

These sober letters tell us a lot about him and also about Marie as we catch glimpses of her in what he writes to her, and, incidentally, about things that historians of our time will lose because of the telephone. Pierre Curie would have been ruined if international communication by telephone had already existed then!

She wrote first, and he answered immediately:

August 10, 1894

Nothing could have given me more pleasure than to receive news of you. The prospect of not hearing from you for two months was extremely unpleasant to me—which is to say that your note was welcome.

I hope you are laying in a supply of fresh air and that you will come back to us in October. As for me, I don't think I will travel, I am staying in the country, and I spend all day in front of my open window, or in the garden.

We promised each other (didn't we?) that we would at least have a great friendship. I hope you haven't changed your mind!

Because promises can't be binding, these things are beyond our control. Yet it would be a beautiful thing, something I don't dare believe, to spend our lives near each other, obsessed by our dreams—*your* patriotic dream, *our* humanitarian dream, and *our* scientific dream.

Of all these dreams, I believe the last is the only legitimate one. What I mean is that we are powerless to change the state of society, and even if we could, we wouldn't know what to do, and if we were to take some random action we would never be sure that we weren't doing more harm than good, by slowing down some inevitable development. Where science is concerned, on the other hand, we can claim to do something—here the ground is firmer and every discovery, no matter how small, remains our own.

See how everything is connected. . . . It is right that we should be great friends, but if you leave France in a year, this friendship will really be too platonic—the friendship of two people who won't see each other any more. Wouldn't it be better for you to stay with me? I know this question makes you angry, and I won't talk to you about it any more—and anyway, I feel so unworthy of you, in every respect . . . .

I had thought of asking you to let me meet you *by chance* in Freiburg. But it's true, isn't it, that you will only be staying there one day, and that day you will necessarily belong to our friends the Kowalskis.

Your devoted
P. Curie

It would make me very happy if you would be so kind as to write me and assure me that you intend to come back in October. Letters will reach me more quickly if you write directly to Sceaux: Pierre Curie, 13 rue des Sablons, Sceaux (Seine).

And four days later:

Now that it's too late, I'm sorry I didn't go. . . . Are you fatalistic? Do you remember mid-Lent day? I suddenly lost you in the crowd. It seems to me that our friendly relations will be just as suddenly broken off without either of us wanting it. I'm

59

not fatalistic, but this will probably be a result of our characters. I won't know how to take action at the right moment.

Anyway, this will be very good for you, because I don't know why I thought I could keep you in France, exile you from your country and your family, without having anything good to offer you in exchange for such a sacrifice.

I find you a little presumptuous when you say you are perfectly free. We are all, at the very least, slaves of our affections, slaves of the prejudices of the people we love, we must also earn our livings and, because of that, we become cogs in the machinery, etc.

Most painful are the concessions we have to make to the prejudices of the Society we live in: how many concessions we make depends on whether we are feeling strong or weak. If we don't make enough concessions, we get wiped out. If we make too many, we are behaving in a vile way and we become disgusted with ourselves. Here I am, without a lot of the principles I had ten years ago: at that time I thought I had to go to extremes in everything I did and make no concession to the social environment. I wore blue shirts like the workers, etc.

Finally, as you can see, I turned into a very old man.

In another letter dated September, he talked to her for a long time about his brother Jacques, with whom he had just spent several days in Auvergne. What did she write back to him? Whatever it was, it worried him, and he advised her "urgently to return to Paris in October. It would distress me very much if you didn't come back."

Apparently Marie had become involved with Poland and her friends in the Flying University again, and had written passionately about how widespread social injustice was, how selfish it would be to accept the situation, how imperative was one's duty to try to change it. For Pierre answered:

What would you think of someone who decided to try to knock over a stone wall by throwing himself head first against it? There might be some very beautiful feelings behind that notion, but in fact it would be foolish and absurd. I believe that certain problems require a general solution, and don't allow of a local solution right now, and that when one starts down a road that is really a dead end, one can do a good deal of harm. I also believe that justice is not of this world and that the strongest or rather the most economical system is the one that will prevail. A man may wear himself out working and yet live in utter poverty: this is a revolting thing, but that won't be why it ceases to exist. It will probably disappear because man is a sort of machine and there is some advantage, from an economical point of view, in making any machine function at its normal speed, without forcing it.

You have a surprising view of selfishness: when I was twenty, something terrible happened to me, I lost a childhood friend in dreadful circumstances—I don't have the courage to tell you about it. . . . Afterwards I lived day and night with one obsession, there was a certain pleasure in torturing myself. Then, in good faith, I vowed that I would live like a priest, I promised myself I would no longer take any interest in things and that I would no longer think about myself or mankind. I have often asked myself, since then, if this renunciation of life wasn't simply a way of allowing myself to forget.

Is correspondence uncensored in your country? I very much doubt it, and I think it would be better, in future, not to turn our letters into dissertations which could be wrongly interpreted, even though they are purely philosophical, and could make trouble for you.

You can write to me, if you want to, at 13 rue des Sablons.

Your devoted friend.

His previous letter had gone unanswered. Remarking on it with surprise, he added in a postscript that it hadn't contained "anything special." "I asked you if you wanted to rent an apartment with me; it's in the rue Mouffetard and the windows look out on some gardens; it can be divided into two independent parts." This was nothing special?

But these lines do show that he understood how highly Marie prized and always would prize her independence, and also how little concern she had for conventions.

On September 17, he was reassured. "At last you are going

61

to come back to Paris and that gives me great pleasure. I very much want us at least to become inseparable friends. Don't you agree?"

And he slipped in another remark: "If you were French, it would be easy for you to teach in a *lycée* or *école normale* for girls. Would you like that sort of profession?" And if she married a Frenchman she would become French.

This time, Pierre signed the letter "Your very devoted friend," and added as a postscript: "I showed my brother your photograph. Was that wrong? He thinks you're very nice looking. He added: 'She seems very determined and *even stubborn*.'"

And how stubborn she was!

Pierre may have thought the idea of sharing an apartment was a good one, but Marie was wary of going ahead with it. She returned knowing that a room would be available to her in the apartment that Bronia had rented in the rue de Châteaudun for her consulting rooms. Having no rent to pay, and being frugal, as always, she could wallow in her work at the laboratory at the Sorbonne, where she was grappling with experimental physics. Pierre's affairs were not advancing.

Then the "gentle mule," as his father called him, told her he would follow her to Poland, if that was what was keeping her from marrying him. He launched an offensive in Bronia's direction, asking her to intercede with her sister. He persuaded Marie to meet his parents.

"The poor foreigner," as she called herself, who had been so hurt by Casimir Zorawski's parents, was not inclined to repeat the ordeal. Certainly Pierre was thirty-six years old and free; but he was also deeply attached to his parents—he had once said to her, "They're remarkable." As it happened, they were immediately affectionate toward this exotic young woman their son was so obviously in love with.

France had its kindly face, which the Curies in some sense represented, and Marie was very comfortable with it. She was to discover later that it had another, and less kindly, face.

Dr. Curie still bore the scar left by the bullet that had entered his jaw when he had been part of the crowd of rioters in 1848. More than twenty years later, he had been an ambulance driver during the Commune, and he and his two young boys had hunted for the wounded on the barricades. He would have liked to devote himself to research, but he had had to earn a living. For some years he had been practicing in Sceaux, and there, in a cozy house surrounded by greenery, he and his wife lived a simple life in the mahogany and velvet setting typical of a bourgeois interior. Here books abounded, roses were brought in from the garden where neighbors came to play *boules* or chess on Sundays. The cooking was good, the conversations lively.

A hot-headed Republican, the doctor would become indignant, then furious, then violent, trying to interest Pierre in the debates that were shaking the heart of the political world—the Parliament. At that time everyone was talking about the violent quarrel that had broken out in the Chamber between a Socialist deputy, Jaurès, and a government minister, Louis Barthou. The quarrel had been followed by a duel.

An artillery captain accused of being a spy for Germany had been condemned to prison and exiled for life. He had been spared the death sentence because the Constitution of 1848 had eliminated capital punishment for political crimes. Strangely, his trial had been held behind closed doors. In the Chamber, Jaurès had become indignant: this was caste justice, class justice, he said. They should have applied Article 76 of the military code of justice so that the felon would be excuted. But the government was protecting its traitors!

The newspapers were full of the insults exchanged by the minister and the deputy and the pistol duel that followed. In saving the captain—whose name, incidentally, was Dreyfus— "the enormous pressure of the Jews was far from ineffective," Jaurès declared to reporters afterwards.

This sort of thing was not likely to interest Pierre. When, three years later, a court-martial acquitted the real criminal, Commandant Esterhazy, and Charles Péguy, a former student who had converted to socialism, circulated a petition in protest, Pierre Curie certainly signed it. That was before Jaurès became pro-Dreyfus himself. But the political jousting his

63

father loved only made Pierre retreat into his daydreams: "I don't know how to get angry," he said.

The meeting between the young, intellectual Polish woman and the old French Republican, the consequences of which would play such a decisive role in Marie's career, was a success. The two were delighted with each other.

Marie and the doctor were both present in the small lecture room of the Sorbonne the day Pierre defended his doctoral thesis on magnetism.[2] Listening to him argue with the three professors—Bouty, Lippmann, and Hautefeuille—who were conducting the oral examination of the future doctor of science, Marie was deeply impressed. "The little room," she wrote, "held some very lofty thinking that day, and I was filled with the sense of it."

But lofty thinking was not well paid. At the age of thirty-six, Pierre Curie was earning thirty-six hundred francs a year at the Ecole de Physique. According to figures made public at the time, the annual incomes of Paris households were analyzed as follows:

Poor	(77%):	1 070 F
Comfortable	(16.2%):	5 340 F
Rich	(5.3%):	15 500 F
Multimillionaire	(0.1%):	385 000 F

With an annual salary of thirty-six hundred francs, what Pierre was proposing to Marie was not a very well-to-do life.[3] The small sums he received as rights for the use of the re-

---

[2] Among other things, Pierre Curie discovered that the coefficient of magnetization varied inversely with temperature. This was known as the "Curie Law." His work with magnetism opened an area of exploration for French science that would end in the awarding of the Nobel Prize to Louis Néel in 1970 for his research on antiferromagnetism.

[3] Today this would be equivalent to 36,000 francs or about $4,600.

search instruments he had invented—a scale that had been bought by a chemical products company, a lens bought by an optical company—did not even bring in enough to pay for the equipment he needed. And so, in January 1895, he accepted a position as consultant to that same optical company, which gave him a monthly income of one hundred francs.

But it certainly wasn't the prospect of living modestly that made Marie leave him in doubt as to her intentions right up to the end of the academic year. Nor was it the unfortunate Lamotte. (He did not give up hope, nor was she finally rid of him, until the day she gave him what, in his last letter, he called the "coup de grâce"—she told him she was getting married.) The only rival Pierre had ever accepted was the one he had just beaten, and that was Poland.

"When you receive this letter," Marie wrote to a girlfriend in Warsaw, "your Marya will have changed her name. I'm going to marry the man I told you about last year in Warsaw. It is very painful to me to remain in Paris forever, but what can I do? Fate has caused us to be deeply attached to each other, so that we can't bear the idea of separating."

And this was how it happened that in July 1895, Marie began secretly studying a new kind of subject with Bronia. How did one make a roast chicken? French fried potatoes? How did one go about feeding a husband? With the little seamstress Bronia had unearthed, she designed the wedding dress that was to be a gift from Casimir's mother, Mme Dluska. What she wanted was something "sober and very practical so that I can wear it afterwards when I go to the laboratory."

M. Sklodowski and Hela came from Warsaw for the ceremony, if such could be called the brief stop at the Sceaux town hall where Pierre Curie and Marie Sklodowska were pronounced man and wife. A marriage without wedding rings or a benediction.

Pierre's mother must have ordered a leg of lamb to celebrate her son's wedding and receive the Polish family in an appropriate way, but we know nothing about it. What we do know is that a cousin had the good idea of sending a check as a present, that this check was exchanged for two bicycles, and that "the little queen," a brand new invention that had become the darling of France, was the vehicle on which Pierre Curie and his new wife—wearing a hat pinned to her blond chignon—went off on their honeymoon.

GENIUS

seven

Traveling by bicycle, they were free to do as they liked. There were no rigid schedules to keep to, no planned itineraries. This was an adventure, a wandering in search of new discoveries, just the sort of thing Pierre liked.

Never would two cyclists ride, within the space of a few years, along so many little roads smelling of hazelnuts, past so many acres of heath, through so many valleys and over so many hills, as these two.

In September 1895, they were exploring the forest near Chantilly. Bronia and Casimir had rented a large house in the area and M. Sklodowski, Hela, Mme Dluska, Pierre, Marie, and Lou, Bronia's little girl, had gathered here for the holidays. Warsaw had been re-created in Chantilly. Pierre was very happy here, and out of love for his wife he started learning Polish. Marie relaxed, and Bronia ran things.

Sometimes Dr. Curie came to lunch with his wife. He liked to initiate his new friends into the subtleties of French politics, two of whose basic principles at the time were active colonialism and alliance with Russia. Colonialism. If only it would bring with it education and medical care for the indigenous population. The alliance with Russia was more perplexing to the Sklodowskis.

Ten years later, during the 1905 uprising, Marie would send money through her brother-in-law to the Russian revolutionaries.

In August 1914, on the eve of the Battle of the Marne, she was one of the members of the Polish colony summoned to the Russian Embassy in the rue de Grenelle to try to dissuade them from supporting Marshal Pilsudski's legion. This Polish legion had joined up with German troops in the hope of

69

liberating Poland, and was threatening the flanks of Russia, whose offensive was impatiently awaited by the French general staff.

But in September 1895, no one in the house at Chantilly was thinking of war. There was good news: at last Pierre would be promoted to the status of professor. This was indirectly thanks to Lord Kelvin. The old British master had been the first to see the possible applications of piezoelectricity. He had come from London to talk about this with the young French physicist, had paid tribute to him in a science journal, and had obviously thought so highly of him that a professor in the Collège de France, Mascart, was impressed and intervened with the director of the Ecole so that at last he would be given a teaching position. It must be said, in fact, that at every stage in the careers of Pierre and Marie Curie, official recognition of their true value always came by way of foreign countries.

With a salary of six thousand francs a year, they were more comfortable. Marie went to work on her plan. She would prepare for the competitive examination that would qualify her to teach in a *lycée* the following year, and at the same time she would look for paid research work, fix up the little apartment they had rented near the school in the rue de la Glacière, and organize her life so that she wouldn't waste either time or energy. There would be no furniture to wax, no picture frames or knickknacks to dust, no tablecloths to wash. She always kept her sense of priorities. This interior, whose decor she had reduced to what was strictly necessary, did not look like a typical Warsaw home or a typical French one.

Pierre didn't mind. He was happy just to see trees from his window, to have flowers on the deal table where they worked across from each other, to have a library for his books, and a bed.

"Little by little I am arranging my apartment," Marie wrote to her brother in November 1895, "but I intend to keep it in a style that won't cause me any trouble and won't require any maintenance because I have very little help. A woman comes in for an hour a day to do the dishes and the heavy work. I do the cooking and the light housework myself." She did her marketing before she went to work in the morning. Marie's attitude toward cooking was consistent with her character. Pierre was hardly aware of what he ate. But as soon as she undertook anything, she had to do it well. She would always pride herself on knowing as well as anyone else how to light a wood fire or take care of a stove. She bought a cookbook called *Bourgeois Cooking*, and its margins are full of her annotations.

We don't know if she also had the talent for cooking that the finest cooks have. Clearly, however, she made it a point of honor and attacked it with determination. She was thrifty in this as in everything, and her thrift was in keeping with the times. For in those days, of course, credit was unknown, and if you were reduced to borrowing you appealed to a family member or a friend. You saved as much as possible, when you had very little, for fear of illness, or, when you had plenty, because it was considered better practice, in the great bourgeois families, to live on the income from your income than to chip away at your patrimony.

However unusual Pierre Curie was in consistently showing as much respect for his wife's work as for his own, he had probably never held a broom in his hands. One might have thought that he would occasionally go out for bread when she had forgotten to buy any, or that he would make the bed now and then. But no. For one thing, Marie never forgot anything. And for another, he didn't know how to make a bed because he had never been in the army: like all young men who went into teaching, he had been exempted from military service. But in the evening, on their way home, they would go together to the *crémier*, the baker, the grocer.

They saw no one apart from the Dluskis and Pierre's parents, whom they visited regularly, but they were perfectly happy. In the evenings, by the light of the kerosene lamp, Pierre prepared his courses and Marie helped him plan them. At first he had divided the lessons between crystallography

71

and electricity; then, "recognizing more and more the usefulness of a serious theoretical course in electricity for future engineers," as Marie told it, "he devoted himself entirely to this subject and succeeded in developing a course of study (in 120 lessons) that was the most complete and the most modern in Paris at that time." His clarity, his precision, his infectious curiosity, remained a vivid memory for his students.

Pierre and Marie spent their days at the Ecole. The director, Schützenberger, known as Papa Schütz, did not resent Pierre for having refused to allow himself to be proposed as a candidate for decoration by the Ministry of Education ("I am quite determined never to accept any decoration of any sort," he had said), and he had authorized Marie to work in the laboratory of the Ecole on condition that she would assume the cost of the work she wanted to do.

Her first venture was in the field of magnetism, where Pierre was already an authority and could therefore mark out a course for her based on his long theoretical and practical experience.

She could obtain the metal samples she needed free from metallurgy companies. An eminent professor in the Ecole des Mines, Henri Le Châtelier, was prepared to help her in her analyses. Marie was therefore firmly established.

Her paper on the variations in the magnetic properties of certain hardened steels was not to be truly innovative. But the completeness, the perspicacity, the sureness of her work, proved one thing—that a woman could have the power of concentration necessary for performing meticulous laboratory work and could operate in what was a male preserve par excellence, the field of scientific research. Even if she, and Pierre too, had never had any doubts about this, at least where she was concerned, it was still a "first." None of the very few female physicists working in laboratories at that time were at such a high level.

At the same time that she was carrying out this study, Marie had been preparing for the competitive examination. Of course she passed, with the highest marks.

Once again the Curies were off on their bicycles, this time to Auvergne. And by the beginning of 1897, Marie was pregnant. She had no regrets, but she was not feeling very well.

"I'm expecting a child, and this expectation has a cruel way of manifesting itself," she wrote to a friend in Warsaw. She was dizzy, constantly tired. "I'm becoming very weak, I feel incapable of work and in a bad spiritual state."

She dragged herself along until July, "suffering the whole time," affected by the condition of her mother-in-law, who had breast cancer, and then she allowed Bronia and the men to decide for her—her father would come from Warsaw and take her on a holiday to a hotel in Brittany, while Pierre finished his courses in Paris. This was their first separation in two years. Because of it, we have some of the letters they wrote each other—and they rarely wrote, since they were hardly ever apart.

These letters, which started with "My dear little child I love so much," "My little girl so dear, so sweet, whom I love so much," "My dearest little child," "My dear husband," allow us to catch something of the tone of their relationship at this point in their lives, when Marie was still the young wife of a thirty-nine-year-old man with a solid reputation in the only field she admired, and for whom she was at once a love object and an intellectual collaborator.

"My little girl, so dear, so sweet, whom I love so much," wrote Pierre, "I received your letter today and I'm very happy. Here there is nothing new to report except that I miss you very much—my soul has run off with you."

Sometimes he wrote to her in Polish, a language which he had resolutely learned, as though henceforth no part of Marie should be strange to him. He sent her some baby shirts by parcel post, along with some technical information provided by a certain Madame P., who had knitted them: "The small size is good for knitted shirts that can stretch, but the cotton ones have to be slightly larger. You should have both sizes of shirts."

He writes again: "I think of my darling who fills my life, and I would like to have new mental powers. It seems to me that if I concentrate my mind exclusively on you, as I have just done, I ought to be able to see you, to follow what you are doing, and also to make you feel that I belong to you completely at this moment—but I can't manage to get a picture."

Strangely enough, though Pierre was a scientist, he believed in parapsychic phenomena, in turning tables, in mysteries which he would have tried to explain if he had had the time.

As for Marie, she was apparently regressing completely now, at the end of her pregnancy: "My dear husband," she wrote him in Polish, "the weather is beautiful, the sun is shining, it is hot. I am very sad without you, come quickly, I wait for you from morning to night and I don't see you coming. I am well, I work as much as I can but Poincaré's book is harder than I thought. I have to talk to you about it and we have to look at it again together and see what has given me so much trouble."

It seems indiscreet to read and publish these letters, which are still warm with intimate tenderness. But Pierre and Marie are only dust in the Sceaux cemetery now, where their coffins lie one on top of the other, the way Marie planned it. And it is good to see that they were bound together by more than just the common interest of their work.

The letters Marie later wrote in such great numbers to another man she loved, in a faultless French that was nevertheless not so free as her style when she wrote in Polish, would one day do her such serious, dramatic, far-reaching harm, that when the time comes it will be impossible to say nothing, here, about their contents.

At the beginning of August, Pierre wrote to her: "Mama is so sad when I speak of leaving that I still haven't had the courage to fix on a day." But finally he came. Soon Marie felt better, and, eight months pregnant, coolly mounted a bicycle to go with Pierre from Port-Blanc to Brest. The result could have been foreseen—Marie had to be taken back to Paris by train.

Where was Bronia? On holiday somewhere, too far away to get there in time. Dr. Curie delivered Marie of a girl she called Irène. A few days later, Pierre's mother died.

On the day of her confinement, September 12, 1897, Marie wrote down in her account book under the heading "Unusual Expenses," Champagne: 3 F. Telegrams: 1.10F. Under the heading "Illness," Pharmacy and sick nurse: 17.50 F. "Total expenses for September: 430.40F." This was underlined twice. Pierre earned 500 francs a month.

Did she want this child, or do we have to interpret this constantly painful pregnancy and her exploits on her bicycle as signs of rejection? On the other hand, physical problems do exist. And we do know that six years later she ardently wanted her second child. Nowadays, she would no doubt have planned the birth of the first one. But there it—or rather she— was. Marie breast-fed "her little queen," tended her, took her for walks, got up in the night when she cried, worried when she lost weight, wrote to her father that she was afraid she would be forced to hire a wet-nurse "in spite of the sorrow it causes me and in spite of the expense—I wouldn't for anything in the world want to hurt my child's development."

The idea of interrupting her work for any length of time because she had a child did not, however, occur to her or to Pierre. Nor to anyone else who knew them—the Dluskis, Dr. Curie, the scientists they came into contact with in their work. The obstacles Marie had to overcome were material ones. She soon needed a nurse with good milk for the baby and more substantial help with her domestic duties, which the presence of a child had increased. She was burdened with household expenses and complications.

She was not recovering her strength. On the contrary, she grew thin and pale, she did not look well. Bronia became worried, Pierre's father insisted on a visit to the family doctor who, like Casimir, was afraid there might be a tubercular

lesion on her left lung and recommended a stay in a sanatorium. It was hard not to think of Mme Sklodowska. And
tuberculosis was ravaging Europe at that time, the cause of
one out of every seven deaths.

Marie listened politely and refused to take any further
interest in the matter. Her cure for all ills was to work. Besides, it wasn't clear that her lung was really diseased. For
women who tend to be depressed anyway, the period after
childbirth can be difficult. But radiography, which could have
confirmed or denied the presence of a dangerous lesion, didn't
yet exist. Or rather, it had just come into being and wasn't yet
operational.

There had been a real uproar, a sensation, when, at the
beginning of the preceding year, in January 1896, a German
physicist presented the results of an observation to a conference: he had photographed the hand of an anatomist, with
the man's permission, and then showed the proof of the photograph to the people in the room—the bones of the hand
were clearly visible. Wilhelm Roentgen had just given the
first demonstration of a phenomenon which was caused by an
unknown factor—whence the name he gave to the mysterious
rays he had discovered by chance during an experiment:
X rays.

Actually, nothing is discovered by chance.

Chance must have caused a number of apples to fall on a
number of heads before Newton discovered gravitational
force and thought of linking all the objects in the material
universe by one single mechanism. And he was no doubt not
the first to wonder why, if objects fall to the ground, the moon
does not.

By chance, we witness a phenomenon. Every phenomenon
has a cause. Even children know this. They ask us, "Why?"
They ask, "Do those little boats moving on the water have
legs, Mama?" By chance we witness an unexplained phenomenon that has been caused by a combination of circumstances. But it is the conjunction of knowledge, curiosity,
intuition, and—in the greatest discoveries—intellectual

76

boldness that transforms the phenomenon into an object of observation, considers the observation itself an effect of the phenomenon, and seeks the cause of this effect. At least when one has a scientific mind.

An anecdote told about Marie Curie during a trip to the United States in the early twenties shows this sort of scientific mind in action. One day everyone was waiting for her in the dining room. She didn't come and a girl was sent to get her. The girl found her in her cabin standing motionless in front of the closet. The closet light was on, and the well-trained Marie didn't want to leave the cabin without turning off the light. But there was no sign of a light switch. She was late because she was looking in vain for the source of the light so that she could turn it off. "The light goes off when the closet door closes," the little girl said.

This was a nice explanation, but Marie had to verify it before she would accept it. How could she do that? As the girl lost hope of convincing her, Marie examined every part of the closet. At last the girl had an idea: "Get into the closet," she said. "I'll shut the door and you can see whether or not the light goes off."

Madame Curie stepped into the closet, came out satisfied, and went off to dinner. The unknown phenomenon, the awakened curiosity, the search for the cause—it was all there.

Roentgen had darkened a certain room, in order to make sure the black cardboard he had put around a cathode tube was perfectly opaque, and he had noticed a gleam of light. The box was perfectly opaque. Then where was this light coming from? From a small plate nearby coated with a barium-based chemical compound, as he found when he lit a match. He disconnected the tube—no more light. Connected it again—light. And yet no light was leaking from the tube.

All that remained was to verify which subtances the unknown ray could pass through, to discover that it passed through the most surprising substances, including human flesh; to find out exactly what its properties were; and to find out what caused these properties.

77

A number of European scientists set to work to find the answers, while the public reacted with both enthusiasm and amazement at this spectacular phenomenon, this violation of the human body, which was for once—a rare event in the field of science—easily perceived, if not easily understood.

No one could know what significance Roentgen's ray was going to have, or that one day not so far in the future the whole edifice of physics and even of philosophy would be shaken by it. But even if the unimaginable had been imagined, this would never have held back the progress of research for very long.

The whole scientific world of Europe had become involved. During this period the British physicist Thompson wrote to a friend: "The world seems to be in the grips of a two-fold delirium—the bicycle and X rays. As for the latter, I confess I am already seriously taken with the game." A young New Zealander, Ernest Rutherford, who would later attract a lot of attention, also set off down the same road.

In laboratories everywhere, people examined the problem, made calculations, observed reactions, interpreted signs, published articles and books, added their contribution to the theory of the phenomenon, attempting to be the first to work it out.

As it happened, Marie was looking for a subject for a thesis and she was watching the movement closely. The origin and the nature of X rays was still far from being explained. But she didn't join the movement, because the gods had mapped out another route for her.

eight

Fifty years ago, the events that took place over the next four years would have been summarized as follows: "Pierre and Marie Curie worked together in a wretched laboratory and yet they were happy because they loved each other, and they discovered radium. Thanks to this discovery, made by Pierre Curie with the help of his wife, there is now a cure for cancer." The history of science has another way of looking at that story. And, on another level, so does the author of this book.

One day in February 1896, a French physicist named Henri Becquerel, who specialized in fluorescence, decided to conduct an experiment. Fluorescence is the emission of light rays by certain bodies after they have been exposed to light. Becquerel wanted to find out if this phenomenon was accompanied by the production of the new rays discoverd by Roentgen. It was true that when an electrical charge was passed through the tube, the sides of the X-ray tube became fluorescent. He wrapped some photographic plates in black cloth, covered them with a sheet of aluminum, and placed on this sheet crystals of uranyl sulfate and of potassium which had been previously exposed to the sun.

After developing them, he saw that the plates were cloudy; there had therefore been an emission of a penetrating radiation.

On Thursday, February 26, Becquerel prepared a new experiment. But because the sun wasn't shining, he put the wrapped plates, the sheet of aluminum, and the crystals away in a drawer. On Friday and Saturday, the sky was still overcast. We don't know why Becquerel opened his drawer on Sunday, took out the photographic plates, and developed them. Where the cristals had lain, the plates had retained an image, they were muddy.

The next day, Monday, at the weekly meeting of the academy, Becquerel told his colleagues about his discovery: uranium salts emitted rays which, like X rays, could pass through matter. They listened politely and went on to the order of the day.[1]

Which one, Marie or Pierre, drew the other's attention to Becquerel's observation, which he subsequently discussed in several articles? It doesn't matter.

No other woman in the world had ever decided to become a doctor of science. Marie knew that in order to establish relations of equality with men she would have to hold the same titles they did, and she would have to earn them all on her own. A doctoral thesis defended by a woman would need an original and substantial contribution derived from her research work. She thought the phenomenon discovered by Becquerel might provide her with a fertile field, one that had barely been explored, and Pierre agreed with her. This phenomenon was none other than radioactivity, as she was soon to name it.

Today, when you go to look at Marie Curie's laboratory notebooks, you must first sign a form releasing the Bibliotèque Nationale from responsibility for any "possible risks of radioactivity." The risk involved in reading these notebooks is slight. But they are radioactive and will be, if not forever, at least for thousands of years.[2] Marie was thirty when she began exposing herself to radioactivity, without knowing that the ray detected by Becquerel was the manifestation of then unsuspected forces concentrated in the very heart of the

---

[1] According to Pierre Auger, Roentgen's discovery was "inevitable" at the moment it was made because of the number of physicists who were working with Crookes tubes at that time, but Becquerel's was not, and half a century could have gone by before it was made.

[2] The radioactivity of radium decreases by only half over a period of thirteen centuries.

atom, forces that were at the origin of what we now call atomic energy.

On the practical side, things were satisfactory. The Curies had moved to the boulevard Kellermann, into a small house surrounded by a garden. The interior was done in "Marie style," with the addition of a sideboard and a few armchairs brought from Sceaux when the doctor, who had stopped practicing when his wife died, came to live with them. Now Marie had not only a flexible schedule; she also had an easy mind. When she was gone, she didn't worry about Irène—the doctor was not only watching out for his granddaughter but also introducing her to the wonders of life. A servant did the heaviest of the domestic work, which no machine was yet capable of performing. Marie took care of Irène in the morning, feeding her and dressing her, but she no longer had to return at noon to give her lunch, and she could go out in the evening after bathing her and putting her to bed. The good, intelligent, lively old man, who continued to inform himself about all sorts of things, had saved her from the choice women are faced with: sacrifice either themselves or someone else.

In order to work, Marie needed a laboratory. Papa Schütz, another good and intelligent man, unearthed for her, on the ground floor of the Ecole, a storeroom that was also used as an engine room. Professor Curie's wife, a proper young lady, was rather frail now; her health was delicate, and she was clearly in danger of suffering from the dampness of the place. But she said no, if the dampness caused any problems it would be because of the experiments she was planning, but she would take it anyway, and was grateful to Monsieur le Directeur. She said this briefly, for she talked very little, and only to say very precisely what had to be said.

She also needed equipment, and she planned her research around what she could get free: the piezoelectric quartz electrometer invented by Pierre, which he had kept in the laboratory of the Ecole. She also needed a sample of uranium, and with the electrometer she began to measure the quantities of

81

electricity formed in the air by the rays of uranium—electrical charges that Becquerel had demonstrated.

Marie's hands were very skillful, and over three years she had acquired a certain practical experience. Meticulously, following an orderly intellectual plan—which was to become her basic method of work—she made her measurements. Then she collected from the various professors and engineers she ran into in the Ecole other metal samples, other bits of minerals, in order to see if substances other than uranium would cause the air to conduct electricity. She very quickly found that this was the case with thorium. She concluded from this that thorium emitted a ray similar to the one detected by Becquerel.

This intriguing property had to be given a name. She baptized it radioactivity. She returned to her electrometer to measure the intensity of the current created by uranium compounds and thorium compounds. She observed that whether they were in powder form or in pieces, whether dry or wet, whether or not they contained foreign elements, the activity of the compounds depended only on their uranium content.

Marie had just confirmed indisputably what Becquerel had guessed: radioactivity was inseparable from the atoms of certain special elements like uranium and thorium, and resulted from a phenomenon occurring within the atom itself. It was on the basis of this discovery that the mysteries of the structure of the atom would be explained in the course of the twentieth century.

Marie did not immediately suspect the consequences of her observation, which she made several weeks after beginning her work. She measured other minerals, including pitchblende and chalcocite. A physicist in the Ecole, Eugène Demarçay, had provided her with samples. These were radioactive, but their activity seemed abnormal to Marie: it was much stronger than one would have thought, given their uranium or thorium content. Marie then started from the beginning again with a series of experiments to make sure she had not made a mistake. She was seeking an explanation for the latest surprising phenomenon she had observed.

And she suggested a bold hypothesis: that the minerals with uranium content that she had examined had to contain another substance, one much more radioactive than uranium or thorium, and that this substance had to be a new element ("new" meaning one that was not present in the table of chemical elements drawn up by Mendeleev, in which he had left some of the boxes empty for future researchers, each unknown element theoretically corresponding to an unknown metal).

At the end of each day's work, Marie naturally told Pierre how her research was progressing, but he did not take part in it. At the beginning of 1898, the chemistry-physics chair at the Sorbonne became vacant; he applied for the position, and he was rejected. "How can you expect to win," wrote Professor Friedel, who had supported him, "against a *normalien* and against the prejudices of the mathematicians?"

In the time he had left after he had fulfilled his duties at the Ecole de Physique, he worked—still in a corridor—on the crystals that continued to fascinate him.

Indifferent, as we have seen, to the joys and sorrows of competition, and intellectually rigorous, Pierre advised Marie not to publish a memorandum on the results of her observations. He didn't see that there was any urgency. It was never good to be hasty, and why do it? For the pointless satisfaction of being first?

Marie loved her husband for this too, because in all situations his attitude was that of "a superior man, one who has reached the highest degree of civilization." But this was *her* work, this was *her* hypothesis. She decided to write a brief note to the Académie des Sciences which would then be printed, according to custom, within the ten days following her presentation, and circulated in scientific circles. This note had to be presented by a member of the academy. Her former professor, Gabriel Lippmann, presented it in the name of Mme Sklodowska-Curie on April 12, 1898.

She had been right to present it quickly. Unfortunately, someone else had been even quicker. Two months earlier, in Berlin, a German had published his observation that thorium, like uranium, also emitted rays. But Marie's memorandum contained something more; this was a sentence in which, noting that pitchblende and chalcocite had higher radioactivity than uranium, she added, with the prudence demanded by the scientific code when a hypothesis hasn't yet been verified: "This is a remarkable fact and leads one to believe that these minerals may contain an element that is much more active than uranium."

Even though they were accustomed to taking this prudence into account and reading beyond it, the physicists remained indifferent. Perhaps it would be too easy to say that they would have been more eager to go and see this for themselves if the memorandum had been presented in the name of a man.

The fact is that afterwards, Marie had the patience to take all the time she needed. Infinitely more time than she had ever imagined spending on the verification of this bold hypothesis of hers—a hypothesis that was all the more surprising considering the fact that she was only thirty years old and that six years before she hadn't even known enough to start her second year of study for her bachelor's degree.

nine

How DID she live in the year 1898? Under the date of February 26, in her first little black laboratory notebook, we read:

> Broke and adjusted the apparatus.
> [a number, then:] Waiting a little.
> [another number, then:] Waiting a little.
> Shake off the excess powder.
> Nothing.

During the same period, at the top of a page: "Temperature in the cylinder: 6.25° C!!!!!!" The six exclamation marks indicate that this was also the temperature of the room she was working in.

The same year, she wrote in her cookbook: "I took eight pounds of fruit and the same weight of granulated sugar. After boiling ten minutes, I strained the mixture through a rather fine strainer. I obtained fourteen pots of very good nontransparent jelly that set perfectly." She had made jam for the winter.

The same year, on August 15, she wrote in a gray notebook: "Irène cut her seventh tooth, bottom left. . . . For three days now, we have been taking her to bathe in the river. . . .

"She stands for half a minute by herself. She screams, but today (her fourth bath) she stopped screaming and played, slapping the water." They were on vacation in Auvergne.

In a green notebook labeled "M. Curie, Uranium, 1898," she wrote:

> "Artificial chalcocite
> "Layer of very wet Im, 1.0 . . . etc."

Seven teeth, four baths, eight pounds, one half minute, one half millimeter, fourteen pots, eight pounds.

And in her account book:

One pair of large socks for Pierre for bicycling, 5.50 F.
Two bicycle tires, 31 F.
Laundry, 4.50 F.

She made a note of everything, but never wrote, "It is cold, Irène has a fever, I'm tired."

Cold could be measured, fever too. Emotional states could not be expressed in numbers, nor could weariness. If she wanted to note that she was tired, she would write: "I climbed twenty-two steps and I had to rest." She didn't describe things, she observed them and noted them down scientifically. She had always been afraid of her excessive sensitivity, and she would not betray it in writing until much later, when it would be sharpened by grief.

What could be more exciting than the discovery of a new element? It was so exciting, in fact, that Pierre interrupted his own work to help his wife. Temporarily, he thought.

On April 14, 1898, they were weighing a sample of pitchblende together. The composition of this mineral was known through chemical analysis. They expected to find one percent of new radioelements, of new substances, in it.

Until then, the Curies would sometimes go out in the evening to the theater or to a concert or to dinner with Bronia and Casimir. The two sisters would sit together on Sundays sewing dresses for their little girls—Marie always made Irène's clothes herself. But amnesty had been declared in Russian Poland and the Dluskis would at last be able to go home. This was a terrible wrench for Marie; she was extremely lonely.

She wrote to her sister:

You can't imagine the hole you have left here. When I lost you two I lost everything I care about in Paris besides my husband and my child. Now I feel as though Paris doesn't exist outside of our house and the school where we work.

Ask Mother Dluska if the green plant you left here should be watered and how many times a day. Does it need a lot of warmth and sunlight?

Irène is turning into a big kid. She is very difficult to feed, and except for tapioca pudding she will eat almost nothing regularly, not even eggs. Write me what sorts of foods children of that age should be eating."

In the laboratory, her black notebook was filled with notes and numbers. Here and there, as we look through it, the orderliness of a page is disrupted by Pierre's quick handwriting. He scribbles, draws attention to an observation with several words written at a slant: one can't help noticing the intermingling of these two handwritings.

Their work method consisted of separating the various components of pitchblende, then measuring the radioactivity of each of these components. These were long, meticulous operations, each stage of which was recorded in the black notebook. In it one can follow the procedures and observations almost day by day.

And so we can picture them, silent, absorbed, bent over Pierre's long-fingered, skillful hands, Marie's delicate, small hands, the hours passing while they don't even dream of lifting their heads or eating anything, then pausing to consider a result, conferring, beginning again, either disappointed or elated, and then trembling with excitement on June 13 when Marie, measuring the radioactivity of a precipitate, finds that it is "150 times more active than uranium," as she recorded it in the black notebook with her sharp pencil.

The same day, as they were heating some lead sulfide to 300° C. in a tube that eventually shattered, Pierre noted that a deposit of black powder was forming in the tube. Together they measured the radioactivity of this powder and found that it was 330 times greater than that of uranium.

87

In spite of this, on Sunday they stopped work. Could they sleep a little longer in the morning? No. Irène would wake them up. She was a difficult child. Even though Marie took perfect care of her, was attentive, was a good mother, as they say; and even though Pierre adored his little girl and spoke to her in a loving voice, Irène must have sensed that in the laboratory there was another offspring, something that was gestating and that needed them, just the two of them, together and alone in the world.

After each separation, after each purification, they obtained a substance that was more and more active. And on July 18, 1898, they were at last sure enough of themselves to announce the discovery of a new element, a new metal.

Poland never has any luck. Polonium, the element named after it, is too active and has too short a life to be extracted on an industrial scale. Its fame was to be eclipsed by its brother, radium. But one characteristic of polonium was to give it its own kind of triumph thirty-four years later.

Whereas radium emits several rays, polonium emits only one, the high-energy alpha ray. In 1932, using a source of polonium, James Chadwick discovered the neutron, one of the three elementary particles of the atom that he had been trying to find for ten years. He had been inspired by reading the results of an experiment performed by Irène Curie and her husband Frédéric Joliot in Marie's laboratory, using a source of polonium.

Why were the Curies so tired when they and Irène, who was cutting her seventh tooth, arrived in Auroux, where they had rented a house for the summer? It was an effort for them to swim in the river and ride their bicycles. And the tips of Marie's fingers were cracked and painful. Neither of them guessed that they were beginning to suffer from being exposed to the radioactive substances they had been handling.

The following December, the word "radium" appeared for the first time on an undated page of the black notebook that bore Pierre's handwriting. It appeared in the middle of the page and was preceded by a question mark:

> therefore radium sulfate
> more soluble in H_2SO_4
> than barium sulfate.

Very few people were allowed into the Curies' laboratory. One of them was Eugène Demarçay, who was raptly following the Curies' progress. He took a sample of the substance that Pierre and Marie had obtained to his laboratory, where he had a spectroscope. And there he succeeded in photographing a spectral ray. As the Curies provided him with purer and purer samples of the new substance, the ray he photographed was more and more intense.[1]

On December 26, 1898, the Académie des Sciences heard a memorandum, again presented by Lippmann, which stated that "The various reasons we have just enumerated lead us to believe that the new radioactive substance contains a new element which we propose to call radium." The note was signed by three people—Pierre Curie, Marie Curie, and G. Bémont.

We know nothing about Georges Bémont's part in the discovery of radium except that as head of works at the Ecole, he was the chemist on the team. He had a red beard and his nickname was Bichro. His handwriting appears several times in the black notebook during May 1898. No doubt he was a very modest man.

What remained was to prove that the new element existed. "I would like it to have a beautiful color," Pierre said.

Pure radium salts are colorless. But their radiation gives a bluish-mauve tint to the glass tubes that contain them. In sufficient quantity, their radiation produces a visible glow in the dark. When this glow began to radiate through the darkness of the laboratory, Pierre was happy.

---

[1]Every element emits a series of characteristic rays. They constitute its "signature."

ten

"It was like a stable or a root cellar, and if I hadn't seen the work table with its chemical equipment, I would have thought this was a practical joke." This was how a German chemist interested in the Curies' work described the place where radium was isolated and its atomic weight calculated, four years after Marie announced her hypothesis of its existence.

According to Jean Perrin, "Pierre Curie, who was perhaps more of a physicist, was especially interested in the properties of radiation itself. He was less convinced of the necessity of making the effort to isolate the new substance and obtain 'a flask' of it, as chemists say. This effort was certainly a result of Mme Curie's stubborn and persistent desire to do it. And today it is no exaggeration to say that this was the cornerstone on which the entire edifice of radioactivity rests."

The fact that Jean Perrin felt he had to emphasize this so firmly shows how difficult it was to dispel the image of Marie as "the great man's collaborator." And this image may persist even today.

Nothing, however, was further from the truth, not only as regards the part Marie actually played in the work they did together, but also as regards their relationship. Even at the beginning of their marriage, when she hadn't yet had much practice performing experiments, Pierre never said to Marie anything like what Sartre said to Simone de Beauvoir—"I will take you in hand"—and Marie never felt this was his attitude toward her.

Both their characters contributed to this rare combination—a man and a woman who didn't dominate each other. It was the result of both Pierre's "high degree of civilization" and Marie's calm certainty of her own worth. Our awareness of that accomplishment should be inseparable from our awareness of their scientific successes. It is distressing to read entries like the following in contemporary French dictionaries: "CURIE (Pierre), French physicist (1859–1906). With his wife Marie née Sklodowska, he devoted himself to the study of radioactivity . . . ," with no other mention of Marie. It is not only distressing because it violates the rights of women, but also because Marie and Pierre themselves would have been outraged.

Between 1899 and 1902, the couple were apparently in perfect balance. Marie no longer suffered from the "attacks of nerves," as they were called at that time, that had occasionally troubled her in her twenties. Now thirty-two, she was gentle, tender, and happy with her husband. She wrote to Bronia in 1899: "I have the best husband anyone could imagine. I never even dreamed I would find one like him. He is truly a gift from heaven, and the longer we live together, the more we love each other."

Her house was tidy, but she never allowed herself to become possessed by the craze for domestic science that had infected bourgeois Frenchwomen of that time. Hygiene had been discovered. The ideal of the expert "mistress of the house" had replaced the ideal of the expert lover. The job of being an expert lover was now left to a different category of females— loose women and prostitutes. Other women studied the art of arranging cupboards, the art of polishing floors, crystal, and silver. As for Marie, she made her own jam and her daughter's clothes in order to save money, not because she loved to do it.

When a colleague or student of Pierre's dropped by the laboratory, she was always reserved and silent. But one of them observed that her silence could be as imperious as someone else's speech, and that however little she spoke, it was she who led the theoretical discussions that Pierre started, standing in front of his blackboard. Pierre believed she was a better mathematician than he was, and he said so. What she admired in him, on the other hand, was "the sureness and rigor of his arguments. . . . The surprising flexibility with which he can change the object of his research. . . ." Each of them had a very high opinion of the value of the other.

But starting now, their work was going to involve even more perseverance, drudgery, disappointment, and purely physical exertion—even as their health was being broken by radioactivity. What radium demanded of the Curies could only be accomplished by the stubbornness of a woman like Marie.

There was radium as well as uranium in pitchblende, but only infinitesimal quantities of it. To obtain a few milligrams of radium pure enough so that its atomic weight could be established, tons of pitchblende had to be treated. And this was an expensive mineral. At that time, factories existed for the extraction of uranium from pitchblende. For the extraction of radium from pitchblende there was only one woman in a shed.

The largest of these factories was in Bohemia. After an appeal by the Austrian government, which had been contacted by the Academy of Sciences in Vienna, the management of the factory agreed to sell its pitchblende residues, which were stored in a pine forest, to the Curies at a low price. Sacks of brown powder mixed with pine needles arrived and were piled up in the courtyard of the Ecole. Where would they be treated?

On the other side of the courtyard, across from the small room where Marie had worked up till then, there was an abandoned shed that had once been used as a dissection room by the students in the Ecole de Médecine. When it rained, water came in through the glass roof, and when the sun shone, the shed became as hot as a greenhouse. The floor was asphalt.

This was where the Curies set up their equipment—a few old tables holding some ovens and gas burners. They were

92

simply relieved that the new director of the Ecole, with whom Pierre didn't get along very well, had given them permission for the move.

No one who saw Marie in action there ever forgot it. She would delve into a sack, take out pounds of pitchblende, and pour as much of it into a basin as she could lift. Then she put the basin on the fire, dissolved the pitchblende, filtered it, precipitated it, collected it, dissolved it again, obtained a solution, decanted it, and measured it. Then she began again.

"Sometimes I would spend the whole day stirring a boiling mass with an iron bar almost as big as I was," she wrote. "By evening, I was dead tired. . . . It was exhausting work, carrying the containers, decanting the liquids and stirring the boiling matter for hours in a cast-iron basin."

The purification operation required the use of hydrogen sulfide. It was a toxic gas, and there was no exhaust hood over the tables. As often as she could, therefore, Marie would carry her basins out to the courtyard. Otherwise, all the windows of the shed had to be left open.

If a mote of dust or a particle of coal fell into one of the bowls where the purified solutions were crystallizing, days of work would be lost.

Pierre, who was still teaching and overseeing the work of the students in the Ecole, was not allocated any help in his own work. His laboratory assistant, Petit, tried to make himself useful whenever he could, but it was Marie who swept, cleaned, and tidied. There was order, discipline, silence in the lab—she couldn't tolerate noise—and happiness too, real happiness.

The chemist Georges Jaffé, one of the privileged few occasionally allowed into the laboratory, reported that he had the feeling he was witnessing the celebration of some cult in a sacred place. In different words, Marie said the same thing: "In our shed, poor as it was, a great tranquillity reigned; sometimes, as we watched over an operation, we would walk up and down talking about present and future work; when we were cold, we would cheer ourselves with a cup of hot tea drunk by the stove. We lived with an unusual preoccupation, as though in a dream."

And she added: "We would sometimes come back in the evening after dinner to look in on our domain. Our precious products, for which we had no shelter, were set out on tables and boards; we could see their faintly luminous silhouettes all around us, and these glowing lights, which seemed to be suspended in the darkness, always thrilled and delighted us all over again."

The precious products also made them mysteriously tired. Pierre began to have pains in his legs. The family doctor attributed them to rheumatism brought on by the dampness in the shed. He put Pierre on a diet, forbidding him to eat meat or drink red wine. Marie became translucent. Was it tuberculosis? Her father-in-law insisted that she be tested, but the tests were negative. Both of them sank into periods of lethargy. At this time, Marie wrote to her brother: "We have to be careful, and my husband's salary isn't quite enough to live on, but up to now we have had several unexpected additional sources of income each year, which means we have no deficit."

She was probably referring to the small sums Pierre received now and then from the various companies that were using his inventions. In the same letter, however, Marie worried about the money they would have to put by "to safeguard our child's future," and she added: "I want to get my degree, and then I will look for work." In the meantime, in March 1900, Pierre took a position as teaching assistant at the Ecole Polytechnique in order to add two hundred francs a month to his salary. By the summer, he was at the end of his strength.

At the laboratory, things were no better. The temperature rose to 37.9° C in Paris, and the shed, with its glass roof, became intolerable. Undaunted, Marie refused to stop, and on July 23, she believed she was done.

"Pure radium in the dish," she wrote in the black notebook. On the twenty-seventh, she noted the weight of an atom of radium: 174. On the following page there is a series of calculations, then the words, "It's impossible."

And it was true that this couldn't be right. She had spent nearly two years repeating the same operations over and over on eight tons of pitchblende. Now she had to begin again.

She was sure of her method, but her resources were absurd.

Although France had not completely ignored Pierre Curie, and although the Académie des Sciences had twice, at an interval of two years, awarded Marie one of its prizes, recognition of their value and true support came, as always, from abroad.

At the Physics Congress of 1900, the attention of both French and foreign physicists was on the new radioactive substance the Curies had been talking about for so long. The Curies had been giving samples of the substance to everyone who was exploring the subject, the most important of them being Henri Becquerel, who had taken a renewed interest in the rays he himself had discovered.

And now the dean of the University of Geneva arrived in Paris with an extremely attractive offer: the university wanted to give Pierre a physics chair, an annual salary of ten thousand francs, a housing allowance, and the directorship of a laboratory "whose credit would be augmented after agreement with Professor Curie and which would be served by two laboratory assistants," as the offer stated. In addition, "After examination of the resources of the laboratory, the collection of physics instruments would be made complete." Marie would be given an official position in the same laboratory.

Pierre accepted the offer and told a friend about it. He and Marie made a quick trip to Geneva, where they were warmly welcomed. The die was cast. But several weeks later, the dean of the University of Geneva received a letter of resignation full of all the proper excuses.

What had happened? According to Marie, "Pierre Curie was very tempted to accept [the Swiss offer] and it was the immediate interest of our research into radium that finally made him refuse it."

In fact, he had accepted it. But everything we know about them and about the events of the summer leads us to think that this time, too, she was the one making the decisions—after, perhaps, a moment of discouragement.

We don't know how Henri Poincaré learned that the Curies were going to leave France, but the fact is that when he heard of it, he applied pressure on his colleagues until he made sure that the teaching position in P.C.N. (Physics, Chemistry, and Natural Sciences) that happened to be vacant at the Sorbonne was offered to Pierre. All Pierre had to do was apply for the position, which he did with remarkable speed.

At the same time, the vice-rector of the Ecole Normale Supérieure de Jeunes Filles informed Marie that in response to her proposal, she would give the physics lectures to the first and second years during 1900–1901. Now they would not have to worry about the family budget, at least.

But the conditions under which Pierre and Marie conducted their research did not improve. In fact, they grew worse. While in foreign laboratories everywhere there was intense competition in the field of investigation the Curies had opened up, Marie at this point had to prepare the classes she gave twice a week at Sèvres while going there on the tramway; Pierre had the burden of preparing two courses in two different places and overseeing the research as well. The following year when, worn out, he applied for a teaching position in mineralogy that had become vacant at the Sorbonne, he was once again rejected in favor of a more highly qualified candidate.

Did he at least have a real laboratory at his disposal, now that he had the P.C.N. teaching position? No—all he had were two miserably small rooms in the rue Cuvier which were useless for Marie's work. And while he was writing, running here and there, taking on more and more work, scientists whom the Curies had generously provided with sources of radioactive matter—matter that Marie had with great effort collected and purified—were working in properly outfitted laboratories abroad. This was quite in keeping with both their moral position and the scientific spirit of the time.

But their moral position did not require them to let themselves be beaten by their competitors.

Robert Reid quotes a letter Ernest Rutherford wrote to his mother on January 5, 1902, from Canada, where he was working: "Right now I'm very busy writing up some notes for publication and doing new experiments. I can't stop, there are always people trying to overtake me. My most formidable adversaries in this field are Becquerel and the Curies in Paris, who have done very important work on radioactive bodies during the past few years."

And the work really was very important, despite all the obstacles in its path. Pierre Curie had observed that the increasingly pure samples of radium that Marie obtained spontaneously gave off heat. And what heat! He estimated this energy to be 100 calories an hour for one gram of radium!

Now for the past two thousand years it had been believed that a certain law governed the universe, and scientists of the late nineteenth century were loath to begin questioning it: it stated that energy could neither be created nor destroyed, that matter was inert, and that atoms, the smallest particles of the physical universe, were indivisible. Hence their name.

Pierre and Marie were to suggest the hypothesis that radioactive atoms had properties that other atoms did not have, that this could be the source of the mysterious energy. But this hypothesis, they said, was only one of several possible explanations. It was Ernest Rutherford who would pursue it and discover, with Frederick Soddy, that radioactive atoms disintegrate spontaneously. An extraordinary phenomenon! A phenomenon that Marie would call "the cataclysm of atomic transformation."

Rutherford was a first-rate scientist. So was Pierre Curie. If he had been able to make full use of his rich imagination and his time, would he have outstripped Rutherford?

At this time he was apparently inclined toward the hypothesis that the source of the energy emitted by the radioactive atoms was to be found in radiation from the sun. In a letter he wrote to Berthelot he said that he dreamed of finding chemical reactions capable of capturing and using solar energy. If Rutherford is to be believed, "M. and Mme Curie never had more than a very general notion of what the phenomenon of radioactivity really was." But Pierre did not worry about his potential rivals.

As for Marie, no one was competing with her in her obsessive pursuit of the proof she intended to furnish, "the sort of proof the science of chemistry requires, the fact that radium is an authentic element." And neither her excessive work load nor her worn fingertips nor the fatigue that continued to puzzle Dr. Curie would be able to lessen her determination.

And so here they were again in their shed in the fall of 1900, after a vacation in Poland. All the Sklodowskis had gathered in Zakopane, where Bronia and Casimir were building a sanatorium.

Things had changed somewhat for the Curies. An aura had grown up around them that attracted people and impressed them. Young researchers were drawn to them by their work, by Pierre's influence, by Marie's intensity and her strength (which was all the more touching as she seemed more and more delicate), by the kind of couple they were, and by the almost religious spirit of their scientific commitment, their asceticism.

They had formed some professional relationships that had turned into friendships. A physicist named Georges Sagnac, who signed one memorandum with Pierre; a sculptor named Georges Urbain, who kept his own hours; the physicist Aimé Cotton, all turned up regularly at the house on boulevard Kellermann, where on Sundays former students of Pierre's, including Paul Langevin, came to spend the afternoon.

At about this time, a disheveled chemist named André Debierne entered the lives of the Curies. According to those who knew him, he was deeply in love with Marie. Whether that was true or not, he never stopped making himself useful to her; he was always there, everywhere, in her shadow, until the day she died. What did she give him in return for this constant ardor? Did she at some point give him more than her mere presence? People said she did, but this is rarely acknowledged, in the same way that people are still evasive about the relationship that surrounded her with scandal a few years after her husband died.

Behavior that might be considered mystifying today was, after all, quite conceivable at a time when a woman's honor was staked entirely on her chastity and when, to quote the striking words that were spoken in the Chamber in the 1880s by a deputy, a woman "should be in her body as though she weren't there."

We want Marie to be both saint and martyr. From all indications, she was neither, not in a sexual sense anyway. She was a young woman at a time when most women wavered between remorse and hysteria, when they had no choice but to be either guilty or "outside of their bodies." When we try to turn her into a saint and a martyr, we not only falsify her but we take away another of her dimensions, her experience of guilt and the drama into which this reticent and modest woman was plunged when her private life was exhibited publicly.

We don't have any precise information about André Debierne or the other mathematician whose name comes up when people who knew her talk about Marie Curie. If there is something to know, she took care that no evidence of it would remain. But if she had not weathered the storms of love, she wouldn't have been able to write, in her last years, "I believe it is unsatisfactory to let all one's interest in life depend on feelings as stormy as the feelings of love." This was also one of her dimensions, and not the least of them—that she never let all her interest in life depend on love.

André Debierne, a modest, self-effacing man who had difficulty expressing himself, but who was an excellent chemist, began working with Pierre on radioactivity, and he quickly discovered a new, important radioelement which he named actinium. Jean Perrin, who was running the chemistry and physics laboratory at the Sorbonne, had made room for him there.

Marie had finally established the method for extracting radium. When the chemical products company that was working the patent of one of the scales invented by Pierre proposed that they try to apply Marie's method using less primitive means, Pierre and Marie accepted gratefully. Debierne took on the job of supervising the process.

With her teaching activities, Marie's universe had expanded. When she began her job as lecturer at the Ecole Normale Supérieure at Sèvres, she was the first woman ever to occupy that position. The school had been founded to train teachers for the *lycées* for girls. The courses were therefore taught by highly qualified teachers. One of them was Jean Perrin. He was roughly the same age as Marie—three months younger—and he had a sparkling wit.

As always, Marie had mixed feelings about the prospect of teaching at this level—she was afraid of doing badly, but she was confident about her abilities, and she wanted to prove what she could do. In addition, there was her feminism: clearly, the fact that the students at Sèvres were girls and not boys meant that they would not enjoy the best working conditions or the best opportunities to increase their knowledge. One of her students described her this way: "She didn't dazzle us, she reassured us, attracted us, and enchanted us by her simplicity, her sensitivity, her desire to be useful to us, the sense she had of both our ignorance and our possibilities. . . . She was the first one who ever established human relations with us."

Until then, the students at Sèvres had never even touched a piece of equipment. Marie doubled the length of her class, which was supposed to last an hour and a half, in order to introduce them to experimental work. She was the one who

100

brought differential and integral calculus into the Sèvres curriculum. In short, she didn't take the job lightly—but then she had never taken anything lightly.

Although this teaching, and also Pierre's extra courses, encroached on the time they had for their research, at least it kept them away from sources of radioactivity. But whenever they had a moment, they returned to their real work. Marie no longer handled tons of pitchblende. The first stage in the extraction of radium was now carried out by chemists she had trained, who worked under the direction of André Debierne: this first stage consisted of deriving ten to twenty kilos of barium sulfate from pitchblende residues, then transforming these sulfates into chlorides. The chlorides still contained only a small proportion of radium—about three parts per 100,000.

What Marie was determined to do was to separate radium from barium by the method of fractional crystallization that she had conceived and perfected. Radium salts became concentrated in the crystals. After each crystallization, a measurement of the activity indicated the progress of the purification. By the time Marie finally gave Eugène Demarçay a sample of about a decigram of purified radium salts in order to make sure it did not contain more than a negligible quantity of foreign matter, she had performed several thousand crystallizations. She had also lost more than fifteen pounds in four years.

But she wasn't interested in her weight. What she cared about was what she wrote in the black notebook on March 28, 1902: "Ra = 225.93. The weight of an atom of radium."

This marked the end of an adventure unprecedented in the history of science. It also marked the end of a certain kind of happiness: once something is achieved, it has also in some sense been destroyed.

A few days later, between arguments about the production of *Pelléas et Mélisande* at the Opéra Comique and the electoral campaign in which the Republicans were opposing the Clericals; between insults exchanged on the subject of the Dreyfus affair; and between comments by enlightened amateurs on the exhibition of a Spanish painter named Picasso who, according to the *Figaro* critic, was "alert, witty, gay and gifted in his use of color, which is very fresh and very brilliant," Paris salons buzzed with talk about radium. Because radium could cure cancer.

The Académie des Sciences opened a credit account of 20,000 francs for the Curies "for the extraction of radioactive substances." A form of therapy, an industry, and a legend had been born.

eleven

WHEN THE first reporters entered the shed where radium had been discovered and made it known that the miraculous cure had been found by a well-bred young woman, a wife and mother, after four years of work in a wretched hovel, people's imaginations went wild.

It was true that Marie had worked hard. But at the same time, the French Parliament had decided that an eleven-hour day, with one hour of rest, would be the legal working day for women and minors under eighteen years of age. Eleven hours. At that time, no one dreamed that there might exist some sort of uniformity among members of the female species that could make women's work in the factories just as respectable as, and more arduous than, a woman's work in a laboratory. When, as the law had anticipated, the eleven hours were reduced to ten and a half in 1902, employers reduced salaries proportionately.

A quarter of the working population of women (who numbered as many then as in 1970) were employed in factories where their male colleagues found it quite normal that, in a metal clasp factory, for example, a male cutter would earn 5.70 F a day while a female cutter earned 1.50 F. (At that time, a kilo of sugar cost 1.15 F.) It wasn't until 1910 that women had a right to keep their salaries instead of being legally obliged to turn them over to their husbands. Equal salaries? A handful of female workers dared to demand it, but they were quite alone. What was more, they were being watched.

When the garment workers from the big fashion houses demonstrated in February 1901, in the rue de la Paix, because they wanted to be paid six francs a day, the managements of Worth, Paquin, and Doucet made their workers eat lunch on the premises so that they wouldn't be tempted to join in the demonstrations.

Among the bourgeoisie of finance, fashion, and literature, the women's struggle was becoming heated, but on another level. The relation between economic quality and equality plain and simple was still far from being understood, but an important bastion was attacked the day one of France's seventy-seven female doctors took the entrance examination for a hospital residency and was admitted.

Two successful women novelists who until then had hidden behind men's names in order to be taken seriously—Daniel Lesueur and Henry Gréville—mounted a campaign to be elected to the Comité de la Société des Gens de Lettres. Their action provoked the following response from the very famous Octave Mirbeau: "Woman is not a brain. She is a sex and that is much more beautiful. She has only one role in the world— to make love, which means to perpetuate the species. Woman is unsuited for anything but love or motherhood. A few women—very rare exceptions—have succeeded in giving the illusion of possessing a creative power in art or literature. But these are abnormal beings or simply reflections of men. And I prefer what people call prostitutes because they, at least, are in harmony with the Universe."

When people learned, therefore, that "an abnormal being" named Marie Curie had discovered the cure for cancer, it caused an even greater sensation. For the Curies' fame, between 1902 and 1904, had two sides to it.

In scientific circles, no one doubted any longer that radium was an element. What was overwhelming, in the proper sense of the word—since it upset the law of the physical universe— was radioactivity and the phenomenon that it implied. This was what captivated the imaginations of the researchers.

But even today, how familiar is Rutherford's name to the general public? Or Niels Bohr's? Fleming is known, because of penicillin. If the Curies are known throughout the world, it is because their name was immediately associated with the cure for cancer. Soon, a few quacks would even be boasting that radium cured everything.

> The most wonderful discovery of the century
> Rezall RADIUM LOTION
> For the Prevention of Hair Loss
> No more thinning hair
> No more baldness
> No more gray hairs

This was typical of the sort of advertisement that appeared in the newspapers at that time.

In fact, two German researchers announced that radioactive substances had physiological effects. Right away Pierre deliberately exposed his arm to a source of radium. He was happy to see a lesion form. And he communicated the results of his experiment to the academy:

> The skin became red over an area of six square centimeters; it had the appearance of a burn, but the skin was not, or was hardly, painful. After some time, the redness began to increase in intensity, though without spreading: on the twentieth day, it formed crusts, then a sore which we treated with dressings; on the forty-second day, the epiderm began to grow again at the edges, reaching the center, and fifty-two days after the action of the rays, there still remained a sore of one square centimeter which had a grayish look to it, indicating a deeper mortification.
>
> We should add that Mme Curie received similar burns while carrying a few centigrams of very active matter in a small sealed tube, even though the small tube was enclosed in a thin metal box.
>
> Apart from these extreme effects, we have had various other effects on our hands during research carried out on very active products. Our hands have had a general tendency to peel; the tips of the fingers with which we have held tubes or capsules containing very active products become hard and sometimes

very painful; for one of us, the inflammation of the fingertips lasted about two weeks and ended in the skin dropping off, but after two months the painful sensitivity has still not completely disappeared.

Henri Becquerel, who had carried a tube containing radium in the pocket of his vest, was burned too. And he was furious. He told the Curies what had happened to him and exclaimed: "Radium! I love it but I'm also angry with it!"

His observations were published at the same time as Pierre's, on June 3, 1901. Becquerel had also noticed that a shield of lead rendered radium harmless. But one had to want to protect oneself.

The doctors began to take action. Dr. Daulos began to treat his patients at the Hôpital Saint-Louis with tubes of radon lent to him by the Curies. Radium really did destroy the diseased cells in a skin cancer—when the epiderm destroyed by its action grew back again, it was healthy.

All that was left now was to begin extracting radium from ore on an industrial scale.

The Curies certainly took satisfaction in being recognized by their peers. What was more, it was "fair"; what had revolted Marie about Pierre's treatment by official France was not the wound to her vanity—she had no vanity, only pride—but the fact that it was an expression of an injustice.

Would this injustice at least be made good now that they were photographed, interviewed, sometimes disturbed in their work; now that they even had to accept one or two invitations to dinner?

At Mascart's insistence, Pierre let himself be persuaded to stand as a candidate for the Académie des Sciences. The physics section of the academy announced that it was unanimously in favor of his candidacy and the outcome of the election seemed a foregone conclusion. But first he had to submit to the customary protocol—mount a campaign, run

106

here and there, flatter people, make himself agreeable, state his claims, display his merits. He was completely incapable of this. And so he was not only defeated—by 23 votes to 20—but also unhappy with himself, bitter, discouraged.

Actually, he was undoubtedly much more affected by the radioactivity that he and Marie continued to expose themselves to, in the shed, than by this setback—because it is true that radioactivity also affects one's morale, one's life force.

As for Marie, she had received a blow from which she had difficulty recovering. Her father had died after an operation, and she had arrived in Warsaw too late to see him alive—the body had already been put in the coffin. She had demanded that the coffin be opened, and there, on her knees, leaning over the beloved face, she had accused herself over and over again—of having abandoned him, of having remained in France out of selfishness, of having broken her promise. Bronia had to tear her away from this lugubrious confession.

Strong though she was, she could not tolerate death, not even the idea of death, which shocked her, as though nature were thumbing its nose at science.

Now she would sometimes get up in the night and wander around the sleeping house. These bouts of insomnia alarmed Pierre. But sometimes he was the one ravaged by pain and prevented from sleeping. Marie would sit up with him, uneasy, helpless. And when morning came and it was time to go to the Ecole or the laboratory or Sèvres, they were exhausted.

"This life we have chosen is a hard one," Pierre remarked once.

After spending one Sunday at boulevard Kellermann, Georges Sagnac was so struck by the way they looked that he wrote a ten-page letter to Pierre:

April 23, 1903. Thursday morning. I beg you to remember that I'm your friend, your friend, your young friend, true, but still your friend. This is why you will read my letter, I hope, with patience and thoughtfulness.

When I saw Mme Curie at the Société de Physique I was struck by the change in her features. I know that she worked too hard while she was writing her thesis, that she has certainly had some rest since, and that once she is done with her defense she will be able to rest more peacefully. But this made me realize that she does not have enough resistance to be able to live a life as purely intellectual as the one you both are leading and what I am saying also applies to you. I would have been six feet under long ago if I had abused my body the way you both have abused yours. I will give you an example to illustrate my point. You hardly eat at all, either of you. More than once, when I have had the pleasure of eating at your table, I have seen Mme Curie nibble at two slices of sausage and then wash them down with a cup of tea. Well, just think about it for a moment, I beg you. Don't you think that even a robust constitution would suffer from such an insufficient diet? . . .

The indifference or stubbornness with which she might respond to you should not be any excuse. I can also foresee objection: you will say, "She isn't hungry! And she's old enough to know what she's doing!"

But she isn't! At the moment she is behaving like a child. I say this to you with all the conviction of my reason and my friendship. And it is easy to see how she is drawn into this stupid behavior. You don't leave enough time for your meals. You eat at any hour, and in the evening you have dinner so late that your stomachs are nervous from waiting so long and finally refuse to function. Of course a piece of research might occasionally make your dinner late; it's excusable once. But you have no right to make a habit of it. . . .

Don't you love Irène? I don't think it would ever occur to me to read a paper by Rutherford that stopped me from swallowing what my body needed, instead of looking at such an agreeable little girl. Give her a good hug for me. If she were somewhat older, she would agree with me and tell you the same thing. So think of her. . . .

The Curies' friends were upset and indignant at the conditions in which Pierere and Marie had to work. And during the course of the year, the new dean of the Faculté des Sciences,

Paul Appell, wrote to Pierre and asked him "as a favor" if he would agree to be proposed for the Legion of Honor in the July 14 list of nominations. He also wrote to Marie, asking her to "use all your influence to make M. Curie agree. The thing itself obviously isn't important, but when you take into account the practical consequences—laboratories, credit accounts, etc., it is very important."

Pierre Curie's respone to Dean Appell: "Would you please be so kind as to thank Monsieur le Ministre and inform him that I do not need to be decorated but that I do need a laboratory very badly."

In the flood of correspondence that they received every day now and that Pierre made a point of answering even though he was beginning to have trouble holding a pen, a letter arrived from Buffalo, New York. Some American engineers had decided to start a radium plant and asked for the necessary information. That day, Pierre consulted Marie before answering. She was the one who had invented the technique for extracting and purifying radium. If the Curies took out a patent, they would receive rights on all future manufacture of radium throughout the world.

Marie thought it over, and then she said no. No, they wouldn't take out a patent. Physicists always published the complete results of their research, the Curies would also communicate the complete results. Her process was to be available to anyone who wanted to use it.

This decision was not the most realistic one the former positivist could have made. People would eventually make immense fortunes from radium, and one of the first to do so was the industrialist who had had the idea of providing the Curies with free premises and free ore so that chemists could proceed with the first series of extractions, while Marie, in her gratitude, wore her fingers out obtaining salts pure enough to be used in medicine. The spirit of enterprise was responsible for earning that fortune.

By the early twenties, the price of one gram of radium had reached $100,000 (1 million francs at that time, 7 or 8 million today). Then the Mining Union of Upper Katanga discovered uranium deposits in the Congo (today's Zaire) and soon controlled a monopoly: the richness of the deposits and the low cost of labor in the Congo put it out of reach of the competition. The price of a gram of radium went down to $70,000. The discovery of other uranium deposits in Canada in the thirties caused a price war, followed by a cartel agreement in 1938 that fixed the bottom price at $25,000.

This gives some idea of what the Curies could have earned. But the decision Marie made in 1904 conformed both to her basic principle—disinterest—and to the scientific spirit. In the twenties, when she realized that money was not another name for the devil but a necessary tool for research, she fought to have the League of Nations admit that scientists should have "property rights" over their discoveries. Later we shall see what came of this.

Scientists had always taken out patents on their inventions, even Pierre Curie. But these patents covered various instruments, not fundamental scientific discoveries, which were always circulated through the scientific world without restriction. A great deal of resistance had to be overcome in order for nuclear fission and the principle of chain reaction—on which the French, the Americans, and the Germans were working at the same time—to be kept secret. But that was in 1939.

Another letter came, this one from London. The Royal Institution would be pleased if M. Pierre Curie would come and give a "Friday Night Lecture." This lecture was part of a tradition unknown in France—that of endeavoring to make science available to the uninitiated public. Robert Reid tells us that the Friday lectures were so successful that the street on which the Institution stood had to be converted to a one-way street, and that it was the first one-way street in London. The cream of British physics, considered at that time to be the best in the world, was present at these lectures: the men came in tuxedos, the women in evening dresses with all their jewels on display, and the greatest scientists were invited to create the best popularizations.

Pierre Curie already had a reputation in Great Briatin, where Lord Kelvin, in particular, and also James Dewar, had recognized the importance of the work he was doing with piezoelectricity, magnetism, and symmetry long before the discovery of radium. But radium was now science's main attraction, and it was about radium that Pierre was asked to speak to the public at the Royal Institution.

As he went on stage in the lecture hall, to the warm applause of the audience, it was clear that he was ill. His legs trembled, his hands hurt. He had needed help to button the vest of his suit, the black suit he wore when he taught and which Marie had carefully steamed for the occasion. But even though he spoke in French—slowly, as his British colleagues had advised him—he was a stunning success. He knew how to address the laymen in the audience, and how to introduce visual elements into his discussion, as he had been asked to do. Radium lent itself to this. He produced an image on photographic plates that were wrapped in black cloth, and asked that the lights be turned off so that the spectators could see the radiation of the mauve light. He pulled back his sleeve and displayed the sequelae of the lesion he had caused. History doesn't tell us if he amused himself by testing the authenticity of the diamonds that sparkled at the necks of a few pretty women in low-cut dresses. False diamonds can't pass the test of radium.

But we do know that he inadvertently spilled a little of the radium in his tube: fifty years later a decontamination team had to be called in because the radium could still be detected in the hall.

During the talk, Marie was sitting next to Lord Kelvin dressed in her "formal dress." She had had the same "formal dress" for the past ten years—it was black, with a discreetly scalloped neckline. It was actually a good thing that she wasn't fond of clothes, because she had no taste at all and

111

never would have. Black, which singled her out because people didn't usually wear black, and gray—the two colors she had adopted for the sake of convenience—solved a lot of problems and set off her ash-blond hair nicely. Then again, in this area even more than in others, she was, as always, unusual, and attractive in her difference. And she had recovered her glow—she was pregnant again, this time without feeling very ill, and it suited her.

There were many women in the hall. The Royal Institution had wanted large numbers of women to come to the Friday Night Lectures. But measures had been taken "to avoid the possible presence among the subscribers of unsuitable individuals of the female sex."

Yet the worthy organization had not imagined for one moment that Marie might appear on the stage next to her husband. He talked, and she listened. At this event, Marie was to discover a fellow sufferer—Hertha, Professor Ayrton's wife, who eventually became her friend. Hertha was a very brilliant scientist whose presence was always welcome—as long as she kept quiet.

Six days later, the situation was reversed, as "Madame Sklodowska-Curie" defended her doctoral thesis before a jury composed of Professors Lippmann, Bouty, and Moissan. The ceremony took place in a small hall at the Sorbonne. It was truly unprecedented—no woman had ever done this before. As Marie understood very well, it was a real event: from now on the world of physicists and chemists would have to include a woman among their number, and she was that woman.

The little hall was packed, because of her and because of her subject: "Research on Radioactive Substances." She had invited Jean Perrin, Paul Langevin, and her students from Sèvres. And of course, next to Pierre and Dr. Curie, there was Bronia, who had come from Poland and who was even more moved than Marie.

She was very striking—pale, young, with her helmet of blond hair, delicate in her black dress, answering in her soft Slavic accent the questions of the three examiners in coattails. What was more, it was clear to at least some people that she knew more than the examiners did about the subject being discussed.

The ceremony ended in the time-honored manner. The president of the jury announced that "The Université de Paris confers on you the title of Doctor of Physical Sciences . . ." with a "very honorable" mention. But he added something that was less common: "In the name of the jury, Madame, I would like to congratulate you." This was Gabriel Lippmann. He was to receive the Nobel Prize in 1908—after Marie.

Another potential Nobel Prize winner (besides Jean Perrin) had just missed being present at Marie's triumph. This was Ernest Rutherford. He was passing through Paris, he wanted to meet the Curies, and so he stopped by the laboratory, where he was told that Mme Curie was at that moment defending her thesis. He arrived too late to hear it, but Paul Langevin invited him to a small dinner at his house in Marie's honor.

That evening, in the dining room of the house in rue Gazan, very close to boulevard Kellermann, where Langevin had come to live with his family, Marie was surrounded by a constellation of famous men—Ernest Rutherford, Jean Perrin, Paul Langevin, Pierre Curie. Pierre, who at forty-four was the oldest, looked like the figure of authority, even though he lacked the official titles for it. Creatively, however, he had made his mark.

Jean Perrin was thirty-two. He had been one of the first to demonstrate the nature of the electron, that minuscule speck of electricity at the periphery of the atom that revolves around the nucleus at considerable speed. And he had just articulated modern atomic theory.

A long time ago, in 1803 to be exact, the atomic hypothesis of matter was formulated by an English chemist, John Dalton. But since that time an entire sector of scientific thinking, the most powerful one, had relentlessly opposed the idea—incompatible with positivism—that there could exist structures inaccessible to our perception.

Jean Perrin would also be the first to say why the stars

shone and why the sun gave heat and light to the earth, and he would suggest the use of rockets for interplanetary travel. This was before 1910. Comical, spirited, enthusiastic, dynamic, never still for a moment, he looked like an elf with his curly red hair. He had also moved near the Curies, into the house next door. They could speak to each other from their gardens. Henriette Perrin, his wife, was the only woman ever allowed to call Marie by her first name. Their friendship was unshadowed.

At thirty-one, Paul Langevin was the youngest. Tall and upright, with a crewcut, a curly moustache, a gentle gaze, he knew thousands of lines of verse by heart and was happy to recite them, loved life, and was the picture of the charming Frenchman as depicted in those days. "Langevin looks like a cavalry officer," Anna de Noailles said of him. This was a compliment.

In fact, Langevin was a pure product of secular and republican France, which believed in the virtue of hard work and social betterment through education. Just as Pierre Curie's career had been that of a marginal figure, a vagabond of the imagination living outside the norms and conventions—to the extent permitted by the rigid mores of the time—so Langevin's career was a typical one for a poor, gifted child of his century.

His father was a journeyman locksmith. Langevin had gone to a *lycée* only because after his elementary school education was finished a teacher had said to his mother, "If you can manage it, he absolutely must continue." She couldn't manage it, and yet she had. Then there had been a professor who, at the end of his *lycée* education, had said, "If you can, you absolutely must become an engineer." And he had taken first place in the entrance exam at the Ecole de Physique, where he had paid for his studies by giving private lessons. This was where he became the admiring student of Pierre Curie.

Then another professor had said to him, "Go to the Ecole Normale." He didn't know Latin, he didn't have the background he needed to take the exam; he acquired it in four

114

months, was admitted at the top of the list, and was also subsequently first in the competitive exams for teaching posts. He had received two grants, one for a period of training abroad—he chose the most famous physics laboratory, the Cavendish at Cambridge—and the other for preparing a thesis on the ionization of gases. Mascart, who occupied the chair in experimental physics at the Collège de France, noticed him and took him on as substitute and then as assistant. An impeccable career.

The great scientists, including Pierre Curie, were not always naturally the best in their classes, and were often not even good students. "By your very presence, you have a bad effect on the attitude of the class toward me," one professor had said to the young Albert Einstein before he failed the entrance exam to the Zurich Polytechnic School. People said he "couldn't care less."

Sometimes they didn't care, and this was the case with Ernest Rutherford, of whom it would be said, in the fifties, that he and Niels Bohr were the physicists who came closest to the man who had set the model for genius—Albert Einstein. The evening of the dinner given by Langevin, whom he had known at Cambridge and whom he loved—"a hell of a good guy," he called him—Rutherford was thirty-two years old. He was a dynamic person, superbly gifted, the son of an odd jobs man. He made no secret of loving money and wanting to earn money. He also loved fame and was certain he would become famous. In Cambridge he was one day heard proclaiming, "This is the heroic age of science! This is the Elizabethan age!" And one witness added that "there was no doubt about who Rutherford saw taking the part of Shakespeare." He was also credited with a nice retort: when he was told that some mean-spirited person had said to him, "The lucky devil! Always at the crest of the wave!" he answered, "Well, naturally. I'm the one who made the wave!"

Very soon after Becquerel's first observation on the emission of rays by uranium, Rutherford discovered that there existed different types of rays, alphas and betas—"my" alpha

115

rays, he called them. Next, with a young chemist named Frederick Soddy, he made the most important discovery in the history of radioactivity since Marie's isolation of radium. And he was immediately aware of this when, with Soddy, he found that as radioactive elements emitted their rays, they split into a series of new elements; the radioactive atom disintegrated spontaneously, and there was no way of speeding up or slowing down the rhythm of this disintegration, which was different for each radioactive substance. But the evening of the dinner, he did not talk about what progress he was making.

This first meeting between the reserved and distant woman who had just been crowned queen of radioactivity and the loud-voiced man who intended to be king of the same field should have been a disaster. But instead, it was the beginning of a reciprocal friendship that never lapsed. Rutherford was the one who later spoke out against some scientists who had been irritated by Marie's haughtiness, and said, "Madame Curie is a hard person to handle. She has at once the advantage and the inconvenience of being a woman." He understood her right away.

He was brusque, as one is with an equal, rather than gallant. She was simply herself, which meant that she was charming without attempting to charm. And Rutherford was always moved by "the absurd way she dressed."

The evening was animated, lively, a great success. Although Paul Langevin was not rolling in money and already had two children, he was extravagant and generous, without any inclination to asceticism, and the wines with which Marie's success was celebrated were no doubt as carefully chosen as the cheeses. And there was plenty to talk about, argue about.

It was June and the weather was beautiful. When night had fallen over the garden, Pierre took a small tube containing a solution of radium out of his pocket. He had coated half of the tube with zinc sulfide. Now, in the darkness, the sulfide glowed just as brightly as the radium. As Pierre performed this trick with the enthusiasm of an adolescent before the fascinated group, he said, "Look . . . this is the light of the future." But his painful, reddened fingers were having more and more trouble holding the tube.

It was vacation time. Marie went ahead to rent a house in Brittany. Once again she went off on an ill-fated bicycle ride. This time it was too late to take her back to Paris. She gave birth to a premature baby who died a few hours after it was born.

In those days no one understood the cause of the accident, even though the latest experiments Pierre had carried out, with two doctors, had revealed that when mice and guinea pigs were exposed to radium emanations they developed extreme pulmonary congestion and a modification of their white corpuscles.

Worn out, Marie had to spend the summer on her back. Pierre, the Doctor, and Irène kept her company, along with a student of hers, the future Eugénie Cotton, whom she had invited for the vacation, and the faithful Debierne. She looked very good as she lay on her couch, but she wrote to Bronia: "I had become so used to the idea of this child that I can't get over it. Write me, please, if you think I should blame it on being generally tired, because I must confess that I haven't spared myself. I trusted in my constitution and now I bitterly regret it, because I have paid for it dearly. The child, a little girl, was healthy and alive. And I wanted her so much!"

The crowning blow was the news from Poland that Bronia's younger child, a little boy, had died within a few days of contracting tubercular meningitis.

"I can no longer look at my little girl without trembling with fear," Marie wrote to her brother. "And Bronia's sorrow is tearing me apart."

Unwell, obsessed by death, which had struck three times within the past year close to her—in her—Marie returned to Paris and caught "a sort of grippe," as she called it, that she would not be able to get over.

She decided not to go to London with Pierre to accept the Davy Medal which the Royal Institution was awarding them.

117

And in December, it was the French representative in Stockholm who stood in for the Curies and accepted the Nobel Prize in physics in their name from the king of Sweden. Pierre and Marie were sharing it with Henri Becquerel, who was the only one of the three to attend the ceremony.

Pierre wrote to the Perpetual Secretary to the Academy, Professor Aurivillius, to ask the academy to postpone the lecture which, as Nobel prizewinners, they were supposed to give.

"We can't be away at this time of the year without greatly disrupting the courses we are each giving," he wrote. "Also, Mme Curie was ill this summer and is not yet entirely recovered."

Kept secret until the official announcement, the news of the distinction awarded to the Curies broke on December 10, 1903, assuming truly extraordinary proportions. This was the third time the Swedish Academy had awarded prizes. Roentgen had been the first physicist to receive one. Because the jury deliberated after consulting the most renowned scholars in the international scientific community, its decisions already aroused great interest. But this event had an added dimension: the heroine was a woman, a frail, blond woman; what she had discovered was a miraculous substance that could save human lives; what the Nobel Prize was honoring was a project that had been carried out by a husband and wife in a miserable shed. How romantic it all was!

The whole world would be touched by this unprecedented story for a long time. Overnight, Marie and Pierre Curie had become famous. This turned out to be a sore trial. With the exception of stage stars—whose job it was, after all—the Curies were the first in contemporary history to endure the torture of the limelight.

FAME

twelve

"THE DISRUPTION of our voluntary isolation caused real suffering for us and had all the effects of a disaster," Marie was to write. At a certain point, disdain for honors begins to seem affected, and it is tempting to think that Marie Curie had reached this point when she complained, in effect, of having been given the Nobel Prize. But there is no doubt that the couple suffered more from the ordeal of being famous than from that of being poor and unknown.

The seventy thousand francs that accompanied the Nobel Prize, along with the Daniel Osiris Prize shared by Marie (who received sixty thousand francs) and Edouard Branly (forty thousand francs), certainly relieved the Curies from any fear that they would "run out of money."[1] Some of the money was loaned to the Dluskis for their sanatorium, some to Pierre's brother, some was spent on presents, and some on a modern bathroom for the house. The rest was prudently converted into French bonds and shares in the city of Warsaw. But as we know, it is the same with money as with health: we only realize how precious it is when it is gone.

As for the rest, they say that Albert Einstein, invited by Chaplin to go with him to see *City Lights*, was suddenly panic-stricken by the crowds of people hemming in their car and staring at them and shouting their names. "What does this mean?" he asked, flabbergasted. Chaplin answered, "Nothing."

This was exactly Pierre's point of view, quite apart from the fact that he truly detested all sorts of honors. The very notion

---

[1] Daniel Osiris, who died in 1911, gave his Malmaison castle to the State, and left thirty million francs to the Pasteur Institute.

of classification, hierarchy, even if it was based on merit, seemed quaint and ridiculous to him.

This was not the case for Marie, who was superior because she had resolved to be superior. Her position, as a woman in a society where she would always have to prove herself superior just to be recognized as equal, did not leave any room for this sort of excessive delicacy. And she was in no way spontaneously inclined to such delicacy anyway. Hadn't Marya Sklodowska desperately wanted to become "someone"? She was therefore not indifferent to honors, even if she was superior enough to know that this was not a sign of superiority.

But she admired Pierre's "detachment from every sort of vanity and from those examples of pettiness that one discovers in oneself and in others and that one looks upon with indulgence, at the same time as one aspires to a more perfect ideal"; she admired it too much not to try to follow his example. What was more, she was overcome by an almost pathological panic when she felt trapped by a crowd—a panic that could even result in a physical breakdown. It suited her to be known. To be recognized terrified her.

For different reasons, then, nothing was more disagreeable to the Curies than to show themselves, to become the objects of public curiosity, to be photographed, caricatured, stared at, transformed into exotic animals. And this was what they were suddenly exposed to—they were besieged at the laboratory, besieged at home, spied upon, approached, solicited, hunted down.

The shed, a description of which had appeared in newspapers all over the world, was invaded by curiosity seekers of all kinds, including the President of the Republic, Emile Loubet, who appeared there in person. Boulevard Kellermann, "an attractive house glowing with the happy intimacy of two great scientists," was beleaguered by reporters who questioned the maid, Irène, the cat.

Snatched from their bowl, our two goldfish suffocated and thrashed about. No, they didn't want to be given a banquet; no, they didn't want a tour of America; no, they didn't want to visit the Automobile Show, attend the dress rehearsal of Sardou's new play, say what they thought of the first Goncourt Prize; no, Marie did not want a racehorse named after her; no, they did not want photographs of themselves to surround the gram of bromide radium that *Le Matin* was exhibiting in its lobby, where a fascinated public filed past.

Pierre was agonized by the caricature of him that took up two columns of *L'Echo de Paris;* Marie bristled at the description of her as a "charming mother whose exquisite sensitivity goes hand in hand with a mind that is ever curious about the unfathomable"; they both were shocked by the cabaret sketch in which they were represented searching on all fours for some radium they had lost during a delicate procedure.

Dispossessed of herself, Marie appealed to Jozef, to Bronia, to Hela. "Above all," she wrote to them, "don't forget me!" Like a mutant terrified at seeing scales grow on its skin, she called on her blood brothers to remember what she had been before she became something else—a monster, perhaps.

The whirlwind in which the Curies had been caught up left them haggard and furious, especially when words were put in their mouths about the miraculous effects of radium, which could supposedly cure blindness, tuberculosis, and neuralgia, as well as light streets and heat houses.

Exasperated, upset, violated, pestered, inundated by madmen and snobs, cadgers and society people, unknown inventors and autograph hunters, petitioners of all kinds who were not content with writing but came in person, the Curies tried in vain to build a barricade around themselves.

Invitations poured in, and they couldn't refuse them all. They dined at the Elysée Palace. "Would you like me to introduce you to the King of Greece?" a lady asked. "I don't see the need," Marie answered, then became embarrassed when she saw that the lady was Madame Loubet. She added, "Well, yes, if you like."

And what about the ambassador of Austria-Hungary? It was thanks to his government that they had once obtained pitchblende. What about Countess Greffulhe? No one refused

123

an invitation from Countess Greffulhe, whose salon, in her mansion in the rue d'Astorg, was the most highly regarded in Paris. And what about Madame de . . .? She talked about giving them a laboratory.

For they still didn't have a suitable place to work. Marie was still working in the shed, purifying the radium that more and more doctors were demanding.

After the awarding of the Nobel Prize, the government felt it had to show some interest in the Curies. An announcement was made that a chair in general physics had been created at the Sorbonne for Pierre. But so much time passed between the decision of the Council of Ministers and its implementation that Pierre became sick with irritability, and on top of that, once the chair existed, it was not provided with a laboratory. A credit account for operating costs was established to pay the salaries of Pierre, Marie (she was head of works), an assistant, and a boy. But this was not followed by any credit for equipment. And so Pierre, embittered, refused the chair. Emotion, agitation, interventions. At last an endowment of 150,000 francs was voted by Parliament. What this meant was an enlarging of the cramped spot in the rue Cuvier that had been assigned to the P. C.N. up to now. When this mediocre solution was adopted, Pierre saw that the buildings would absorb such a large part of his credit that he would still be short of equipment. And his mood darkened even more.

During this insane year, his daily life and Marie's fell out of harmony. Exactly one year after the awarding of the Nobel Prize, Marie had had a second child. The confusion surrounding her sudden fame had opportunely removed her from the radium emanations for at least a few hours a week, and she had temporarily stopped teaching at Sèvres in order to conserve her strength, but during this pregnancy she experienced a different sort of distress. She had become stupid, she said. She was always sleepy, when she wasn't hungry. She wanted caviar and she no longer wanted to talk about physics or mathematics or radioactivity. This left Pierre helpless, as though he had been cut off from his own life source. What was wrong with her? The only thing wrong with her was that she

124

was pregnant and this time all her energy was concentrated on the child she was carrying, but she panicked and begged her sister to come.

Bronia came and comforted Marie, reassured her, protected her, nursed her, and helped her pull herself together. A beautiful little girl named Eve was born, and a few weeks later Marie, happy and moved by the new baby, recovered her strength and her enthusiasm and was filled with a powerful love of life. Her animal nature, which had been so tightly restrained for so many years, rebelled.

"We have to eat, drink, sleep, lie around, love each other—I mean, we have to be in touch with the sweetest things in life, and yet not succumb to them completely," Pierre had written, speaking of his "fragile brain." "Yet while we do this, the unnatural thoughts to which we have devoted our lives must remain uppermost and continue on their imperturbable course through our poor heads." That was certainly true, but in Marie's head, natural thoughts were claiming a place among the unnatural thoughts.

Her mornings were taken up by her children and her house. She had gone back to teaching at Sèvres. She was organizing the laboratory in the rue Cuvier. But she also wanted a vacation, she wanted to enjoy herself, she wanted to get away. And she was finding it less difficult to get used to being famous than was her husband, for whom fame was a profitless thing.

Sometimes there is a pathetic note in Pierre's correspondence with his childhood friend, Georges Gouÿ—a correspondence that shows a slightly different aspect of him from what we see in Marie's descriptions.

In July 1905, he writes: "We are still leading the same kind of life—we are very busy and do nothing interesting. For a year now I have done no work and I haven't had a moment to myself. Obviously, I haven't yet found a way to protect us from frittering our time away, and yet I must. It's a matter of life and death, intellectually."

In fact, Pierre did not publish again after he won the Nobel Prize.

"My pains seem to come from a kind of neurasthenia rather

125

than true rheumatism." To fight this neurasthenia, the family doctor gave him strychnine and put him back on a substantial diet. But at the time he took possession of his chair, in November, he wrote to Georges Gouÿ: "I'm not very well, but I'm not very sick either. I tire very easily and I no longer have much capacity for work. My wife, on the other hand, leads a very active life, with her children, the school at Sèvres, and the laboratory. She never wastes a minute, and is much more regularly involved with the running of the laboratory than I am." A very active life. "Her" children.

Pierre and Marie were not estranged, and they never would be. It was simply that life had to be lived, and perhaps Pierre was not capable of going through the motions any more.

The sublime world of the Curies, two solitary lovers, had changed almost imperceptibly. The Curies were seen more often at the theater, where they went to watch "la Duse" and Ibsen plays staged by Lugné Poë. The Paris public, who put on formal dress to go out in the evening, turned their lorgnettes on Pierre's shapeless overcoat and the loden cape Marie threw over her eternal gray dress. The Curies were seen at a concert at the Colonne, where they went to hear Ignace Paderewski, who had become "the most illustrious pianist in the world" since the time when Marie, Bronia, and Casimir were claques in a half-empty hall at his first recital in Paris.

Spiritualism, which had always intrigued Pierre, was the fashion now. The discovery of X rays had inspired the wildest ideas about manifestations of invisible things. Eusapia Paladino, a medium with a large reputation, was something of a celebrity in Paris at this time. One evening Pierre Curie and Jean Perrin found themselves sitting at a table with the beautiful woman between them. She put her right foot on the left foot of one of them, her left foot on the right foot of the other, and asked for the room to be made completely dark. The light was turned off. A sort of ectoplasm appeared, brushed against Pierre's face and then Perrin's. At that point someone thought of turning the light on. Eusapia had slipped out of her shoes without either man noticing, the shoes being weighted down, and was waving a muslin scarf in the air.

126

The Curies were seen at the Salon d'Automne, the shrine of modern painting. At the Grand Palais, Rodin's "The Thinker" was being shown. Marie took a liking to Rodin, whom she had met at Loïe Fuller's house, and she often went to see him in his studio.

Loïe Fuller, an American dancer, was at that time the darling of Paris. She was presenting a show at the Folies-Bergère in which skillfully blended lights played over the veils she used in her dancing. People called her "the fairy of light." She had read in the newspaper that radium was luminous, and one day the Curies received a letter from her asking them how she could coat herself with radium so as to become phosphorescent.

Pierre sent her a kind answer—he answered everyone—without making fun of her ignorance. The young woman was touched and showed her gratitude in a delicate way, by offering to come and dance for the Curies at their house. The dining room of boulevard Kellermann was invaded by the beautiful American's electricians and became the setting for a remarkable evening. Loïe Fuller was delightful. A friendship grew up between her and the Curies, born perhaps of the sympathy that celebrities have for each other, however different their work may be.

Marie would never get used to facing a crowd or dealing with strangers, but her sudden fame had made her more gentle. The only things she could not tolerate were boredom and the least attempt at familiarity. But who would dare to be familiar? Madame Curie was an intimidating woman. She intimidated the people sitting next to her at dinner, she intimidated her students, she intimidated her fellow workers, and she even intimidated the impudent little Marguerite Borel, who had plenty of nerve and who, at the age of nineteen, could wrap the foremost scientists of France around her little finger.

The Curies' circle had enlarged to include the Borels—or more exactly the Borels' circle had enlarged to include the Curies, who began to appear at their house now and then.

Emile Borel was a brilliant mathematician and a handsome, dark-haired man with gold-flecked eyes. His very young wife Marguerite, lively and provocative, was the daughter of the dean of the Faculté des Sciences, Paul Appell. The Borels and the Perrins took turns entertaining their friends once a week, their friends being mainly Emile's and Jean's former schoolmates at the Ecole Normale. Only men came to these parties. The ones who were married, like Paul Langevin, came without their wives. Mathematicians, physicists, and chemists crowded around the piano, the wood fire, the bottles of beer, and the cakes; sometimes writers came too, like Jacques Maritain and Charles Péguy, who turned up a few times, and Léon Blum and Edouard Herriot. The latter challenged all the others to ask him a question he couldn't answer about the poetry of Victor Hugo. Even Langevin didn't know as much as he did about Hugo. Langevin's writer was Balzac.

The intellectual level of these young men's parties moved between the most esoteric sort of scientific discussion and the crudest sort of practical joke. Sometimes Jean Perrin sat down at the piano and sang the "Song of the Grail" in a duet with Langevin. They were both staunch admirers of Wagner, whose operas were beginning to be put on in Paris.

Young Marguerite, charming, coquettish, provocative, fluttered here and there among her admirers. She flirted outrageously with Perrin, whom she called "the Archangel" because of his curly hair, and with Langevin, who had "such beautiful chestnut eyes" and knew how to use them; in this group she played the role of the pretty little idiot and pretended to think that her ignorance was tiresome to these young scholars, just for the pleasure of hearing Perrin say that "flowers don't know anything either."

She would go with them when they went out in the evening to give a talk at an *université populaire,* where they would chat with the audience after the lecture in a kitchen at the back of the courtyard.The audience always included a few bareheaded female workers. (At that time the hat was a symbol of bourgeois status.) Marguerite also knew how to listen, how to be entrusted with secrets, how to sense that a love affair was beginning or ending, how to cook up a plate of scrambled eggs for someone who arrived shouting, "I'm hungry!"

"Sometimes," she wrote, "Pierre and Marie Curie slip in like two shadows. He speaks very little. She looks very young and attractive with her curly hair, and she abruptly enters a conversation about science and talks for a long time about what she thinks. They intimidate me."

But Marie, who was so intolerant of idle chatter, also fell under the charm of this sharp little person, this dedicated feminist who later, with some success, started a publication called the *Revue du Mois:* she even managed to persuade Pierre Curie to write for it. She went on to gain quite a reputation as a novelist, writing under the name of Camille Marbo.

One evening, the Borels met the Curies at the theater. Marguerite, excited by the play (it was one of Ibsen's), talked animatedly about the heroine. Marie, amused by her ardor, kissed her—such a stupefying event that sixty years later Marguerite piously recorded it in her memoirs.

The Borels had dash, style, influential friends, and also strong characters and courage. A few years later, when Marie became the object of a scandal, Borel was brave enough to offer her a refuge, though not without a sense of how dramatic the situation was.

In university circles, there were a few wealthy young men but many more whose parents had "bled themselves white," as people said in those days, so that their sons could enter the Ecole Normale or the Ecole Polytechnique, and who were to become the pride of the Republic. Emile Borel was the son of a minister. Jean Perrin's mother, an officer's widow, ran a tobacconist's shop. And Langevin's father, as we have said, was a locksmith.

They are the sort of people who have nurtured France's tradition of respect for knowledge, its reverence for memory, its predilection for the apt quotation in the midst of a political speech, reminding one that the speaker studied the humanities before he started busying himself with questions of

129

water supply; its veneration for competitive exams, degrees, and common stocks of historical and literary references—and it has taken a long time to realize just how rare this attitude actually is.

In 1904, Jaurès told Aristide Briand the names of the people who were going to write for the newspaper he was starting, *L'Humanité*—Briand himself was to be the political correspondent—and said proudly, "Seven of them have higher degrees!" Briand answered, "But where are the journalists?" He was right to ask.

It didn't matter. At that time the future shone with the light of one idea: that knowledge would belong to everyone and that instead of listening to the Church preach resignation and obedience, the people would possess the means to free themselves. Freedom, then, began with instruction. "Revolution doesn't take place in the factories but in the schools!" said Jaurès.

The Borels and their friends were ardent partisans of the secularization of teaching, and this hardly dismayed the Curies. On the contrary, Pierre and Marie had not baptized their children at a time when baptism was almost a social obligation. Nor had they simply exchanged one form of sectarianism for another. Pierre, however, agreed with Berthelot when he said that "science, the emancipator, has for centuries stooped under the oppressive yoke of theocracy."

If the Curies were not very conscious of the daily turmoil of politics, it was because they were horrified by the violence that went with it and this violence had been rife, even in the churches, ever since the Combes ministry had been elected in 1902. A substantial majority in the Parliament—339 as against 124—supported the government and would keep it in power for thirty-one months, but an active minority was fighting it.

For some, Combes—a former professor of Catholic philosophy, and all the more heretical because he had swung so far in a different direction—was nothing less than the son of Satan, while for others, as his nickname said it, he was "little father

Combes," the father of the people. Not only was Combes dissolving religious congregations, he was also allied with the "reds." The very same day that he obtained Parliament's vote of confidence to carry out "a policy of secularization, social reform, and solidarity," the poet José-Maria de Heredia, receiving Melchior de Vogüé into the Académie Française, congratulated the new member on having come from a line of people who "loved God, the king, their land and war." From then on, no nomination, no promotion of any functionary could take place without the prefects being consulted about the Republican loyalism of the person concerned.

The birth of the secular state, sanctioned in 1905 by the separation of church and state, was not accomplished without pain and hatred. One day Marie herself was to suffer from its aftereffects.

For the moment, she was less interested in the outcries of the Clericals against the Republic and the daily scuffles that accompanied the Republic's dissolution of the religious congregations than she was in the Russian uprising.

Bronia and Jozef had written her that this time, at last, Poland would be rid of its oppressor.

"If only this hope isn't disappointed," Marie wrote to her brother. "I long for it ardently and I never stop thinking about it. In any case, I think the Revolution must be supported. I will send money to Casimir for this, since I unfortunately can't give any direct help."

For the time being, their hope was disappointed.

But a different hope, which Marie had never stopped nourishing, was realized—Pierre was admitted to the Académie des Sciences. He had been asked to be a candidate again, and this time, after a brief struggle, he consented and even inflicted on himself the ordeal of paying the ritual visits, though we don't know why.

"My deal Curie," wrote Mascart, "manage it any way you can, but before June 20 you must make the sacrifice of a final round of visits to the members of the Académie, even if you have to hire a car for the day."

131

Pierre Curie made himself do it, but his attitude is rather hard to understand. Impossible to understand, even if we take into account Marie's influence. True, it was the first tribute—and the only one—Pierre Curie would receive from his fellow countrymen. And nobody's perfect.

But once he was elected, he wrote to Georges Gouÿ about what was bothering him:

> I find myself in the Académie without having wanted to be there and without the Académie wanting to have me. . . . Everyone told me that it was agreed I would receive fifty votes. That's why I almost didn't get in.
>
> . . . What can I say? In this place they can't do anything in a simple way, without intrigues. Quite aside from a very well run little campaign, the lack of sympathy on the part of the Clericals and the people who thought I hadn't paid enough visits worked against me. . . .
>
> . . . Really, I ask myself what I am doing here. The meetings are not at all interesting. It is very clear to me that this is not my sort of circle.

His election resulted in an interview with Marie in *La Patrie*. Was she expecting a similar reward for her own work? "Oh, I'm only a woman, nothing but a woman, I will never have a seat under the Coupole." Her only ambition, she added, was to help her husband with his work.

But the readers of *La Patrie* hardly had a chance to appreciate this healthy feminine modesty when a stinging denial from Marie said that this was a "purely imaginary" speech. The editor sheepishly admitted it and apologized.

After two postponements, the trip to Stockholm for the ceremony required by the rules of the Swedish Academy took place. It was a relatively happy event. The Swedes had planned the ceremony in a simple way, without ostentation, without crowds of people, and without excessive publicity. Most of the people Pierre and Marie met were scientists. Because Marie could speak German and English, they had plenty of people to talk to. Also, June in Sweden was beautiful, and the Curies still loved nature.

Every Nobel laureate was supposed to give a speech about the work for which he or she had been given the prize, and of course Pierre was the one who gave it, even though Marie shared the prize equally. He stood on the stage; she sat in the audience.

He had just gone through eighteen months that had been difficult in every respect, as well as scientifically unproductive, but he had a more acute sense of the meaning of research. He still believed in what he told his students over and over again when they were talking about social problems: "It isn't worth worrying about. Physicists will solve these problems quite simply by doing away with them, because they will create enough wealth for everyone."

But he ended his talk by saying, "It is also conceivable that in the hands of criminals, radium may become very dangerous, and here one may well ask oneself if mankind benefits from knowing the secrets of Nature, if we are mature enough to take advantage of them or if this knowledge isn't harmful to us. The example of Nobel's discoveries is typical: these powerful explosives have allowed men to perform admirable works. They also constitute a terrible means of destruction in the hands of the great criminals who are drawing the people towards war."

And he concluded: "I am one of those who believe, as did Nobel, that mankind will derive more good than ill from these new discoveries." But he could hardly say anything else to the academy founded by the inventor of dynamite.

Pierre Curie was the sort of scientist who devoted himself to science in the same spirit that some people devoted themselves to art, in order to escape the bleak despair of daily life. But radium had opened up an abyss in the path along which he was feeling his way, and in the abyss he saw the mystery of mysteries, which at once fascinated and horrified him—the mystery of matter. Yet it was another scientist who later used

133

radium—used these radioactive elements—to split the nucleus, which had once been thought to be indivisible.

The Curies were only one of the links in the chain of scientific discovery in which a person says, "I've found it" only days, perhaps, before someone else would have found it, someone who hesitated or got off the track, or who was so shackled by his knowledge that he took too many facts for granted and lost the intellectual agility to prove them wrong.

Max Planck later admitted that in 1900, when he proposed his unlikely hypothesis involving "quanta," it was an "act of desperation" for him to introduce it into the theory of energy. It was a hypothesis that completely overturned physics, one that no one was willing to admit, and that he himself fought when Einstein applied it to light five years later.

Henri Poincaré, who in 1896 suggested to Becquerel that he perform the experiment that proved so crucial, and who had spoken of the "principle of relativity" in 1904 and given evidence of surprising premonitions about it, showed himself to be, in Einstein's words, "simply hostile to the theory of relativity, and despite all his acumen, he hardly seemed to understand what we were doing" (at a conference six years after Einstein—who was an examiner at the Berne Patent Office—had described the theory).

In a letter intended to support Einstein's candidacy for a position as professor in Zurich, Poincaré wrote, "Since M. Einstein is exploring all sorts of avenues, one must expect that most of them will be dead ends, but at the same time one must hope that one of the directions he has pointed out will be the right one." But Poincaré also added, "That is good enough. It is certainly the way one must proceed. The role of mathematical physics is to pose the questions well; only by experiment can they be answered."

At the same time that Pierre Curie was giving his speech in Stockholm, Einstein was proposing his famous equation, $E = mc^2$, which would be verified by experiment thirty years later, and given concrete form in 1945, with the bombing of Hiroshima. It would also be manifested in the form of nuclear power stations furnishing the "new source of energy renewing itself with almost no labor," which Marcelin Berthelot saw as the fundamental problem of the twenty-first century.

As we can see, Pierre Curie's speech did more than simply express the sort of unrelieved pessimism that may be characteristic of an optimist who is physically debilitated.

thirteen

O N April 15, 1906, Marie was in the country with the children. The summer before, she had rented a house close to Paris, in Saint-Rémy-de-Chevreuse.

Pierre came to join them there.

Easter Sunday and Monday were to be the last two days the family would be together. Apparently they were pleasant days, if perhaps a little melancholy.

The Curies' dreams had shrunk to more human proportions, and so had their work. And they had had to make a considerable effort to achieve a new balance now that they were both famous. In the eyes of the public, their performance had been faultless, with Pierre consistently taking pains to "give his wife all the credit," as one of his English colleagues put it. But he had decided to give up radioactivity and go back to his work on the physics of crystals, and that was no doubt significant.

After a spring which had been so rainy that in Paris the Seine had risen to a dangerously high level, the weather was beautiful. As they had done when they were younger, Pierre and Marie took long walks in the countryside, picked newly opened flowers, and laid a big fire in the fireplace. They talked about the future. Pierre thought about different teaching methods. He dreamed of an education for his daughters, for all girls and boys, in which science would be incorporated— without it, how could twentieth-century culture mean anything?

He took the train back to town Monday evening, carrying a bouquet of buttercups with him. Marie returned Wednesday evening. In Paris, it was raining again. At the dinner of the

Société de Physique, which always took place in the Foyot restaurant, Pierre started a discussion with Henri Poincaré on educational reform. The next day, Thursday, he had to attend a luncheon for professors from the Faculté des Sciences, which took place in the Hôtel des Sociétés Savantes; then stop by Gauthier-Villars, his publisher, to correct proofs of an article; and then go on to a meeting at the Académie.

The rain had stopped, and after lunch he walked down the boulevard Saint-Germain. At Gauthier-Villars, he found the doors locked; the employees of the print shops had stopped work. The great wave of strikes of May 1906 had begun. He turned into the rue Dauphine and walked toward the quays and the Institut.

The rain started again, and he opened his umbrella. The street was narrow and crowded. He stepped out into the street from behind a hackney carriage, and ten seconds later his head was crushed on the muddy pavement.

A truck pulled by two horses had been coming up the rue Dauphine from the quays. Just as it met and passed the hackney carriage, the driver had seen a man in black holding an umbrella appear suddenly in front of his left horse. The man had staggered and tried to catch hold of the horse's harness. Entangled in his umbrella, he had slipped between the two horses while the driver tried with all his strength to rein them in. But the weight of the truck, which was five meters long and loaded with military equipment, had carried it forward. The left rear wheel struck Pierre's head and crushed it.

A mob formed, people began to abuse the panic-stricken driver; other people intervened, said they had seen the accident, and that the man had thrown himself under the team. A scuffle broke out; the police stepped in. Someone stopped a cab. The driver refused to take the body of the man in black because he didn't want to get blood all over the seats of his cab.

At last a stretcher arrived. The man in black was carried to the nearest police station, in the rue des Grands Augustins. In his jacket pocket they found visiting cards bearing the famous name. The boulevard Kellermann address was on some, the address of the Faculté des Sciences on others. A police inspector telephoned the Faculté.

Outside the police station, the news began to spread. Pierre Curie had been killed by a truck driver! This time, the crowd was ready to tear the driver limb from limb. The police took him away, along with his truck and his team of horses, who were nervously pawing the sticky ground. The driver's name was Louis Manin. He was thirty years old. He sat crying on a bench at the police station while a doctor counted the fragments of what had been Pierre Curie's skull and cleaned up his face, which was dirty but intact.

A former lab assistant, Pierre Clerc, arrived from the Faculté and burst into tears when he saw the gaping wound, which the doctor quickly covered over with a bandage. "Do you recognize M. Curie?" the police inspector asked him. And he picked up the telephone. It would have irritated Pierre Curie to know that he was important enough, even in death, for the minister of the interior to be informed right away, but he no longer had the ears to hear about it.

A messenger from the President rang the doorbell of the house in boulevard Kellermann and asked for Mme Curie. The maid answered that Madame hadn't come home yet. The messenger left. The doorbell rang again and Dr. Curie answered it. When the old man saw the distraught faces of Jean Perrin and Paul Appell, the dean of the Faculté, he did not ask them anything, but simply spoke four words: "My son is dead." They told him how the accident had happened. And the Doctor, overcome, murmured, "What was he dreaming about this time?"

Marie came home late that day. She opened the door with her key and went directly into the room where Perrin and

The first Solvay conference, which took place in Brussels, October 29–November 3, 1911, and was attended by the greatest names in international physics. Standing, l. to r.: R. B. Goldschmidt, M. Planck, H. Rubens, A. Sommerfeld, F. Lindemann, M. de Broglie, M. Knudsen, Hasenohrl, Hostelet, Herzen, J. H. Jeans, E. Rutherford, H. Kamerlingh Onnes, A. Einstein, P. Langevin. Seated: W. Nernst, M. Brillouin, E. Solvay, H. A. Lorentz, O.H. Warburg, J. Perrin, W. Wien, M. Curie, H. Poincaré.

Close-up of a famous detail from the above photo: Marie Curie between Jean Perrin (on her right) and Henri Poincaré (on her left). She was about to turn 44.

Marya, Bronia, and Hela Sklodowska with their father in 1890. "How was he to make ends meet?"

Marie and Irène in 1908 after Pierre's death.

Jacques and Pierre Curie with their father and mother. "My parents are remarkable."

Pierre Curie at about age 40. A "high degree of civilization."

Pierre and Marie Curie in 1895. Making their way at once "through the realm of the sublime and through the realm of theoretical physics."

Setting off on their bicycles after the wedding. "Without wedding rings and without a benediction."

Irène (eight years) and Eve (one year). Always dressed by their mother.

The house at Boulevard Kellermann.
"The wisteria, the hawthorns, and
the iris are beginning."

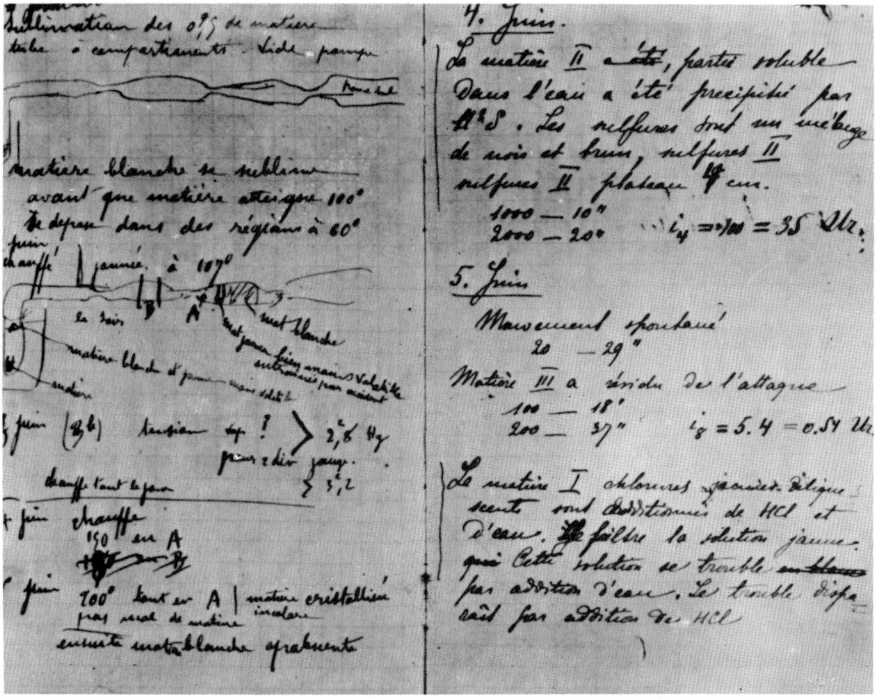

Two pages in the black laboratory notebook. The two handwritings mingle.

The laboratory where radium was discovered. "Like a stable or a root cellar."

Marie at her work table. The temperature in the room would sometimes fall to 6.25° C.

Paul Langevin in 1902, aged 30.
"A thunderous boy."

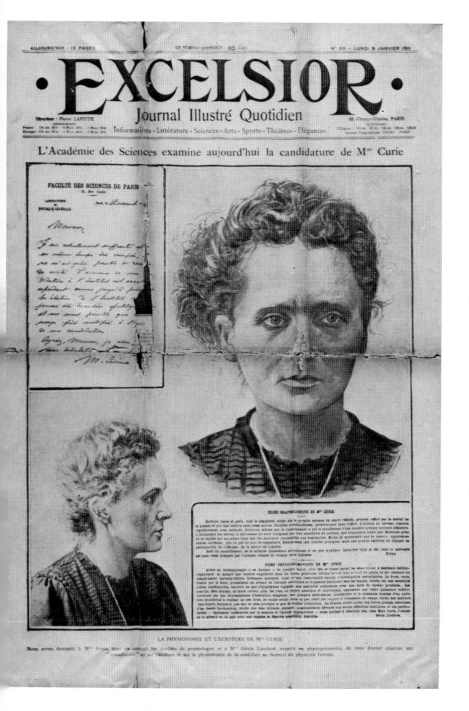

The front page of *L'Excelsior*, January 9, 1911.

The "little Curies" on display in the courtyard of Les Invalides. 1,100,000 radiographs were taken in 1917–1918.

Marie at the wheel of her radiology
Renault. She drove in all kinds of
weather at speeds up to 50 km/hr.

With American industrialists in Pittsburgh in 1921. "The anti-star bombed."

At the White House with President
Harding. "Dignifying science."

With Albert Einstein in Geneva.
"His work is absolutely first rate."

Jean Perrin.

Henri Becquerel.

Ernest Rutherford.

André Debierne.

Appell were waiting for her with the Doctor. They told her very plainly what had happened.

Marie froze. Then she asked, "Pierre is dead? Is he really dead?"

Yes, Pierre was really dead.

Pale and mute, she seemed to close in on herself.

Did she want an autopsy to be performed?

No.

Did she want Pierre's body to be brought back to boulevard Kellermann?

Yes.

A telegram was sent to Bronia, then a message to the Perrins, where Irène was playing, asking them please to keep her there. Marie went out into the garden, where the rain was still pouring down, and sat down and waited. She waited one hour, then two.

A police inspector brought her Pierre's keys, wallet, and undamaged watch. Then the ambulance arrived, accompanied by André Debierne. Marie showed the stretcher-bearers into a room on the ground floor, watched impassively as the dead man was laid out, and then shut herself in with him.

The next morning, when she saw Jacques Curie, who had hurried from Montpellier, she broke down for a moment and then pulled herself together again.

The doorbell kept ringing. There was a succession of visitors. Telegrams flooded in from all corners of the world, letters piled up; some of the condolences came from royalty, some from republicans, some from scientists; some were formal and some were simply emotional and sincere. Pierre Curie was a famous man. He was also a man people had liked.

Who would make the customary speech? Who would represent the government? The Académie? While people were discussing this, Marie moved the date of the funeral forward. Pierre had died on a Thursday afternoon; he was buried Saturday morning, without ceremony, in the Sceaux cemetery where his mother lay. Only his friends were present. The minister of public education, Aristide Briand, had discreetly slipped in among them.

Le Journal of April 22, 1906, carried the following report:

> On the arm of her father-in-law, Mme Curie followed her husband's coffin to a grave that had been dug at the base of the cemetery wall in the shadow of the chestnut trees. There she remained motionless for a moment, with a fixed and hard look on her face; but when a spray of flowers was brought up to the grave, she took it suddenly and began pulling out the flowers one by one and scattering them over the coffin.
>
> She did this slowly and deliberately and seemed to have completely forgotten the other people gathered there, who were deeply impressed and did not make a sound.
>
> The master of ceremonies, however, felt obliged to warn Mme Curie that she would have to receive the condolences of the people present. Then, without saying a word, she let the bouquet fall to the ground and rejoined her father-in-law.

From now on, Marie was known as "the famous widow." She was thirty-eight years old. Pierre had just turned forty-seven. They had been married for almost eleven years. Eleven years was a long time, long enough for the roots of love, if the tree was robust, to plunge so deep that they would survive forever.

Marie had not only lost the man who had been with her day and night, who had shared her work and her success. She had also lost her security. She had lost the man who had loved her whether she was proud or dejected, inspired or stubborn, shy or categorical; he had loved her because she was his very heart.

Now she would go into mourning not only for Pierre but also for herself as she had been, supremely young and in love with a great man: this young Marie had died with him and no one would ever be able to bring her back.

She was also going to torture herself, punish herself for all the times she had been distracted from him.

Marie left an account of the days immediately following Pierre's death in a gray notebook where her small, clear, and regular handwriting suddenly becomes disordered. This was a sort of laboratory notebook of grief.

> Pierre, my Pierre, you are there, calm as a poor wounded man sleeping with his head wrapped up.
>
> . . . Your lips, which I used to call greedy, are pale and colorless. Your little beard is touched with gray. Your hair is hardly visible because the wound starts there, and above your forehead, to the right, is the bone that has been broken. Oh! How you were hurt, how you bled, your clothes were soaked in blood. What a terrible shock your head suffered, your poor head that I stroked so often, taking it in my two hands. . . . I would kiss your eyelids, which you would close so that I could touch them, bending your head down to me with a familiar gesture. . . .
>
> . . . We put you in your coffin Saturday morning and I held your head while you were moved. We kissed your cold face for the last time. Then we put into the coffin a few periwinkles from the garden and the little portrait of me you loved, the one you called "the good little student."
>
> . . . Your coffin was closed and I couldn't see you anymore. I couldn't let them cover it with the awful black cloth. I covered it with flowers and sat down next to it.
>
> . . . They came to get you, an unhappy group, I looked at them, I didn't talk to them. We took you back to Sceaux and we watched you go down into the large, deep hole. Then there was a frightful parade of people. They wanted to take us away. We resisted, Jacques and I, we wanted to watch till the very end, they filled up the grave, they put sheaves of flowers on it, it was all over, Pierre was sleeping his last sleep under the earth, it was the end of everything, everything, everything.

Two weeks after the funeral, on May 7, she wrote: "My Pierre, I can't stop thinking about you, my head is bursting and my mind is confused. I can't understand that from now on I have to live without seeing you, without smiling at my life's sweet friend."

And on May 11: "My Pierre, I get up after having slept quite well, relatively calm. Hardly a quarter of an hour later and here I am again wanting to howl like a wild animal."

If only she had been able to howl.

The day after the funeral, she went to the Perrins' house. Irène, who was seven now, had to be told that her father was dead. She was playing with Aline Perrin. She didn't seem to understand, and went on playing. "I understood it more quickly," Aline Perrin tells us, "and I heard Mme Curie saying to maman, 'She's too young, she doesn't understand.'"

Nowadays Marie would have known that children are never "too young." As soon as she left, Irène burst into tears and begged to be taken back to her mother's house.

"She cried a good deal at the house, then she went off to her little friends' house again, to forget. . . . Now she doesn't seem to be thinking about it anymore." Marie wrote in her gray notebook.

"Arrival of Jozef and Bronia. They are good."

"Everyone is talking. And all I can see is Pierre, Pierre on his deathbed."

In the midst of the unhappy confusion that had filled the house, she was preoccupied, tense, silent. The two families were worried. A woman alone with two children. What would become of her?

Pierre's friends thought of taking up a public subscription. With one word, Marie nipped the plan in the bud. Repugnant. The government informed Jacques Curie that Marie would receive a state pension, like Pasteur's wife. She refused to accept it. She knew how to work and she would work.

In that case, where would she work? How? What did she want? She didn't want anything. "I don't even want to kill myself," she wrote in the gray notebook.

Jacques Curie and Georges Gouÿ talked it over with Pierre's friends. The ministry was alerted. The council of the Faculté des Sciences had a meeting. At last an offer was made: if Marie agreed, she could occupy the chair in general physics that had been created for Pierre.

This was the sort of offer she could listen to: never before had a woman been admitted into the upper-level teaching positions. As had happened in other fields, the first woman to be admitted was coming in on the shoulders of a dead man.

This time, would she agree? "I'll try," she said. She was appointed assistant lecturer on May 13, 1906, with an annual salary of ten thousand francs, effective May 1. She wrote in the gray notebook: "My little Pierre, I want to tell you that the laburnums are in flower, and the wisteria, the hawthorns, and the iris are beginning—you would have loved it all. I would also like to tell you that they've given me your chair and some imbeciles even congratulated me on it."

Jacques Curie, Georges Gouÿ, and Jozef were reassured and went back home, leaving Marie worn out but calm. In a letter he sent her on May 9, Georges Gouÿ thanked her for being willing "to shake off your sad thoughts for a while in order to occupy yourself with the scientific matters that were so dear to Pierre," and gave her some information about an experimental electrical circuit. In 1898, Georges Gouÿ had discovered that Brownian movement was a manifestation of heat.

"Everything is dismal," Marie noted on June 16. "Life's preoccupations don't even leave me time to think in peace about my Pierre."

Except for a few fragments, the contents of the gray notebook are going to remain secret until 1990. We know, however, that Marie did not even tell Pierre, who would never read it, about the gruesome scene that Bronia described thirty years later.

Bronia was about to leave to go back to her husband in Zakopane, when her sister called her into her room one evening. There was a fire burning in the fireplace even though the spring was mild. "Bronia," said Marie, "you have to help me." She locked the door, took from the wardrobe a package wrapped in thick wrapping paper, picked up a pair of scissors, crouched down in front of the fire, motioned to her sister to sit near her, and undid the package.

The package contained a bundle tied up in a sheet. She untied the sheet and Bronia saw a tangle of clothes stiff with dried mud and blood. They were the clothes Pierre had been wearing when he fell in the rue Dauphine. Marie had been keeping them in her room for the past month.

Methodically, she began to cut Pierre's jacket into pieces which she threw one by one into the flames, then she stopped and began wildly kissing the soiled cloth. Bronia tore the scissors and the clothes out of her hands, and threw away the paper, the sheet, and the napkin with which she had wiped Marie's hands and her own.

"I couldn't bear to have anyone else touching them," Marie said. "Do you understand?"

And suddenly, clinging to her sister, she sobbed, cried out, hiccuped: "How am I going to live now? What am I going to do?"

It took a long time for Bronia to undress her, put her to bed, and calm her down.

Now it was summer. The sunshine is painful when inside you everything is black.

"I spend every day at the laboratory," Marie wrote in the gray notebook. "I can no longer think of anything that gives me any personal happiness, except perhaps for scientific work—and yet not even that, because if I were successful I couldn't bear it that you wouldn't know."

But she would be successful, and she would be able to bear it, because that is the way life is.

fourteen

B Y NOON on November 5, 1906, a crowd had already started to invade the Place de la Sorbonne and trample the ground in front of the closed gates, even though the meeting wasn't scheduled to begin until one-thirty in the afternoon. At one o'clock, the small physics lecture hall was taken by storm, then the doors were immediately closed again. "The front rows looked like the orchestra seats of a theater," *Le Journal* reported. "Formal dresses, a profusion of large hats; fortunately, the hall is built in tiers!" Sitting between Jean Perrin and Paul Appell was the Countess Greffulhe, who could be identified by her toque. She made her own hats, and she had just started a craze for toques.

About fifteen students from Sèvres had come to watch this memorable performance by "the first woman to join the Masters," as one of them put it, and they were astonished to see that there were more society women, artists, photographers, and members of the Polish colony than students in an audience that had come to hear a talk about the ionization of gases.

The custom was for the dean of the Faculté to "induct" the new holder of a chair, and for the latter to thank the ministry and the Faculté and to speak in praise of his predecessor. At one-twenty, Paul Appell got to his feet and said that in keeping with Mme Curie's wishes, there would be no official induction and no eulogy. At one-thirty, Marie slipped furtively into the hall. As she put her papers on the table and rubbed her worn fingers together, she was greeted by an ovation. She waited with lowered eyes for the applause to die down, then began speaking in a flat voice, her r's resounding: "When we consider the progress physics has made over the last ten years,

145

we are surprised at the way our ideas about electricity and matter have changed." She was resuming Pierre's course just where he had left off.

She was so wound up, she was on the point of collapsing. She couldn't be heard very well. Her voice was weak, her delivery too rapid. She was addressing a public that wouldn't have understood her anyway—she might as well have been speaking Chinese. And yet something was happening here that made people's eyes grow dim, their throats tighten, that kept the entire audience right up to the highest rows rigid with emotion before this small black figure. She finished in a storm of applause, picked up her papers, and slipped away. It was fifteen years to the day since the small Polish student, newly arrived from Warsaw, had crossed the courtyard of the Sorbonne for the first time.

"A curved forehead like a Memling virgin," said one man, describing the impression Marie made on him that day. Another wrote that she had "a strange face, ageless. Her light and deep eyes seemed tired from having read too much or cried too much." And the columinst from *Le Journal* called the event "a great victory for feminism. . . . For if a woman is allowed to teach upper-level courses to students of both sexes, what does that say about so-called male superiority? I tell you, the time is very near when women will become human beings."

At some point during the few months after Marie's lecture, a successful novelist named Colette Yvert published a book called *Princesses of Science*. The heroine of the novel is Thérèse, a doctor's daughter who follows in her father's footsteps. She gets married and has a child while continuing to practice medicine. What happens? The silver no longer shines, the cook takes another job on the side, her husband's collars are badly starched, and the child dies while still an infant.

Now the husband goes off looking for consolation and affection in the home of an indolent young widow. Thérèse finally understands that instead of imitating her father, she should have imitated her mother, and that it is high time to renounce her profession and help her husband's career by giving dinner parties for his friends.

In other words, if Mme Curie had stayed at home, her husband wouldn't have died in an accident, most likely wearing a shirt that was missing a button. After all, when servants aren't watched, they become careless.

At the end of the year, *Princesses of Science* was awarded the Prix Fémina by an all-woman jury. Feminism still had a long way to go.

More serious—but also more stimulating—was Lord Kelvin's attack. The eminent old man, who was now in his eighty-third year, had come to Paris to attend Pierre's funeral, and he had been very affectionate and attentive to Marie. But he had gotten it into his head that radium was not an element, and he chose to publicize this on the first page of the London *Times*, in the famous letters column. Naturally, this caused just the sort of stir the venerable and illustrious Lord Kelvin had hoped for.

His hypothesis—that radium was probably only a molecular compound of lead and helium—contradicted not only Marie Curie's hypothesis, but also Rutherford and Soddy's theory of the existence of something called "atomic energy." The old lion of British physics, who was beginning to be irritated by these young people, had to be licking his chops over this.

During the summer of 1906, the *Times* became the site of a furious battle that spilled over into the specialized magazine *Nature*. Sooner or later, all the most famous scientists of the time became involved in it.

"I don't see the point of fighting Lord Kelvin's theory," wrote Marie haughtily; she was supported in her opposition to the old guard by scientists representing modern radiochemistry. She was right. Once "doubts had been expressed by people to whom the atomic hypothesis of radioactivity did not yet appear to be obvious," it was useless to argue. The hypothesis had to be proved.

147

To prove it, she had to produce, not salts of pure radium, several centigrams of which she had managed to obtain after four years of work and a few thousand procedures, but the metal itself. Marie was the only one who could to it. And from now on her laboratory was to benefit from considerable material help from a new source—Andrew Carnegie.

Carnegie had made an enormous fortune in the steel industry and was now the enthusiastic patron of all sorts of enterprises, though he remained personally very austere. He had met Marie in Paris shortly after Pierre's death, when she was surrounded by an aura of melancholy fame which she bore soberly. He had been touched to the heart by the simplicity of her manner and the exactness of the objectives she had set for herself. He had decided to finance her research, which he was able to do very elegantly. When he arranged the procedure for this financing with the vice-chancellor of the Académie de Paris, he proposed that the foundation created for this be named, not the Fondation Carnegie, but the Fondation Curies. "The plural," he added, "included Madame, which I want very much." As it turned out, the plural had to go; the money stayed, of course.

In her newly reorganized laboratory, with its new equipment and staff, where she would soon be training a generation of young researchers in the methods she had invented, Marie, assisted by André Debierne, undertook to demonstrate that Lord Kelvin was mistaken. She was to spend four years doing it. Four years performing painstaking, exhausting procedures that were not feasible with the minute quantity—ten centigrams—of radium salts that she had at her disposal.

"The operation presented great difficulties," was all she said when it was over. By electrolyzing a solution of radium with a cathode of mercury, she had succeeded in condensing an infinitesimal but indisputable particle of white metal—"her" radium, whose melting point she gave as 700°C.

During the same period, she settled an account with a German chemist, Willy Marckwald, who, after performing operations that were just as arduous as Marie's, thought he had discovered a new radioactive substance that he named radiotellure. Rightly convinced that this radiotellure was none other than "her" polonium, Marie had proceeded, after ten months of observations, to tear the unfortunate chemist's discovery to pieces. She even took the trouble to publish a memorandum in German on the subject. Marckwald acknowledged defeat.

Lord Kelvin did not have to submit to the same humiliation. He died before finding out that the charming Mme Curie had proved he was wrong. In a certain sense he had helped her. Nothing is as valuable as a challenge, so long as one has the strength to accept it; Marie drew that strength from her pride, which never failed her. In the eyes of the international scientific community, the young widow who had discovered radium with her husband—no one was sure exactly what part she had played in that romantic collaboration—had emerged as a formidable figure, one unrivaled in her field, and because she was a woman, a unique star in the constellation that shone in the sky of science at that time.

She had lost the bloom of youth, but when she became animated, she glowed with a strange, emaciated beauty that was sparked by intelligence and that captivated everyone who had the rare honor of meeting her. Yet she could also be cold, completely unattractive—unbearable, in fact. This was how she appeared to the American physicist Boltwood. In 1908, he had asked if he could compare his solutions of radium with those Marie had obtained, and he was summarily refused.

"Madame hadn't the least desire to make this comparison," he said to Rutherford. Her "innate" ill will prevented her from "doing anything whatsoever that could directly or indirectly help a researcher working on radioactivity." Boltwood immediately joined the ranks of those who maintained—and there are people who continue to say this—that Mme Curie's reputation was unfounded, even though they trembled at the idea of having to confront her whenever a group of scientists came together.

Her enemies said she took too much advantage of her delicate health, declaring herself to be in a state of "nervous exhaustion" whenever it suited her to interrupt a discussion by leaving the meeting; she would then return to the attack the next day, and would always end up by imposing her will on men who were exasperated, and quite furious, later, at having given in.

The conference held at Brussels to reach an agreement on the definition of an international standard of radium was particularly disagreeable. This standard had become indispensable as much to researchers as in the therapeutic use of radium, in which the doses of radium to be used had to be precisely measured. Once there existed a standard, then each country could produce its own.

It was agreed that Mme Curie would be the one to establish the standard because she was an authority on the subject. Someone suggested naming the unit of measurement a "curie" and Marie deigned to say she found that satisfactory. But what would the unit of measurement be? "The quantity of emanation in equilibrium in one gram of radium," Marie said. She refused to discuss it, left the room, and did not appear at the dinner that closed the conference, saying she had a cold. Jean Perrin and Rutherford had some trouble persuading their colleagues that Marie's health really did require some attention.

Her definition was adopted. Later, Rutherford had to use all his charm to convince Marie that an international standard could not remain in her laboratory. With regret, she parted from the little tube of glass containing the twenty-one milligrams of pure salt that she had precipitated, and deposited it with the International Bureau of Weights and Measures after sealing it with her own hands.

Only the great Rutherford knew how to deal with Marie, because he wasn't awed by her—he liked her. Ever since the conference, when he had had to leave the opera one evening in the middle of a performance to take her, staggering, back to her hotel, he had felt sorry for her, too. "Her nerves are not well," he had been told by several doctors who were attending the conference. Nerves are never ill. They simply tell you that some part of your body is ill. But in 1910, no one knew the results of Dr. Freud's analysis of Dora.

Marie was uncompromising with her colleagues, except when she felt they were of a high enough caliber so that she could discuss things with them. On the other hand, with her "laboratory children," as she called them—to them she was "the boss"—she was kind, though demanding. A Norwegian student, Mme Gleditsch, left the following account of Marie in the laboratory:

> "There wasn't a lot of room, there were only five or six of us workers. Marie Curie came every day and spent hours and hours there. . . . There was no question that she was good at administration. . . . But what was most important and most precious was the close contact between the students and the heads. . . . She had a thorough knowledge of the work each student was doing, and was always very interested in all the details. In the laboratory, her face, which was usually closed and slightly sad, became animated, she smiled often, and she even laughed with a fresh, young laugh. . . . And every student was struck, from time to time, by the extent of her knowledge, the luminous clarity of her mind, as she always grasped the essence of a problem, no matter how complicated it was.

Marie would go home in the evening exhausted. There she was gentle but reserved. She didn't cry, but she wasn't very cheerful either. It would be many years, still, before her daughters were old enough so that she could talk to them about what she had done during the day.

She had once enjoyed the greatest of privileges—a coherent life. She had fulfilled a dream: she had joined together the life of her heart, her mind, and her senses. Now she had been split in two the way a rock is split in two by a stream of water.

After Pierre's death, she left boulevard Kellermann and moved into a house in Sceaux with the old Doctor, the two girls, and a young Polish woman Bronia had sent to manage the house. Her views about the education of children were

151

very decided and, for that period, revolutionary. The first principle was to keep them healthy by having them live in the country, far away from the noxious atmosphere of the city. Then they should be hardened by being put outdoors in all kinds of weather, exercising on bicycles, trapezes, rings, a rope. They should be introduced to different sorts of manual work, since everyone should know how to use his hands, and use them well. Finally, they should receive early training in science.

What about school? "I sometimes have the feeling," Marie wrote to her sister Hela, "that it would be better to drown children than to shut them up in the sort of schools we have now." Strengthened by this conviction, which her father-in-law shared, she managed to persuade her friends Henriette and Jean Perrin, Paul Langevin, and the sinologist Edouard Chavannes and his wife, who were neighbors in Sceaux, that there was an alternative to allowing their little group of a dozen children to waste their time in school. The plan they devised was simple—there would be one lesson every day, and no more. They would draw the teachers from the faculties of the Sorbonne and the Collège de France: Jean Perrin, Paul Langevin, and Marie would share chemistry, mathematics, and physics; Henri Mouton and the sculptor Magrou, who joined the experiment, would take charge of the natural sciences, drawing, and modeling; French, literature, history, and visits to the Louvre would be covered by Henriette Perrin and Mme Chavannes. When word of this plan got around, there were people who didn't think much of it. One gossip columnist wrote: "This little group, which hardly knows how to read or write, is given complete freedom to perform experiments, construct apparatuses, test reactions. . . . The Sorbonne and the building in rue Cuvier haven't blown up yet, but all hope isn't lost!"

The plan was effective, however, to judge by the children's glowing memories of it, and it lasted two years. After that, they had to return to the ranks of ordinary schoolchildren.

Marie clearly had no liking for public education: she put Irène, and later Eve, into a private school.

She did everything she could for her daughters. She toughened them, she educated them in all sorts of fields, she developed their special aptitudes without going against their different temperaments and tastes. Irène was never made to say hello when she met people, and she never did learn to do it, whereas Eve was never scolded for charming everyone and everything.

Both girls learned to speak foreign languages, cook, ski, sew, ride horseback, and play the piano. Marie was uncompromising where mathematics was concerned, and strict about moral lessons. She turned the two into independent young people who knew that they would have to earn their own livings and enjoy doing it, which was just as unusual for that period as it was to let the children go out alone as soon as they turned eleven. She protected them without crushing them, she loved them without smothering them, she treated them both exactly the same, and when the charming Eve decided that she didn't know what she wanted to do—except that she certainly didn't want to go into physics, medicine, or anything to do with what Marie had respected most since her childhood—Marie wasn't in the least critical of her.

She never neglected a cavity, never forgot a birthday. If she gave little time to her children, it was because she didn't have much time. If she did not seem very warm, it was because she didn't know how to show warmth. If she did more equations during the holidays than she gave kisses, it was because she had never been allowed to kiss her own mother.

She never talked to them about their father; she had forbidden his name to be spoken. Open wounds bleed easily, and she would not bleed in front of her children, or in front of anyone. Her rule was to keep quiet in order to remain in control of herself, and she enforced it. This didn't make communication any easier.

In February 1910, Dr. Curie, who was eighty-two years old,

153

died of pneumonia. The day of his funeral, Marie had Pierre's coffin placed on top of his father's, thinking ahead to the day when she would join him. The impenitent rationalist who never set foot in the cemetery was no longer there to tell her that these wooden boxes contained nothing, nothing but insignificant little piles of bones. She did not go into mourning, but only because she had never come out of mourning.

When later that year Marguerite Borel, who was having dinner at the Perrins' house, saw her arrive wearing a white dress with a rose through her belt, and looking younger and more luminous than she had for some time, she perceptively concluded that at last Marie had started living again.

fifteen

TWENTY-EIGHT votes for Mme Curie, twenty-nine for Edouard Branly, one for Marcel Brillouin.

On January 23, 1911, an election was being held in the large hall at the Institut to choose a successor to the chair of the physicist Gernez. The public was roaring. A man was overcome by the heat and fainted. "We will proceed to a second round of voting," the president of the meeting announced in the midst of the din.

For two months, the public, aroused by a terrific newspaper campaign—one that was unprecedented for an academic election—had been waiting for the day of the election to see whether or not the doors of the Académie des Sciences would open for a woman. The Institut de France included five academies of unequal prestige: the Académie Française, the Académie des Sciences, the Académie des Inscriptions et Belles-Lettres, the Académie des Beaux-Arts, and the Académie des Sciences Morales et Politiques. Would it have occurred to Marie to try to enter the academy just because it was the only remaining honor which she hadn't yet been the first woman to receive? Or did Henri Poincaré, Lippmann, and Bouty have to persuade her to present herself as a candidate?

She had just published an exhaustive *Treatise on Radioactivity.* According to Rutherford, it was quite sufficiently academic. He wrote to Boltwood: "Reading her book, I would have thought I was rereading something I myself had written, supplemented by some research done in the last few years. . . . It is very funny to see the trouble she goes to at certain points to claim that French science was first, or rather that she herself and her husband were first. . . . And yet I can sense that the poor thing has worked enormously hard. . . ."

155

Even so, the international scientific press and Rutherford himself published respectful reviews of the book.

Accustomed to recognition from her peers, Marie had no doubt that she would be elected. For once, she was presuming too much. It was not that she lacked the qualifications or the talents. She had more of both than anyone else in that august assembly, which was traditionally composed of an almost constant number of men so mediocre that one had to ask oneself what could possibly have allowed them to think they belonged there, unless it was the mediocrity of the people who brought them in in the first place.

The Académie Française had elected a certain M. Saint-Priest over Balzac, and twenty-two candidates in succession over Zola. The Académie des Sciences had elected a certain M. Amagat over Pierre Curie in 1903, before finally and grudgingly giving him their votes. Marie knew enough about the ways of academe to be aware that although merit was not always a handicap, if often was. But apparently she and her friends thought that her singularity would guarantee her winning the election. And in the beginning it actually looked as though they would be right.

As soon as Le Figaro announced on November 16, 1910, that she was thinking of trying to enter the Academy, the national daily press, which at that time had a circulation of more than four million (or ten times that of today, for a population of thirty-one million), featured the event.

"Along with her fame she has such nobility and beauty—nothing is missing, not even the poignant poetry of grief, from the pure and perfect image we have of her," wrote Le Figaro, devoting three columns to Marie which were signed with the name Foemina.

The circulation of Le Figaro, which was the organ of the "society people" and was run by Gaston Calmette, was not very large but it prided itself on setting the fashion and in many ways did, since the prestige of a newspaper depends not on its circulation but on the level of education of its readers and on the nature of their interests.

L'Excelsior, which had recently been started by Pierre Lafitte and which had a revolutionary format—immense news photographs with large captions—spread a picture of Marie down the entire length of the front page and printed alongside it a facsimile of her handwriting and an analysis of it. *L'Intransigeant* asked its readers to help make up a list of the women they thought most deserved to sit under the dome of the Institut. Colette headed the list, but many people named Marie. Even *Le Temps*, whose circulation consisted only of men, joined in on December 2, singing Marie's praises.

In a letter to the editor-in-chief of *Le Temps*, Marie confirmed her candidacy and asked that articles and commentaries be henceforth suspended. She also wrote to *L'Excelsior:* "The announcement of my candidacy for the Institut is correct; however, since the Institut's elections have never before been discussed publicly, I would be upset to see this custom changed because of my candidacy." For several days she was allowed to think she could lay down the law to the press the same way she did to scientific conferences.

Until the end of the year, newspaper columns were filled with other topics: the rising of the Seine, the death of Tolstoy, the "antimodernist" oath demanded by the Vatican and taken, in the Saint-Roch church, by the curés of Paris and the suburbs; the new minister, Briand; the exhibition of the first Rolls-Royce in the Salon de l'Automobile; the campaign against abortion—the "national crime"—launched by *Le Matin* (circulation 350,000) and taken up by the rest of the press.

But once the first shock had passed, the academicians recovered and took action. No woman, even if her name was Mme Curie, would ever cross the threshold of the sacred precinct. Pierre Curie's one-time successful rival, Gabriel Amagat, became the dragon at the temple door.

The mathematician Gaston Darboux, perpetual secretary of the Académie des Sciences, took a different and more courageous position. A woman? he said. Why not? And making use of the "open forum," which in an unprecedented gesture *Le*

157

Temps had offered him, he published on December 31 a firm and well-documented article explaining the purely scientific advantages a researcher would gain from belonging to the Académie and the benefits the Curie laboratory would derive from it.

On January 4, the Institut brought together its five academies to discuss the basic principles. Describing the arrival of the 150 academicians as they hurried in, the *Figaro* reporter wrote: "I see wrinkled old gentlemen go by with gray handkerchiefs in their hands; their shoulders are covered with dandruff, their pants are twisted around their thin shanks. . . . There is something both laughable and pitiful about the men that file by, some of them eminent figures but more of them simply decrepit; they are on their way to a meeting at which they will discuss . . . whether or not to admit a woman into their company."

Surprise. A majority voted in favor. The next day, in keeping with the rule, the general physics section of the Académie des Sciences ranked the candidates for Gernez's chair. They ended up with three—Marcel Brillouin, Marie Curie, and Edouard Branly. Marcel Brillouin had no chance at all, even though he was a brilliant physicist. But Marie's enemies had shown themselves to be astute politicians when they persuaded Branly to be a candidate. Sixty-six years old, Branly had already been turned down twice. He was already known publicly as a modest, decent man who had not been properly compensated for his popular invention—the wireless telegraph. He was, in fact, the inventor of the iron-filing coherer that made telegraphy possible.

By achieving radio links, the Italian Marconi had snatched the Nobel Prize out of his hands. Outside France, Edouard Branly's scientific credentials had not received the sanction he might have hoped for, but something had happened that he valued even more: Pope Leo XIII had named him Commander of the Order of Saint Gregory the Great—he did not teach at the University but at the Institut Catholique. Now everyone

158

wanted to know which rival Branly would be fighting against in a battle that was immediately seen as patriotic.

On January 10, *L'Intransigeant*, whose new director, Léon Bailby, was holding to the same nationalist and anti-Semitic tradition as the founder of the newspaper, Henri de Rochefort, began attacking Marie. The cry was soon taken up even more loudly by other newspapers with similar tendencies. What had this woman Curie done, that she should dare to compete with Edouard Branly for the remarkable honor of sitting under the dome of the Institut? She had come to France from Poland and married Pierre Curie, who deserved all the credit for the Nobel Prize. She was a foreigner. As for the weekly lectures she gave—where, ever since the announcement of her candidacy, Marie was greeted with applause by her students—people were bored to tears with hearing her talk about the "dear radium" she claimed to have discovered. Exactly what had been her name before she was called Curie? Sklodowska. An impossible name. Was she Catholic? So they said. But for how long? Didn't she have some Jewish ancestor back there somewhere?

The Dreyfus affair was not far in the past. Nor was "little" Father Combes. Even though Dreyfus had been proved innocent and decorated with the Legion of Honor in 1906, in the courtyard of the military school where he had been dismissed, *L'Action Française* and *L'Intransigeant* still spoke of him as the "Jewish traitor."

The Catholics of the Left, as we call them today, who had been united by Marc Sangnier around *Sillon*, were not interested in academic battles at this point, but in fighting for one day a week of rest for bakery workers. Besides, the Vatican was condemning them for confused thinking. And Sangnier had just given in.

The competition between Marie and Branly, which was dubbed "the war between the sexes" by the liberal press, was really being waged between two different aspects of France. Marie, who knew only one, the aspect of France represented

159

by her friends, had largely underestimated the distaste she aroused in the ranks of the other. She was to underestimate it to the very end.

She spent two weeks climbing flights of stairs—fifty-eight times—to pay the visits that had to be paid according to the ritual. Edouard Branly did the same. On Monday, January 23, the day of the election, idlers and curiosity seekers crowded in front of the doors of the Institut while the president of the meeting and the members of the academy pretended to listen with interest to the announcements on the agenda. At last the clock chimed four, marking the end of the ordinary meeting and the beginning of the electoral ceremony.

"Let everyone enter except for the women!" cried the president to the ushers.

In the large hall, which was packed with journalists and photographers, the excitement was at its height. The president tried to maintain silence while the ushers took the urns around. A moment of calm turned into an uproar when someone shouted that he had seen Gaston Darboux slip a ballot into the hands of another member of the academy, M. Radau. The unfortunate Radau, who was blind, had to explain that because he favored Marie and because he was being harassed by his neighbor, who favored Branly, and because of his "extreme myopia," he had asked the perpetual secretary of the academy to give him a ballot that corresponded to his choice of candidate. This explanation became the subject of a letter to *Le Temps*. There was a steady din in the hall while the votes were counted, and then the president announced the results and said that there would have to be a second round of voting to obtain a majority.

In the cloud of smoke caused by the explosion of a vial of magnesium, the most ardent supporters of both candidates made a last effort to win people over to the other side. One of these partisans walked across the hall to speak to someone— and a ballot that had already been folded was replaced at the last minute by another.

At five o'clock in the afternoon, reporters burst out of the

Institut with the news that Mme Curie had been beaten. She had held onto her twenty-eight votes, but Edouard Branly had received thirty. She heard the results of the election on the telephone in her little laboratory office, where she had been waiting. She said nothing, left her office, and joined her co-workers just in time to see them whisk away the bouquet they had prepared to celebrate her victory. Meanwhile, on the quai Conti, the members of the Académie Française were pleased. Henri Poincaré had the decency to go shake hands with the enemy clan, who had gathered around Amagat, congratulating him on the victory he had won through Branly.

The Institut remained inviolate. If Marie had presented herself as a candidate the following month, when a new seat became vacant because of another death, this time she probably would have been elected, and the Institut would not have waited another sixty-eight years for its first female member. But she wouldn't hear any talk of this, and never again applied for any other seat or distinction. What was more, she never again presented any of her projects to the meetings of the academy.

At the end of that same year, 1911, the jury of the Swedish Academy decided to award her the Nobel Prize for chemistry. This time she wasn't sharing it with anyone. But the news came to her in the midst of a storm compared to which the disturbance over the academy business was nothing. What had happened, in fact, was that in the eyes of the French public Mme Curie had ceased to be an honorable woman.

SCANDAL

sixteen

ONE DAY in March 1914, an elegantly dressed woman named Henriette Caillaux went into the office of the editor of *Le Figaro*, took a revolver out of her muff, and fired it six times at Gaston Calmette, killing him.

Le Figaro had recently begun printing the correspondence of the young woman and her husband, Joseph Caillaux, deputy from Sarthe and former president of the Council who had, people believed, a good chance of being reelected. The murder was merely a particularly sordid episode in a continuing political struggle. The letters, which had been given to the newspaper by the first Mme Caillaux, revealed that before she married the deputy, Henriette had been his mistress.

Attempting to explain her crime, Henriette cried out to the jury of the Assizes: "My poor father always told me that a woman who has had a lover is a woman without honor." She was acquitted. It is important to keep this in mind if we are to understand the climate in which the Langevin affair, as it was called, exploded in the fall of 1911.

At the beginning of the century, bourgeois France was not so much puritanical as prudish. Every day, an average of thirty-nine declarations of adultery were recorded in Paris, and there were so many abortions in the country that in 1910 *Le Matin* launched a campaign to eliminate from the popular newspapers the more or less explicit classified ads in which midwives offered their discreet services. Twenty-four births out of a hundred were illegitimate.

Whether they meet in living rooms, stables, or factories, whenever men and women mix there is always the possibility that they will fall in love, have an affair, and fall out of love. But as they played this age-old game, women now risked

165

losing the only things they could truly call their own—their reputations—because during the nineteenth century the notion of family had been endowed with a new value; it may be the only value that has lasted through the years. But whereas nowadays the family is seen as a fragile entity that requires a determined cooperative effort if it is to last, in the nineteenth century the preservation of the family unit was safeguarded by both written and unwritten laws. Because women were naturally inclined to sin and were birdbrains, they could not be trusted and had to be kept in cages.

The Civil Code and the Social Code took care of this. The latter had established a new feminine model—the Honest Woman—who would hardly have been recognizable to her ancestors, among whom were several very different types: the medieval woman, who was a joyful sensualist; the *précieuse*, an intellectual who delighted in being endlessly courted; and the libertine, who never gave her heart to anyone. Now an upright woman was supposed to regard the giving of herself as a sacrifice on the altar of marriage. And this was often the case, since the wise husband was careful not to awaken his wife's senses, supposing he had the capacity to do it. Otherwise, what a lot of trouble there would be!

Once he had made sure his home was safe, the husband looked for love, or a substitute for love, elsewhere. This was what some sociologists have labeled with the horrible name of "recreational sex." Whether they consisted of brief liaisons or protracted ones, passing fancies or true passions, these irregular love affairs were socially viable, for women "of quality," only if they took place in strictest secrecy. And all the frustrated wives kept a wonderfuly close watch on each other.

This wasn't likely to bother Marie Curie and Paul Langevin. They had known each other for ten years, had worked together, consulted each other. After Pierre's death, Langevin had helped Marie prepare her first courses at the Sorbonne; she had helped him when he succeeded her at the Sèvres school. Their intimacy was therefore not a subject for scandal. It was true that Marguerite Borel's experienced eye had detected something indefinable radiating from Marie, but this only aroused her curiosity, it did not make her turn against Marie.

She herself tended to cultivate ambiguous friendships: she was the privileged confidante of Jean Perrin and a few others, who were happy to find pretty Marguerite in her little yellow drawing room at the end of the day, always available to listen to them. The Borels now lived in the rue d'Ulm, in the apartment attached to the position of science director of the Ecole Normale. It was here that Langevin came more and more often, begging for a cup of tea, confiding that he was unhappy, and delaying the moment when he had to go home to Fontenay-aux-Roses.

Langevin, who had started out as a scholarship student, was now a professor at the Collège de France. He had a solid reputation as a scientist. He was a physicist, but he used mathematics as a tool so confidently that even the mathematicians were impressed. After finishing his thesis, he became inspired by Pierre Curie's experimental work and developed a complete theory of diamagnetic and paramagnetic phenomena *before* the development of the quantum theory. He had presupposed the existence of something that could only be accounted for by the action of quanta.

In 1906, he reached the conclusion that $E = mc^2$, that the mass of a body is equal to its energy divided by the square of the speed of light. This was before a friend of his, Edmond Bauer, told him that someone "named Einstein" was working along the same lines. In 1911, he gave a brilliant lecture to the International Congress of Philosophy in Bologna on how the theory of relativity was upsetting notions of space and time. In short, as Marie would have said, Langevin was "someone." But his work was a mystery to the woman he had married at the age of twenty-two. She was the child of a working-class man, as he had been, and at the time of their marriage she was running a small grocery store with her mother.

What was more, he was generous, extravagant. She was struggling to bring up their four children with never a penny

167

to spare. And when tempting offers were made to Langevin by private industry, she nagged him to accept them and give up the university. "You'll earn four times as much," she would say to him over and over again. His endless money problems irritated Langevin, but he tolerated them because he looked upon them as a sacrifice he owed to science. His wife, however, saw them as the sacrifice she and her children had to make because of an egotist's irresponsibility. In fact, their situation was like that of many other couples, even including the quarrels that broke out between them and the bitter comments of Mme Langevin's mother, who lived with them.

Jean Perrin, whose wife was at once charming and indulgent toward his escapades, and Emile Borel, whose relations with his wife were unusual but remained happy for half a century, felt great sympathy for their friend Langevin, were worried to see him becoming more and more nervous and tense, and tried to distract him by taking him to the theater and then afterwards to Les Halles for onion soup. The Perrins, who were very close friends of Marie's, clearly knew that her intellectual intimacy with Langevin had grown into a love affair. And doubtless the Borels had guessed as much.

It is quite possible that by July 1910, when Langevin rented the small apartment in Paris that was to be the scene of their affair, Marie had already decided to persuade him to leave his wife. It is hard to imagine her tolerating for very long a situation in which she had to compete with Jeanne Langevin. Or with anyone, for that matter. Whatever the case, the crisis Langevin was undergoing, as he confided it to his friends— depicting himself as the researcher torn between science and his wife's craving for money—provided Marie with the best possible excuse for attempting to extricate him from the influence of his marriage, supposing she needed an excuse.

Attending a conference in Genoa with the Borels, she asked Marguerite to come see her in her room one evening. There, curled up on the bed, she talked about Langevin. She was afraid, she said, that he was wasting himself. "And he's a genius!" She grasped Marguerite's hands and begged her:

168

"We have to save him from himself. He is weak. You and I are tough. He needs understanding, he needs gentleness and affection."

Gentleness and affection? It was clear that she loved Langevin as she had never loved Pierre. She did not have the sort of relationship with him that she had had with Pierre, a warm and peaceful relationship in which she was sure of being the only one, the irreplaceable one, the Dear Little Girl cherished by her gentle companion. This was an intense, passionate, and stormy relationship, punctuated by arguments and ultimatums, with an undependable man. Another time, André Debierne was the one who approached Marguerite and begged her to speak to Paul Langevin. About what? To ask him to stop "tormenting Marie with his disillusionment." Debierne went on, "He is worrying her. She can't bear to see him so despondent."

"What do you want me to do?" asked Marguerite. "He comes and complains to me, too."

"Complaining to you is not as dangerous," Debierne answered.

A rumor went around that Langevin and Debierne had had a violent quarrel.

In August 1911, while her husband was in England with his two sons and Marie was in Poland with her daughters, Jeanne Langevin instituted legal proceedings to obtain a separation.

Langevin's older son, André, in a biography of his father which he wrote sixty years later, put it very nicely: "Isn't it natural that a few years after Pierre Curie's death this friendship [with Marie], enhanced by mutual admiration, should have gradually grown into a passion and resulted in a love affair? . . . The home in which we had lived until then was for a time destroyed. My father and mother were to live apart until the First World War." There wouldn't be anything more to say about it if the affair hadn't taken on the proportions it did.

On October 29, 1911, the Solvay conference in Brussels opened. This year, Ernest Solvay, the Belgian industrialist

169

who had founded the International Institute of Physics, had brought together all the great scientists of the day for the first time. In a famous photograph of the occasion, Marie is sitting between Henri Poincaré and Jean Perrin. Standing behind her are Einstein, Langevin, Rutherford, Kamerlingh-Onnes, Max Planck, Maurice de Broglie, Marcel Brillouin, Sommerfeld, Nernst, Lorentz, Warburg, Wien, Goldschmidt, Rubens, Lindemann, Knudsen, Hasehorl, Hostelet, Herzen, and Jeans. The entire world of physics was there. The reigning queen and the man who was going to topple her from her throne.

Apropos of the conference Einstein wrote to a friend:

> Lorentz presided with incomparable tact, incredible virtuosity. . . . On the whole, Poincaré appeared to be simply hostile [to the theory of relativity!].
> Planck is stopped by several undoubtedly mistaken prejudices. . . . But no one really understands. There's something about this whole business that would delight a society of demoniacal Jesuits.

It was after this same conference that Marie wrote in support of something Einstein had done:

> I very much admired the work published by M. Einstein on questions having to do with modern theoretical physics. . . .
> . . . His work is absolutely first rate. . . .
> If we consider the fact that M. Einstein is still very young, we have reason to pin the greatest hopes on him and to regard him as one of the top theoreticians of the future.

Her age—she was forty-three—placed her exactly midway between the older and younger physicists. Maybe it was because of Langevin, who was four years younger, that she had started working in modern physics so early.

While the Solvay conference was taking place in Brussels, readers of *Le Journal*, which had a circulation of 750,000, found the following headline covering two columns of the front page on November 4:

170

A LOVE STORY
MME CURIE AND PROFESSOR LANGEVIN

The article begins with the following paragraph: "The fires of radium which so mysteriously warm everything around them had a surprise in store for us: They have just kindled a blaze in the hearts of the scientists who are studying their behavior with such tenacity—and the wife and children of one of these scientists are in tears."

There follows an interview which the author, Fernand Hauser, claims to have conducted at Fontenay-aux-Roses with Langevin's mother-in-law. It deserves to be quoted in full, because it is such a nice period piece.

"An unlikely rumor is going around Paris," I said. "They say Professor Langevin has left his family for Mme Curie. I am here so that you can deny the truth of this news."

Mme Langevin's mother looked at me for a moment, then put down the child who had been playing with her and said: "What? They already know about it?"

"Does that mean it's true?"

"It's unthinkable, isn't it? Pierre Curie's widow, the great scientist who collaborated in the discovery of radium, who is a professor at the Faculté des Sciences, who was nearly admitted to the Institut de France, the famous, renowned Marie Curie has stolen my daughter's husband, the father of my grand-children!. . . M. Langevin was a student of Curie's. When his teacher died, he put himself at the service of the widow, to help her with what she had to do, with her work; little by little, M. Langevin got into the habit of spending more time at Mme Curie's than at his own house; very soon—a woman's instinct is never wrong—my daughter suspected something; and then, one day, she knew everything. Oh! What frightful hours those were! What terrible days! . . .

"Finally, one morning three months ago, M. Langevin left with his children."

"And with Mme Curie."

"I don't know. But one thing is sure: she left Paris at the same time he did. . . . My daughter wanted her children back, at

171

least; she went to the judge and it was decided that the father and mother would take turns seeing the poor little things, except for this little girl. She's only two and she has been left with us."

"And do you know where M. Langevin is now?"

"We don't know. A few days ago he asked for his books. We've put them in boxes. They're here. No one has come to get them yet."

"Has Mme Langevin begun divorce proceedings against her husband?"

"No . . . . She's hoping her husband will come back to her and that her family will be restored to what it was. You know, when you have children—six children—you hesitate to do something irrevocable."

"But supposing M. Langevin doesn't come back?"

"Then, we'll see. . . . We haven't made any decisions yet."

"They say you have in your possession letters from Mme Curie."

"Oh? You've heard that too? Well, we do have those letters. . . . And they constitute the proof of what we suspected, what we already knew without being able to confirm it yet."

Mme Langevin's mother bowed her head thoughtfully; I interrupted her train of thought and said: "It's unbelievable!"

"Yes," Mme Langevin's mother said, echoing me, "it's unbelievable."

I would have liked to know what Mme Curie and M. Langevin thought of this sad story; I would have liked to hear them cry out to me, "They're wrong, they're making a mistake, there isn't a word of truth in what they've told you." But Mme Curie can't be found, and no one knows where M. Langevin is.

A rather superficial sort of article. Fernand Hauser generously gave Langevin six children instead of four, but it must be said that he was pretty well informed.

What he reported was tailored to please the readers of *Le Journal* and its founder and editor-in-chief, Fernand Xau, who had made a fortune in the newspaper business by being the first to aim his newspaper at a particular audience—society women.

On November 4, while this issue of *Le Journal* was still on the newsstands, the other newspapers were trying to decide how to handle the affair. They sent reporters to the Collège de France, the Curie laboratory, and Emile Borel's house; they tried to find Mme Curie and Langevin, discovered they were at the conference in Brussels, and alerted their correspondents there.

"This is a disgrace!" Marie said.

Langevin admitted that he had left his wife, but he said he had done it to "get away from the jealous scenes that she made for no good reason."

Jean Perrin and Henri Poincaŕe declared that they were "indignant at the slanderous accusations" being made against their colleagues and friends.

Marie sent the reporter from *Le Temps* a statement she herself had written in which she denied that she had "run away" and asserted that she attached no importance to the rumors, which were "pure madness." On November 5, *Le Temps*, which was always favorable to Marie, published her statement on an inside page. The same day, all the dailies published what both parties had said and insisted that they wouldn't have spoken of "this private affair if the attack on these two important personalities hadn't caused a sensation."

But *Le Petit Journal* (circulation 850,000), which was competing with *Le Journal* for the same territory, had discovered where Mme Langevin was and on November 5 published a two-column report on the front page under the following headline:

A NOVEL IN A LABORATORY
THE LOVE AFFAIR OF MME CURIE AND M. LANGEVIN

Le Petit Journal denied that the couple were running away and printed an interview with Jeanne Langevin. She didn't know about the scandal, she said, and disapproved of the publicity, which was hurting her. When the reporter questioned her about her grounds for seeking a separation, she wept and, according to him, confided the following:

173

I know that for the past three years my husband has been having an illicit relationship with Mme Curie, but I only became certain of it and got the material proof of it—which I'm saving for the trial—eighteen months ago or even more recently. At that time, if I had been the sort of woman they have tried to make me out to be in certain places—stupid, jealous and insane—I would have talked, I would have cried out that my husband had betrayed me and that that woman had destroyed my home. I said nothing, because it was my duty as mother and wife to hide the faults of the man whose name I bore. And so I waited, always hoping for a reconciliation, for my husband to return to his senses. Perhaps I would have remained even longer in this horrible situation, knowing I was being ridiculed and hatefully deceived, if a decisive event hadn't taken place last July 25.

Here she told how she and her husband had had a violent scene "over a badly made fruit compote," that he had hit her and then left, taking his two sons with him, and hadn't come back. Her lawyer had then issued a subpoena.

Jeanne Langevin added that two weeks later she had wanted to attempt a reconciliation in the presence of her lawyer and Langevin's: "If my husband had come back to the house, I would have given up my weapons—the proof of his relations with Mme Curie. They rejected all my proposals."

At the end of the article, *Le Petit Journal* printed a paragraph entitled "In Brussels." From the news agency Information had come the following dispatch: "When we informed Mme Curie and M. Langevin of the rumor that was going around about them, they protested indignantly."

Between discussions about quanta, the members of the conference were whispering busily. "It's all nonsense," said Rutherford. But Marie did not attend the closing session, scribbled a note to Rutherford thanking him for his kindness, and returned to Paris without the reporters' knowledge.

On November 6, *L'Intransigeant* chimed in, referring to the well-known quarrels of the Langevin household and printing an open letter to one Monsieur X, physicist, signed by Léon

Bailby, that concluded: "The woman who was once your confidante is now quite obviously your mistress."

This time Marie's reaction was brutal, and *Le Temps* published it: "I find all these intrusions of the press and the public into my private life abominable. . . . This is why I am going to take strong action against the publication of any documents attributed to me. Also, I have a right to demand large sums of money in reparation, and I will use this money in the interests of science."

She obtained an apology from the man who had thrown the first stone, Fernand Hauser of *Le Journal*, and sent his letter to *Le Temps:* "Madame," wrote Hauser, "I am filled with despair and I offer you my humblest apologies. I was relying on similar information from different sources when I wrote the article that you know about. I was wrong. And now I can hardly understand how my professional enthusiasm could have led me to commit such a detestable act. . . . I am left with only one consoling thought—that such a humble journalist as I am could never, by any of his writings, tarnish the glory that halos you nor the esteem that surrounds you. . . . Yours, very distressed, Fernand Hauser."

The following day, November 7, Marie received a telegram: "You have been awarded the Nobel Prize in Chemistry. Letter follows. Aurivillius."

This was a unique situation in the history of the Nobel Prize, the highest distinction that could be awarded a scholar in the twentieth century: Marie Curie had received it twice. It was an extraordinary success, an extraordinary sanction, an extraordinary tribute to French science![1]

That day, Marie might have felt proud. She might also have hoped that when the news became public, this second Nobel

---

[1] Marie Curie remains the only Nobel Prize laureate crowned twice for scientific work, except for the American physicist, John Bardeen, who shared the Nobel Prize in physics in 1956 for the development of the germanium transistor, and then again in 1972 for the theory of superconductivity.

Prize would kill the scandal. But she knew that the proof Mme Langevin had mentioned did exist, in the form of some letters which the latter's brother-in-law had discovered when he broke into a bureau drawer. Accompanied by Marie and by Langevin's lawyer, Raymond Poincaré (not to be confused with Henri, the mathematician), Jean Perrin and Emile Borel went to see the police prefect. Poincaré obtained a sequestration of the documents held by Mme Langevin. If it is true that Raymond Poincaré was guilty of divulging letters from Mme Caillaux with the aim of eliminating a political rival, it isn't clear if he learned something from the Curie affair or if there was simply a remarkable dissociation between the lawyer side of him and the politician.

Poincaré was also the lawyer for the Sydicat de la Presse Parisienne. The president of the syndicat, Jean Dupuy, telephoned the editors of the principal Paris newspapers and asked them to put a stop to the articles on the Curie-Langevin affair. He alluded discreetly to the Nobel Prize, what an honor it would be for France. The big newspapers quieted down.

But there were others. Dupuy had neglected—or thought it pointless—to speak to *Action Française* and *Le Libre Parole* (Edouard Drumont's newspaper, whose motto was "France for the French"), and the articles they printed made it clear that this side was well armed. *La Libre Parole* printed fifty lines on the front page under the headline, "WILL MME CURIE REMAIN A PROFESSOR AT THE SORBONNE?" It shouldn't be hard to guess what the article contained. After mentioning that the action for adultery Mme Langevin was bringing against her husband and against Mme Curie for complicity would come before the Ninth Correctional Chamber on December 7, the writer adds:

> The documents involved in the trial are crushing for Mme Curie. In the summons there are letters written by her . . . that will dumbfound people when they become known. And they will not fail to become known because they will be produced in the presence of the audience.
>
> As is our custom, we would have said nothing about this if it

involved only the private lives of the people concerned. But something more is involved here. Mme Curie occupies a public teaching position which she obtained in circumstances that give public opinion the right to form a judgment, and her students and their families the right to demand that the teacher be what the English call "respectable."

Quiet as the grave about this affair, as far as we know Marie never told anyone how she spent the two weeks that passed between the time the telegram arrived from the Swedish Academy and the time her letters were published. Did she spend it with Langevin? The two of them fighting side by side? It doesn't seem so. Perhaps her lawyer had advised her to be prudent about this. Or was she reproaching Langevin for his carelessness? After all, you shouldn't leave letters from your mistress lying around the house. But she wasn't the sort of woman to blame others for her own actions. Or was she allowing herself to think, for a moment, that Langevin would at last be free to live with her? What we can be sure of, in any case, is that she was obsessed by her image in this.

It is clear that what hurt this image, the wound to her self-esteem, was the only thing that finally struck her where she lived and led her to censor this episode in her life completely.

She retreated to her house, which was surrounded by groups of people. Occasionally a stone bounced against a windowpane, or someone shouted, "Get out, foreigner!" or "Husband-stealer!" Suddenly, on November 23, a red booklet was published by *L'Oeuvre*. The title that appeared on the cover was the following:

The Truth About the Langevin-Curie Scandal:
FOR
A
MOTHER
by Gustave Téry

Gustave Téry, editor-in-chief of *L'Oeuvre*, was to make a name for himself in the newspaper world. *L'Oeuvre* had become a daily in 1915 and was one of the influential news-papers. Its advertising slogan was: *"L'Oeuvre* isn't read by imbeciles."

Téry was certainly not am imbecile. He was worse. He was a bitter man. A graduate of the Ecole Normale, like Langevin, with whom he had been on cordial terms in school, he had abandoned an undistinguished career as a professor of phi-losophy one year before in order to found his newspaper, in which he exercised his intellectual pretensions on an obscene xenophobia and anti-Semitism. These feelings, however, were not out of keeping with the mood of that time.

Small, ugly, and tormented by stomach problems, Téry was loathsome. He was, however, undeniably talented.

His article began in the form of a dialogue.

"One shivers to think that if this ill-fated student had not come from Poland for the express purpose of being present at the discovery of radium, there would no longer be any such thing as French science. . . . And there are still a few patriots obtuse enough to regard the invasion of foreigners as a na-tional scourge. But all that's involved here is the honor of one woman, and so the press should be silent."

"One woman? I thought there were two."

"Only one of them is interesting. As you must have read in all the newspapers, this Mme Langevin is 'a little fool who doesn't deserve her husband and who's as jealous as a little factory worker.' "

"I don't think people are going to base any arguments on the fact that in her letters Mme Curie calls Langevin *tu*. . . . She does, but only as a friend. . . . Everyone knows that's the custom in the laboratory."

"I'm sorry. I didn't know that everyone at the Sorbonne called each other *tu*, the way they do in Parliament and in prison. . . . And no doubt if Mme Curie and M. Langevin only met in the laboratory . . . etc."

Did his article risk making the university look bad? The university had "nothing to do with phenomena of radioactivity, which were quite sufficiently well known before Pierre Curie's discovery."

At this point Téry indulged in some thoughts about the ravages caused by "Nietzschean morality," which he summed up in the phrase, "Act on your desire." He went on:

> If Mme Curie had said: "I laugh at your traditions and your prejudices; I am a stranger, an intellectual, a free spirit. . . . Leave me alone. . . . If Mme Curie had said something like this, we would have said: "It's not French, but it's pretty daring!"
>
> These women who espouse feminist principles at every opportunity have a strange and ambivalent attitude! . . .
>
> Deliberately, methodically, scientifically, Mme Curie set about alienating Paul Langevin from his wife and separating his wife from her children. All this is either cynically recounted or unconsciously admitted in the letters which remain Mme Langevin's only defense now.

Was he going to publish these letters? "Mme Curie and her gallant defenders may rest assured that we won't publish these letters, not so much out of respect for her as for our female readers."

And after this pretty speech, he went ahead and published them. Or rather, with the sort of cunning that even the best newspapers do not scruple to use, he published the writ issued against Langevin by his wife's lawyer, in which these letters were amply quoted.

Imagine Marie Curie, as we now know her, reading this and knowing that people everywhere would be reading it that same day. It begins with the *whereas*'s of the writ:

> Whereas starting in July 1910, Paul Langevin and Mme Curie met there daily and even several times a day (Mme Curie did the shopping herself and stayed there far into the night).
>
> Whereas M. Langevin continually told Mme Curie about his most intimate concerns, asking her for advice and for actual moral guidance.

179

And in support of this, there followed a series of excerpts from the letters. What she wrote was in character for her. It was sober, intelligent, strong, concise, and passionate—though the passion was couched in the most decent sort of vocabulary. What she wrote is also interesting to us, because it reveals her as we rarely see her.

First, we see how she was thinking: "There are very deep affinities between us which only required a fertile piece of ground in order to develop. We sometimes sensed this in the past, but we did not become fully aware of it until we found ourselves face to face with each other at a time when I was mourning the beautiful life I had made for myself, and you had the feeling you had completely lacked this sort of family life."

Notice "the beautiful life I had made for myself." Only she would "make" her own life.

Elsewhere, there is a moment when Langevin was no doubt hesitating because of his children—he couldn't resign himself to separating from them:

"The instinct that has drawn us together has been very powerful. Don't you think that the destruction of a sincere and deep feeling is like the death of a child one has cherished, as one watched it develop, and in some cases isn't such a destruction an even greater misfortune than the loss of the child?"

Clearly, Marie wasn't afraid to write that. She went on: "Didn't everything come from this feeling? I think it was the source of everything for us—good shared work, a good solid friendship, courage in life and even beautiful love children in the most lovely sense of that word."

And finally there is the following passage, which deserves to appear in an anthology of women's letters, and whose last paragraph throws such light on Marie Curie:

One of the first things to be done is for you to go back to your own bedroom. I promised I wouldn't reproach you anymore and you can count on that. I trust you completely as far as your intentions are concerned. More than I can say, I am afraid of events we can't foresee—the fits of crying that you find it so hard to resist, ruses to trick you into making her pregnant.

If she were to have another child, that would mean a final separation because I couldn't accept this dishonor to myself, to you and to other people I respect. If your wife understands this, she will make use of it. So I beg you not to make me wait too long for you to stop sleeping in her bed.

Dishonor! During the course of his life, the unfortunate Langevin proved again and again that he had real courage, but when caught between two women, he was evidently no more courageous than anyone else would have been.

L'Oeuvre greeted his writ with this note: "The Langevin-Curie trial will come before the Ninth Chamber on December 8. There we will see the foreign element of the Sorbonne opposing a French woman, a French mother, the French home. But the Syndicat de la Presse is requiring newspapers to put the lid on the scandal. Why don't they mind their own business?"

In the United States, one of Hearst's daily newspapers gave a concise summary of the *L'Oeuvre* account: "Mme Curie madly in love. The wife? An idiot, she says."

When Jean Perrin, accompanied by André Debierne, arrived at the Borels' at nine in the morning with *L'Oeuvre* in his hand, Emile Borel immediately sent his wife to Sceaux with Debierne to bring back Marie and her children. She would live with them at the Ecole Normale as long as she needed protection. A room should be prepared for her.

The mission was accomplished right away. Marguerite hurried to Sceaux, where she found Marie dumbfounded by the news. Marie did not protest as she and Eve were bundled into a taxi under the stares of the curious who had gathered around the house.

Irène was at a gym class. Debierne took it upon himself to go get her, and found her very upset, absorbed in reading a copy of *L'Oeuvre*. She was only fourteen. Once she reached the rue d'Ulm, she refused to leave her mother. Henriette Perrin succeeded in taking her away. Marie, still silent, was led into a bedroom.

And while Perrin, Debierne, and the Borels thought about what to do, the telephone began ringing. Everyone in Paris had read *L'Oeuvre* that morning. Except for the Chavannes, who had been won over by Henriette Perrin and didn't join in the slaughter, people ceased to visit Marie Curie—she had become one of those women with whom one no longer associated.

"We associate with her to such an extent that she lives with us," answered Marguerite Borel. "Yes, at the Ecole."

Emile Borel was immediately summoned by the minister of public education, Théodore Steeg. He was told that he did not have the right to discredit the university by harboring Mme Curie in the apartment attached to his position. If he persisted in this, he would be dismissed.

"All right," answered Borel, "I will persist."

"Talk it over with your wife," the minister suggested.

At that point Marguerite was summoned by her father, Paul Appell, who was still dean of the Faculté des Sciences. He was putting on his shoes when he saw her. He exploded. Why were his daughter and son-in-law getting mixed up in this? Were they out of their minds? The minister was furious. This was an incredible scandal. The Sorbonne was being attacked right and left. Responsible for order in the Faculté, he had decided to withdraw Mme Curie's chair. He advised her for her own good to resign and go teach in Poland.

"If you ask her to leave France, I will never see you again," answered Marguerite.

Exasperated, her father, who was holding a shoe in his hand, threw it against the wall.

The fact was that this had happened before at the university. The wife of a higher official had recently been enticed away by a history professor. And the wife of a mathematician had gone off with a professor from the Polytechnique. But these gentlemen were merely behaving "like men."

182

While the Borels, the Perrins, and Debierne launched a campaign to rehabilitate Marie among their friends, *L'Oeuvre* and the nationalist press threw off all restraint. The "foreigner" would be spared nothing, not even the words of the driver of the truck that had killed Pierre: "He literally threw himself under my horse!" He would only have thrown himself under the horse if he had good reason to do it. In fact, M. Langevin and Mme Curie were both teaching at Sèvres at the time. Everyone understood.

People had a passion for dueling in those days, and not only with words. They fought often, either to wash away an insult with their enemy's blood or to get themselves talked about. It would be a long time before this tradition died out—duels were still being fought in France after the Second World War.

Insulted in *L'Action Française* because he had criticized the tone of the paper's attacks against Marie and Langevin, the editor of the magazine *Gil Blas* fought Léon Daudet with a sword and inflicted on him a "wound six centimeters deep." Criticized in *Gil Blas* because he had published Marie's letters, Téry challenged the editor-in-chief of the magazine to a duel using swords. Téry called Langevin a "coward" and a "boor" and applied to him the witty epithet that was making the rounds of the cabarets, where Langevin was known as the "chopin de la Polonaise," or "the Polish woman's stooge." Incensed, Langevin went to the Ecole Normale, sent word for Borel to come downstairs, and said to him: "I have decided to challenge Téry to a duel. It's idiotic, but I have to do it."

And taking Marguerite along with him so as to have a soft shoulder to cry on, he went off looking for seconds. Everyone he asked refused, except for the mathematician and future prime minister, Paul Painlevé: he agreed right away and persuaded Haller, head of the Ecole de Physique, who had at first refused, to take part as well.

The episode was grotesque. At ten minutes to eleven on the morning of November 25, the two men, who were dressed in black, with bowler hats and waxed moustaches, met in the ring in the Parc des Princes accompanied by the four seconds,

183

two doctors, and a few reporters, who had climbed to the top of the stands using for the purpose a ladder placed outside the stadium. The seconds had agreed that the duel would be fought with pistols at a distance of twenty-five paces.

At eleven o'clock, Langevin and Téry faced each other with their weapons lowered. Painlevé counted: One . . . two . . . three. . . . Langevin lifted his weapon. Téry kept his arm at his side. Langevin lowered his weapon, raised it again, lowered it again. Téry refused to fire. Langevin had no choice: he had to refrain from firing too. The duel was over. The seconds took the weapons from the duelists and emptied them into the air.

Téry later explained to his readers that he had been afraid of hurting Mme Langevin's cause by killing her husband. And that he had not wanted to "deprive French science of a precious mind, whether that mind worked on its own or preferred to resort to Mme Curie as gracious intermediary."

Shut up in her bedroom with Eve, where she was served her meals, watched over by Henriette Perrin, who kept her from seeing the newspapers, and by Bronia, who had come from Poland with Hela and Jozef, this time Marie seemed completely defeated. If she was forbidden to work in France, then she would go back to Poland with her family, as they were begging her to do, anxious to remove her from this ungrateful country.

According to Marguerite Borel, the Council of Ministers deliberated about this. Whatever the case, the vigorous efforts of Perrin and Borel among their colleagues, and of Marguerite among the wives of the colleagues, as they attempted to persuade them that Marie was the very embodiment of innocence, succeeded in quieting the explosion of virtue in the university community. The Sorbonne prepared a report on the subject.

After a few days, people began to show some sympathy for Marie. Jacques Curie sent some words of comfort, which were precious to Marie, coming from him at a time like this. And strangers, too, sent candy and flowers. Paderewski came to have lunch with her. But she was shattered.

Yet before sinking completely into her illness, Marie would once again find in her reserve of pride the energy to pull herself together.

The most eminent scientists were to meet in Stockholm on December 10 for the official ceremony in which the prizes would be awarded. Sweden was forty-eight hours away by train. Marie was ill. She had to write a speech, deliver it standing before the royal family, the ambassadors, her fellow scientists, the press, and the photographers; she would have to expose herself to the hungry stares of the curiosity seekers who always flock to look at the heroine of a love story, especially when her lover is younger than she is. But she did it. Bronia went with her, and so did Irène—she especially wanted Irène to come.

In the same room where, six years earlier, Marie had sat with the other women listening to Pierre Curie talk, she was now the one talking, standing up straight in her lace dress. And every word she said was carefully weighed.

The prize she had shared with Pierre Curie and Henri Becquerel had officially been awarded for "the discovery of radioactivity." The prize she had just received was officially awarded for "the discovery of radium." Some people, particularly those who had hoped to receive the Nobel Prize for chemistry that year, found the distinction too subtle. One of them was the eternal Boltwood, who had this to say about the Langevin affair: "She is exactly what I always thought she was, a detestable idiot!"

But most of the foreign scientists, shocked by the way the Académie had treated her, were pleased to see her real talents rewarded. And since for the past year, people in France had been insinuating or saying outright that she had taken credit for her husband's gifts, this time she was going to go to great lengths to prove them wrong.

After a nod in the direction of Becquerel, and another toward Rutherford, she went on to make the following statement: "Radium had a decisive importance from the point of view of general theories. The history of the discovery and

185

isolation of this substance furnished the proof of the hypothesis *I made*, according to which, etc., etc." [Italics mine.] And the following: "The chemical procedures whose aim was to isolate radium in the state of a pure salt and to describe it as a new element were carried out specially *by me*." She referred to "bodies *I* called radioactive." She deliberately repeated over and over again, "I used . . . I carried out . . . I found . . . I obtained. . . ."

But she also gave Pierre credit. "This work . . . was closely tied to the work we were doing together. I therefore think I am correctly interpreting the thoughts of the Académie des Sciences when I say that the high honor coming to me is a result of the work we did together and is thus an homage to the memory of Pierre Curie."

There. It was done. Now she could die. And this time she actually wanted to die.

She returned to Paris exhausted at the same time that *L'Oeuvre* put out a new issue with the following headlines on its cover:

THE INVASION OF FOREIGNERS
At the Sorbonne
At the Ecole Centrale
At the Institut Pasteur
At the Faculté de Médecine
Everywhere

On an inside page, an article began: "Foreigners at the Sorbonne. Laboratories invaded by a mob mostly made up of foreign individuals. The numbers of women are constantly increasing, the most commendable of them are there because they are looking for husbands. As for the others . . ."

This was the moment the archdiocese chose to hold a meeting to define what attitude confessors should adopt toward readers of "inferior newspapers." Inferior newspapers were defined as "those that attack the Church, are harmful to mo-

186

rality or propagate anti-patriotic feeling." The confessor should refuse absolution to the assiduous reader of such newspapers, but he did not need to trouble the shareholders of an "inferior newspaper." They could breathe easy. The readers of *L'Oeuvre* and similar literature could feel comfortable about their relation to God too.

On December 29, before she could move into the apartment she had rented in Paris, at 36 quai de Béthune, Marie had to be taken to the hospital on a stretcher. She was in terrible pain and was shivering with fever. It would never be quite clear how much of her pitiful condition was due to radioactivity and how much to her wish to die.

The doctors kept everyone out of her room because her fever was rising and she needed complete rest. After several days she was told about the Langevins' separation decree. Raymond Poincaré had negotiated it very skillfully: the decree did not contain one word about Mme Curie. What she had been dreading the most was that there would be official proof, on record, of her "adulterous complicity."

Unquestionably, the doctors found Marie in better shape that day.

Jean Perrin was able to write to Rutherford:

> The fever has gone down and they won't have to operate on Mme Curie right away, something we were very worried about, in view of her state of exhaustion.
>
> The separation decree between Langevin and his wife makes *no mention* of Mme Curie . . . but the "wrongs" are attributed to Langevin (who did not take the precaution of finding witnesses to the wrongs he could have accused his wife of without bringing Mme Curie's name into the trial).
>
> The two boys eat lunch with Langevin every day (between their classes at the *lycée*). The four children sleep at their mother's, except for every other Thursday and every other Sunday. . . . From the age of nineteen on, the boys will live with him. Lastly, he retains "the intellectual control" of the four children. These are the terms of the judgment (in addition to his wife's alimony, of course).

And now, I hope that we will all be able to get back to work!? . . .

Jean Perrin
(Langevin has appreciated your friendship very much. Mme Curie has also been very touched by your attitude.)

Marie herself wouldn't be able to work for months. She had handed the laboratory over to André Debierne, who was also handling her personal affairs, and she consulted with him about urgent matters, but when she came out of the hospital at the end of January, she couldn't even stand by herself. Her kidneys were seriously damaged. She shut herself up in the apartment on the quai de Béthune and waited to recover enough strength to undergo an operation.

This new apartment was a superb one, with its old parquet floors and tall windows, its fourth-floor view of the Seine and the spur of the Île de la Cité. It was also quite uncomfortable. The building had no elevator and the apartment was immense, riddled with hallways and interior stairways. Marie Curie was to live in it for twenty-two years without ever putting down a carpet, hanging curtains, or adding other furniture to the pieces she had inherited from Dr. Curie, which were lost in the enormous living room. Domestic comfort had never been her strong point. She was insensitive to it.

She could not bear, on the other hand, that a meeting about the international standard of radium should be held in Paris when she was too ill to attend it. She tried to have it postponed, but with no luck. Rutherford, who was more amiable than ever, went to see her but was secretly pleased that Debierne, "the sensible man," was representing Marie at the meeting, for "we will perhaps be able to wrap it up much more quickly without Mme Curie, who, as you know, tends to raise difficulties," as he wrote to one of their colleagues.

The situation was actually a ticklish one. An Austrian physicist, Stefan Meyer, had prepared his own standard. If the one Marie had prepared was not strictly identical, then one of the two would have to be wrong. Rutherford didn't like to think

188

how Marie would greet this suggestion. The committee decided that since Marie wasn't present, Debierne would make the comparison, and miraculously enough, the two standards were the same. Mme Curie was happy to approve of the method after the fact.

After an exhausting operation, she retreated to Brunoy, close to Paris. Bronia had rented a house there under her own name. The address was a carefully kept secret. Marie wrote to Irène using double envelopes, sending the letters through André Debierne. Irène addressed her letters to Mme Sklodowska. The shopkeepers and the mailman of Brunoy were completely in the dark. Marie had sound, objective reasons for wishing to remain incognito. The newspapers were no longer full of the Langevin affair, but people remembered it, and nothing less than a world war would be necessary to erase it from their thoughts. She was therefore still at the mercy of the lowest sort of gossips.

But it was one thing to try to hide from sight by shutting herself away, and it was another to conceal her identity permanently. A name is not something that can be toyed with so easily. There is every reason to suppose that the decision Marie kept to for several months was sustained by a feeling of guilt—the guilt that was so quick to rise up from the depths of her childhood.

She didn't reproach herself with what everyone else was reproaching her with—she didn't see herself as an exotic seductress snatching the scientist from the bosom of his family. She didn't see Langevin as the pitiable victim of a treacherous siren. He would find other, less conspicuous sirens who were happy to console him.

We don't know what Marie thought when the guilty man returned to his family two years later. What was certain was that their friendship survived their passion and remained constant. Many years later, when Langevin, who was in love with one of his former students and had had a child with her, was trying to find a position for the young woman in a laboratory, he asked Marie to take her in. And of course she did.

189

What Marie accused herself of was not that she had transgressed the taboo about illicit love. It was that in doing so she had sullied the name Pierre had given her. The day she had taken his name, she had ceased to be the rejected governess. Now she had inadvertently dragged this name through the mud. She had to mortify herself, and so she declared that she was unworthy of calling herself Mme Curie. It was as Mme Sklodowska that she left Brunoy in June for a sanatorium in the Savoie, and then, at the end of July, went over to England.

Hertha Ayrton and Marie Curie had kept up a sporadic friendship ever since they had met in London in 1903. As soon as the scandal had come out, Mrs. Ayrton had written to Bronia to suggest that Marie should come stay with her.

A physicist, Hertha Ayrton had been no more successful at getting into the Royal institution than Marie had been at getting into the Académie. Her colleagues had refused to acknowledge the fact that although she collaborated with her husband she had also done independent work. But they had been more hypocritical than the French, falling back on the statutes of the institution, which did not cover the case of a married woman.

Hertha was spirited, beautiful, eccentric, and brilliant, and after the death of her husband her colleagues provoked her into becoming an energetic feminist. Although Marie was a member of the International Council of Women, which had at that time about 70,000 members in France, her brand of feminist militancy was in keeping with the character of the organization, which was against noisy demonstrations and concerned with day-to-day efficacy.

Hertha Ayrton, on the other hand, was working closely with Emmeline Pankhurst. She had taken part in the first march of the English suffragettes, to the prime minister's residence, where a policeman had grabbed her by the neck to stop her from going in. The three leaders of the suffragettes had been arrested and sentenced to nine months in prison. They had gone on a hunger strike. An international petition had been circulated to demand their release. When Hertha Ayrton had written to Marie asking for her signature, Marie—who was always judicious about how she used her name—had signed it right away. Hertha was one of the few women she trusted and would continue to trust. It was true that she trusted more women than men. Men were sometimes geniuses, they were sometimes handsome, one could take all sorts of pleasure in them, one could be friends with them and make love to them, but as for trusting them. . . . It was harder than trusting women.

Hertha arranged with Bronia that as soon as she was well enough to travel, Marie would join her in her house in Hampshire. Marie's departure was delayed by a relapse. In the Savoie, she had to undergo a new treatment, and she noted down every aspect of it that was quantifiable—her temperature, how much liquid she absorbed in the morning, in the evening, the condition of her urine, the frequency and intensity of her pains—just as she had noted in her account book, "L. affair, 318 francs."

At last she arrived in Hampshire, thin and drawn. Hertha Ayrton's servants did not suspect that this tired woman with her slight Slavic accent was the notorious Frenchwoman whose amorous exploits had been all over the English newspapers.

Hertha's intelligent friendship was to work wonders. What she provided was not the sort of compassion that seems to violate the intimacy of unhappiness, but rather a supportive companionship. Slowly, as her health improved, Marie saw things more realistically and began putting her life back together.

What had happened to her? Her important friendships hadn't been threatened at all. Her scientific prestige was intact, it was actually greater than it had ever been before. By destroying the image of the grieving wife, she had alienated the sympathy that the public reserves for widows, but she had no use for this sympathy. The report drawn up by the gentlemen at the Sorbonne on her adulterous complicity had been buried when the court had neither proceeded with the offense against Langevin nor mentioned Mme Curie's name. She could go back to teaching whenever she liked. Her laboratory was waiting for her. She had suffered through a terrible upheaval, but she had not experienced an existential breakdown.

She no longer had any "private life," but she was the one who had destroyed it. As far as that was concerned, her pride was intact. Her English biographer, Robert Reid, may have been a little hasty when he said that "there would be no more men in Marie's life." It would be safer and more accurate to say that no other man would play a major part in her life—which is different.

Irène, on the other hand, played a larger and larger part. Her letters already showed the maturity of a serious adolescent. She wrote to her mother in July, 1912:

> I too was very upset by the death of M. Henri Poincaré. As for politics, I'm always interested in it but right now there isn't much I can understand. For example, the causes and consequences of the fall of the Turkish government are things that are too complicated for me. I have vaguely understood that it had something to do with the desertions in the Turkish army and the resignation of the Minister of War or the Minister of the Navy, or of both of them (I'm not exactly sure) . . . .
>
> I've also noticed that every day or almost every day an English minister just misses being killed by the English suffragettes, but it seems to me that that isn't a very brilliant way for the suffragettes to prove they're capable of voting.

Before she left for England, a Polish delegation led by Henry Sienkiewicz had come to beg her to return to Poland.

"Our people admire you," the author of *Quo Vadis* wrote to her—he himself had also received the Nobel Prize—"but they would like to see you work here in your native city. This is the ardent desire of the whole country. If we have you in Warsaw, we will feel stronger, we will lift up our heads, which have been bowed down by the weight of so many misfortunes. May our prayer be answered. Do not push away the hands that are reaching out toward you."

But Marie felt capable of facing Paris now. She could go back, and she did.

When she returned to her apartment on the quai de Béthune in October 1912, it had been exactly a year since she had noted her last observation in her laboratory notebook. The next one appeared on December 3, 1912. She had taken herself in hand again. And she had resumed her teaching.

On the form called "Personal Statement" in the files of the Faculté des Sciences, where her name, occupation, titles, and degrees appear, there is an entry under the heading "Interruptions of Employment" noting that she was absent for reasons of illness from January 1, 1912, to August 1, 1912. She was never to be absent from her work again.

The laboratory report she signed for the year 1912–1913 indicates that she had reestablished her usual relations with the university authorities: in it, she makes vehement demands for more funds.

By now, Marie Curie had nothing more to prove in the domain of science. Her international reputation, which was unprecedented and unrivaled, had continued to grow as more and more successes were reported in the application of radium to the treatment of cancer. But people had barely begun to discover the secrets of radioactivity.

Paradoxically, the phenomenal success of radium left researchers with less money than before. Not only did the price of radioactive substances skyrocket because the demand for them was increasing constantly all over the world and production couldn't keep up, but priority was given to medical institutions and private funds were concentrated on medical research, so that physics laboratories had no funds with which to train and pay researchers or to buy the more and more sophisticated equipment they needed for their work.

The battle of the laboratories, those "temples of the future," as Pasteur had called them, was one in which Marie was to take full part, now that she had recovered her strength. She was clearly determined not to give up one inch of the ground she had broken; on the contrary, she was going to extend it even farther. An agreement between the university and the Institut Pasteur—which operated on private funds—gave her the means to do this.

The director of the Institut Pasteur, who had wanted for a long time to bring Marie in, and the dean of the Académie de Paris, who had no desire to lose her from the Sorbonne, agreed to create and share the costs of an Institut du Radium which would contain two sections—one to be directed by Marie and devoted to research in physics and chemistry, the other to be directed by Dr. Claude Regaud and devoted to medicine and biology. The two wings of the Institut du Radium would be built in the rue Pierre Curie.

There were plans, architects, contractors, and decisions of all kinds to be made. Here was something that required all Marie's attention. She was also able to use her scientific approach to gardening: even before the foundations of the two buildings were laid, she saw to it that lime trees were planted so that they would have time to grow before she moved. And in her estimate of expenses, she included a gardener. During the time the Institut was being built, the workmen would often see her tramping through the worksite, usually in the mud and rain, and climbing the scaffolding.

A young scholarship student at the Institut Pasteur named Lacassagne, later Professor Lacassagne, left the following account:

> In a sort of ritual ceremony, the various contractors would meet on the worksite every Friday afternoon. I had come from Lyon four days before. On November 7 [1913] I accompanied Dr. Regaud to this outdoor meeting. Mme Curie joined us. She was a frail woman dressed all in black and very pale.
>
> She was forty-six at the time—it was her birthday—and yet I was struck by how extraordinarily young she seemed, by the charm and gentleness of her expression.

A trip to the Engadine had put her completely back on her feet. She had gone mountain-climbing with her daughters and a traveling companion who talked to her in German. Irène and Eve were amused by this gentleman, who would walk absentmindedly among the rocks and say to their mother: "You see, Madame, what I need to know is exactly what happens to the passengers in an *elevator* when it falls through the air." The gentleman was Einstein.

She had gone to Warsaw to inaugurate a laboratory and had lectured on science in Polish for the first time there. Then she had gone to Birmingham to receive an honorary doctorate. She happily described the ceremony in a letter to Irène, and also gave her news that the girl had been waiting to hear for a long time: she could write to her mother in London, care of Mrs. Ayrton, in the name of Mme Curie—"The servants know my name now, so there is no problem about our using it."

Exit Mme Sklodowska. Mme Curie had freedom of the city again. A friend of Rutherford's who was present at the Birmingham ceremony with Lorentz and Soddy described his impression of Marie in this situation: "shy, reserved, in control of herself and full of nobility; everyone wanted to see her but very few succeeded. Reporters tried to interview her and Mme Curie skillfully evaded their questions by singing Rutherford's praises. This wasn't exactly what they had hoped for, but it was all they could get."

"I urge the people of England to keep their eyes on Mr. Rutherford," she had said. "His work on radioactivity has surprised me very much. There will probably be some great developments soon, and the discovery of radium will have been merely a preliminary step."

Rutherford had just discovered the nucleus of the atom by using for the first time a procedure that physicists are still using today, and which consists of bombarding matter with radiation. At that time, a young Danish physicist named Niels Bohr was working in the Cavendish laboratory. It was he who would later incorporate the quantum theory into Ruther-

195

ford's model of the atom and establish the "planetary model" of the atom.[2]

Rutherford's experiments were to furnish the first deliberately provoked demonstrations of nuclear forces. And his genius was not yet exhausted. Nor was Marie's.

But other forces were in motion that were to tear both of them away from the intoxicating delights of pure science.

---

[2] According to the quantum theory, the emission and absorption of radiation by matter can only take place in discontinuous quantities of energy.

THE INTERMISSION

seventeen

"**W**HAT we need," said the wife of the President of the Republic, Madame Poincaré, in the spring of 1914, "is to have a good war and get rid of Jaurès."

This decent lady, this animal lover, was going to have her wish. It is only fair to acknowledge that she wasn't really to blame for saying what she did. As is often the case with foolish people, she was only expressing the collective unconscious. A desire for war was pervasive in Europe at that time, even though people still continued to make plans for the future, start families, build houses, plow their fields, and hope for peace.

As for Marie, she was pestering the carpenters who were putting up the last shelves in her office in the Curie wing, which was nearly finished. On Sunday, June 28, 1914, she bought a copy of *Le Temps*, as she did every afternoon, and learned that shortly before noon Archduke Francis Ferdinand, the heir apparent of his great-uncle, Franz Joseph, emperor of the Austro-Hungarian Empire, had been assassinated along with his wife by a Serbian student in a Bosnian city called Sarajevo.

For a few days, Marie and her friends were worried. In the powder keg of the Balkans, Bosnia, which had been annexed by Austria in 1908, was a center for restless Serbian minorities. Was the emperor going to seize on this pretext to send a punitive expedition against the kingdom of Serbia? And if a war began there, where would it end?

But the Viennese court, which had never forgiven the archduke for marrying beneath himself by taking a Polish countess as his wife, only gave him a third-class princely funeral, and on July 4, observers concluded in the Paris press that "All conflict between Austria and Serbia has been avoided."

On July 15, the bourgeoisie of France went on vacation, some to Touquet, some to Biarritz, some to Cabourg. Marie sent her daughters, her cook, and a governess to Brittany, where she was going to join them at the end of the month.

The newspapers were full of the trial of Henriette Caillaux, although a few lines here and there were given to the parliamentary debate on increasing military spending. The sum involved was only what would be needed to change the infantry's field-service uniform, but the debate provoked some surprising exchanges:

"How much time would be needed to get rid of the dangerous red trousers?"

"Three to seven years."

"And what would happen if war broke out between now and then?"

In the Senate, the army's entire administration was violently and specifically criticized, and the senator addressing the government concluded: "If war were declared, our soldiers would go off with one pair of shoes on their feet and half a pair of boots made thirty years ago."

But on July 23, *Le Temps* commented—it was the only newspaper to do so—on "the arrogant tone and the boundless audacity of the demands" contained in the ultimatum Austria-Hungary had delivered to Serbia.

Suddenly, on Sunday, July 26, the Caillaux trial retreated to the second page: Russia had begun to mobilize. Recalling that "the Russian army is admirably well organized, trained, and outfitted," all the French newpapers, whatever their political tendencies, expressed satisfaction "that Russia is not unmoved by the collapse of Serbia." Jaurès alone wrote: "Our only remaining hope is the immensity of the catastrophe that threatens the world." He called upon "all proletarians to unite so that their hearts beating as one may ward off this horrible nightmare."

Parisians gathered on the boulevards in front of the newspaper buildings where the latest telegrams were posted.

On Tuesday, July 28, Serbia rejected Austria's ultimatum.

The first cannon of World War I was fired at Belgrade.

In Paris, grocery shelves were picked clean by housewives laying in stocks of sugar. Shoe stores were invaded by people buying walking shoes.

In the extremely right-wing *La Libre Parole*, Colonel Driant wrote: "I ardently wish, as every Frenchman should, that peace may be kept, but if Germany decides that this is the occasion she has been waiting for so long, if she assumes responsibility for the attack, I say that we have enough confidence to look her in the face." Driant was killed in March 1916.

Le Radical said more or less the same thing: "The storm has begun, but our ship is seaworthy. . . . Each man is at his post, and we are standing by. Hoist the flag!"

And also *La Lanterne:* "However strongly attached one might be to the idea of peace, there are times when one must respond to violence with violence. At those times, war is our most sacred duty."

At the last session of the Caillaux trial, the lawyer for the defense, M. Labori, cried out: "Let us save our anger for the enemies that threaten us from outside!"

In Berlin, the German Socialists organized twenty-nine simultaneous meetings to protest against the possibility of war. But they attributed it to "the prestige politics of Austria and Russia." They weren't implicating Germany. And in Brussels, Jaurès praised the French government, "which wants peace and is working for peace."

The Socialist International had failed. Failed to abolish nationalism even in its own ranks, failed to realize its dream of creating a kind of solidarity among workers that would cross frontiers, failed to substitute the class war for war between different countries, which was a sublime war, a holy war, a war that brought into play the highest values—heroism, self-sacrifice, one's duty to one's country.

These values were so widely shared, nationalist feeling was so fervent, that not one pacifist failed to appear when he was called up. On the eve of the war, the general staff estimated

201

that 14 percent of the total force of mobilizable men would refuse to serve. During the extent of the hostilities, only 1.3 percent of the force would be reported absent.

On July 30, the last windowpane was put in place and Marie toured her new kingdom with André Debierne. Two years before, she had been losing her grip on everything. Now she was back in charge. What could be more symbolic of her resurrection than these rooms—where more than thirty researchers would work under her direction—and this lecture hall, and this solid building with "INSTITUT DU RADIUM, PAVILLON CURIE" written across its facade? If life had any meaning, this was the meaning of her life, and this was the seat of her power over things . . . and over people too.

Of course it was possible that an absurd war would come along and. . . . But she didn't want to believe this. Her friends didn't either. The Borels had gone to Brittany. Jean Perrin was leaving that very day. Marie stopped in at the Gare Montparnasse to reserve a seat for August 1. As it happened, she never occupied it.

On the evening of July 31, Jaurès was assassinated by Raoul Vilain. No one knew whether Vilain's mind had been more effectively poisoned by *L'Action Française* or by Péguy, who was exultant. "How many times have we let Jaurès go unpunished!" he said[1]. The next day, France and Germany mobilized their armies. The iron die had been cast.

The mesh of circumstances that was to drag twenty-seven countries into the war, crush ten million men, kill three emperors, change several borders and a great deal else had been set in motion.

No one in France or Germany doubted that the war would be brief and victorious. In flag-bedecked Paris, the first day of

---

[1] Charles Péguy was killed at the front on September 18, 1914. Jaurès's son was killed in June 1918. Raoul Vilain remained in prison throughout the war, was acquitted, and was killed in 1936 in Minorca by a Spanish Republican.

mobilization had "the gaiety and splendor of a holiday," according to *Le Figaro*. Marie wrote more soberly to her daughters: "Paris is calm and gives a very good impression despite the fact that people are leaving."

But mail was no longer reaching Brittany, where no one knew anything except that the alarm had sounded, women were crying, and men were leaving, saying: "It's for the Serbs." Called up on the second day to be an engineer officer, Jean Perrin got back on the train, disgusted.

Curiously enough, Marie, who was optimistic about the outcome of the hostilities, was immediately convinced that the war would be long and murderous, and that the modern weapons would produce dangerous wounds. Her acuteness is all the more impressive given the fact that on August 11, using information provided by the Ministry of War, the press, in an attempt to reassure families who were worried about certain rumors that were going around, reported that "All [the wounded] agree that the wounds are not painful. The speed with which they are inflicted, as well as their heat, ensure that there is no danger of infection, and the disorders caused by them are for the most part insignificant."

All the men Marie knew—Debierne, Langevin, her nephew Maurice Curie, the boys who worked in the lab, and a large number of students—were going off to their posts. Marguerite Borel was involved in the Secours National, a "sacred union" sort of organization of which her father, Paul Appell, who was too old to fight, had been elected president. He was an Alsatian, and if the Germans took Paris, he was in danger of being shot. "A nice death for an Alsatian in time of war," he declared.

Urged to take part in the organization, Marie answered, "One must act, one must act." She soon found what she had to do.

Except in a few hospitals in Paris, roentgen rays or X rays were not being used with much frequency or effectiveness. The medical units of the army had no facilities and possessed

203

only a single radiology vehicle. The improvised military hospitals had neither equipment nor competent staff.

By August 12, making use of her name, her authority, her connections, Marie had already extracted a mission order from the overworked functionaries of the Ministry of War. Her plan was to form a fleet of cars outfitted with the necessary equipment and staff so that wherever wounded men were being picked up in the combat zone, radiological examinations could be carried out right away. Now all she had to do was to get the cars, the equipment, and the people to operate the equipment. All the suitable cars had been requisitioned.

For obvious reasons, Marie had never shared the French people's infatuation with Russia. When Nicholas II greatly troubled France by announcing that after his victory over Austria, he would "re-form Poland under his authority," she had no news of Bronia, and did not know which side her brother and her brother-in-law were on. Were they fighting with the Russians against the Austrians, who were invading Poland? Or with the Austrians and the legion Pilsudski was forming, against the Russian oppression? But we know that she kept her priorities straight. Asked to give an opinion about "the Polish question," she made an unambiguous statement that was published in *Le Temps*.

Writing from Brittany, Irène begged her mother to let her come back. Not only did she want to "be useful for something," but the people in the country were beginning to look askance at the Curie girls. What language were they speaking with their cook and their housekeeper?

> It means more [Irène wrote] because you yourself were accused of being a foreigner and we haven't anyone in the army. . . . They say I'm a German spy. . . .
>
> I'm not very frightened about all this but I'm very upset. It makes me sad to think people take me for a foreigner when I'm so profoundly French and I love France more than anything else. I can't help crying every time I think about it. . . .
>
> I would 100 times over prefer to be alone with Eve right now than with Walcia and Jozia.

Pierre Curie would have liked Marie's answer: "I was sorry to hear that you're having trouble over your nationality. Don't take these things too much to heart, but do your best to explain it to the people you see. Remember, also, that not only should you endure these little miseries with patience, but that it is actually your duty to protect Joséphine and Valentine, who are foreigners. This would be your duty even if they were German, because even in that case they would have a right to live in Brittany. Darling, try to be more fully aware of exactly what your duty is, as a Frenchwoman, to yourself and to others."

She went on to give her daughter some practical advice, then said: "Have Fernand [Chavannes] do some physics problems. If the two of you can't work for France right now, work for its future. After the war is over, a lot of people will unfortunately be missing. They will have to be replaced. You should both study physics and mathematics as diligently as you can."

As for her, she was making the rounds of all the well-to-do women she knew. Were they patriots? This was the time to prove it. How? By donating a car. "I'll give it back to you after the war," she told them confidently. A few of these ladies agreed, and the ones who didn't gave money instead. Marie had already collected a few cars when a German plane dropped three bombs on the capital, along with a banner that read: "The German Army is at the gates of Paris. The only thing for you to do is give yourselves up."

On September 2, the President of the Republic and the government left for Bordeaux. Everyone who could follow them there did. Marie, too, left in a crowded train that crept along at a snail's pace. She was, as she wrote, surrounded "by people who could not or would not face the dangers of a possible occupation by Germany." They were taking their gold, silver, and jewels with them. Marie was also carrying a bag she could hardly lift. It was as heavy as lead—in fact, it was lead. Forty-five pounds of lead encasing one gram of radium, the only one that existed in France—Marie's radium.

She spent the whole day traveling, horrified at the idea that someone might recognize her and think she had joined the exodus. But when she found herself standing on the station platform in Bordeaux in the middle of the night with a bag she couldn't carry, for the first time in her life she was delighted to hear someone cry out: "It's Mme Curie!" The stranger grabbed hold of her bag and found her a room in a private house in the overpopulated city. The next day, she rented a safe-deposit box in a bank, left her treasure there, and started home again. This time she traveled in a military train headed for Paris; looking distinguished in her alpaca coat, she happily shared a sandwich given her by a soldier. She distinctly preferred these traveling companions to the ones she had been thrown in with on the way down.

Alarming news was spreading through the train. The Germans were in Compiègne.

On September 12, Irène's birthday, Marie wrote a note sending a "kiss to my sweet seventeen-year-old darling." On the fourteenth: "The invading forces are withdrawing and soon you'll be able to return to Paris without too much trouble." On the twentieth: "You have my permission to come back by yourself. . . . If you can bring luggage, take the leather-covered hamper. There isn't much time for taking care of one's clothes here, so if you can, bring them."

Irène had hurt her foot and couldn't go anywhere. She was being nursed by Henriette Perrin. She answered: "I'm beginning solid coordinates because I can't understand differential equations at all." At last she was able to return to Paris, where Marie immediately put her to work.

After calling on the women who owned cars, Marie had gone knocking at the doors of body-shop mechanics to see if they would turn the cars into vans. Then she had gone around to the builders of X-ray apparatus and dynamos to ask them if they would provide the equipment she needed.

When the first radiology vehicle set off toward the front on November 1, 1914, painted regulation gray with a red cross on its side, 310,000 men had already died and 300,000 had been wounded on the French side alone—men who had gone to war in red trousers.

In the car were Marie, Irène, and military staff consisting of a doctor, an assistant, and a driver. Their first stop was to be the military hospital of Creil in the Oise department.

The system Marie had devised was primitive but effective: each car would carry one dynamo, one portable X-ray apparatus, all the photographic equipment needed, a cable, curtains, a few screens, and protective gloves.

The apparatus was set up in a room with windows hermetically sealed by the curtains. It was connected by the cable to the dynamo, which remained in the car and which was operated by the driver.

This was the technical side of it. The subjects of the radiography, however, were men, and they were men in pain, men who in many cases were very badly wounded. "To hate the very idea of war, it ought to be enough to see just once what I saw so often during all those years," Marie later wrote. "Men and boys brought to the ambulance behind the lines filthy and covered with blood." For a person of seventeen who had led a protected life until then, it was a rude shock. Irène felt it, but didn't waver. The fact that she was a Curie required her to do it. And what wouldn't she have done to fulfill her mother's expectations? She had never forgotten the day when her mother was giving her a physics problem and Irène had absentmindedly come up with the wrong answer. Marie had grabbed her notebook and thrown it out the window.

"My mother had just as much confidence in me as she had in herself," Irène was to say later, telling how, at the age of eighteen, she went off alone to install an X-ray facility in the military hospital at Amiens, how she alone assumed responsibility for another facility near Ypres "after carrying out the task—not an easy one—of teaching the methods of localizing projectiles to a Belgian military doctor who was opposed to the most elementary notions of geometry."

On November 1, 1914, it was Irène's turn to learn something new, and she set to work on it. The log book of their car, which

207

they called Car E, shows that on that day the small team carried out thirty examinations.

To train her people, Marie began with simple cases. The first wounded man she and Irène worked on together had received a bullet in his forearm. They put him in position in front of the apparatus. Marie regulated it, obtained a tracing of the image projected on the screen as the doctor dictated his observations, and then took a picture that was developed right away by an assistant.

They encountered many head wounds. In 1911, the minister of war had proposed that soldiers be equipped with helmets, but the Chamber had rejected the idea because "it would look too German." They weren't given helmets until 1915.

Early in the war, surgeons hadn't yet had much experience with radiology. Some of them, especially the older ones, had no confidence at all in this new method of examining patients. In the beginning, it needed all of "Madame Curie's" authority to persuade them. Later, they often operated without even taking pictures first, using the radiological screen as their guide.

Everywhere she went, behind the lines, in her gray Renault, Marie kept in mind the possibility of installing a permanent radiology station, and when she had to, she came back herself with the necessary equipment.

On January 1, 1915, she wrote to Langevin, who was a sergeant in one of the army's workers' battalions: "I have received a letter telling me that the radiology car operating in the Saint-Pol region has broken down. This means the entire North is without radiology facilities!"

The following month there was one car. Then two. Then three. One thing Marie was good at was organizing people. She knew how to do things herself, but she also knew how to get other people to do things.

The twenty cars, which were known as "the little Curies," and the two hundred permanent posts that she succeeded in establishing would perform 1,100,000 radiographies in 1917–1918 alone.

As soon as the front stabilized, life started up again in Paris. Concert halls opened their doors. At the movies, people could see Charlie Chaplin and the *Mysteries of New York*. In March 1915, fashion designers came out with daring mid-calf–length skirts. At the Opéra, Diaghilev's Russian Ballet gave a benefit performance for the British Red Cross. The class of 1916 was called up, and *Le Figaro* wrote: "In the cool spring morning, troops of young men went off toward the stations carrying only duffle bags slung across their backs; their hands in their pockets, their hats or caps tilted over their ears, they called out to each other gaily and the older people, women, and girls who went along with many of them tried not to dampen their youthful high spirits."

But from the Somme, a doctor wrote to Marie: "I am on the go from morning to night. I managed to carry out 588 examinations during the month of July . . . I don't think I can go on assuming this kind of responsibility much longer." Marie put all the available men to work. Then she decided to train women to be radiologists, too.

For several months now, women had been doing all sorts of new jobs. Marguerite Borel had opened a recruiting office for national services in one room of the Ecole Normale and was conducting the first aptitude tests there. She was sending entire railway cars full of women to gunpowder factories, airplane factories. Women were working as mail carriers, hairdressers, market gardeners, railway workers.

This was such a widespread phenomenon and such a staggering one that Deputy Jules Siegfried paid tribute to their courage and dared to suggest to the Chamber that after the war they should be given the right to vote. In an article published in *Le Journal*, the dramatist Eugène Brieux explored the consequences of such a decision: "Women are saying to themselves, 'We are neither so weak, so foolish, nor so inept as men claim we are, and so there are other careers open to us besides marriage. Therefore, if we no longer need men in order to survive, we have the right to choose.'" The Chamber of Deputies was to grant Frenchwomen the vote on

209

May 20, 1919, by 344 votes to 97. But the Senate quickly corrected this momentary aberration, which must have been inspired by quite understandable emotion after the end of the war.

Brieux concluded that after the war, "men will respect women," that "the abominable institution of the dowry will disappear," but that "the competition between the sexes for jobs will be intense."

But at the moment this was certainly not a problem. The army needed drivers and asked for two hundred women. Marie needed radiologists and looked for women capable of acquiring the necessary expertise.

One of her former students, Marthe Klein, took charge of recruiting these women, while Marie implemented a sort of "accelerated training."

Candidates were brought together in groups of twenty in the Pavillon Curie. Here Marie spent two months introducing them to the elementary concepts of mathematics, physics, and anatomy that they would be needing. Then they were sent off to their radiographic positions. One hundred fifty examiners were trained this way.

Characteristically, Marie proved to be both patient with her students and also ruthless. She was patient with the ones who were serious about their work—and most of them were—and she was ruthless with the others, whom she kicked out unceremoniously.

Naturally, she started a new notebook at this point, in which she recorded her students' daily progress. Next to one name, we read: "X . . . idiot." Next to another: "Wanted to quit because of the harmful effects of the rays (???)." This particular "idiot" was quite correct. We don't know how many of the young women, who performed their work with almost no protection—only cloth gloves!—were seriously hurt by it.

At the same time that she was organizing the radiological service, Marie retrieved the radium she had left at Bordeaux. Scientists now knew how to liquefy radium, and in its liquid state it gave off a gas called radon, which had recently begun to be put to therapeutic uses. In Dublin, a certain Professor Joly had invented a way to "milk" the radium of its gas and to enclose the latter in minuscule, hermetically sealed glass tubes which were then slipped into platinum needles. These needles could be implanted in patients' bodies.

Military hospitals were asking for more and more radon for the cicatrization of certain types of wounds. With Irène's help, Marie brought equipment from the rue Cuvier to the pavillion and here created the first French service for the manufacture of tubes of radon, using her gram of radium.

Here, too, women were the ones handling the precious substance; they were more skilled at it. Sometimes, one or another of them would become strangely exhausted, unable to stay on her feet. After a few days away from the laboratory, she would come back. In the meantime, Marie would take her place.

Though she was the director of the radiological services of the army, she was never seen in a uniform. She was Madame Curie, that was all. She traveled about wearing a shapeless round hat, with a badge pinned to her coat.

"Irène tells me you're somewhere near Verdun," her nephew, Maurice Curie, wrote to her. "I stick my head into all the medical cars that go by on the road but I never see anything but peaked caps with a lot of gold braid on them and I can't believe the military authorities would want to regularize the situation of your very nonregulation hairdo."

She dearly loved young Maurice Curie, was afraid for him, and yet obviously did not take advantage of her connections to find him a safe job. But what a pity it was that scientists were put to such poor use. . . .

Jean Perrin had managed to get himself assigned to Marie's service and was in charge of one radiology car. In January 1915, they went north together, had two flat tires, crashed into a tree, stopped to swallow a cup of tea, and wrote to Langevin, who was marking time at the home front:

Here we are at Dunkirk in a modest hotel sitting at a shaky pedestal table drinking tea that is too strong. . . . We are given

211

a good welcome everywhere, mostly because of the presence of Mme Curie.

. . .We are all going through such a difficult period now that someone like you should quickly offer to be useful in ways that only you can be. You can do a lot and you must. Fortunately, you weren't called up during the "statistical" mobilization which pretended that we were all identical. A more "discriminating" mobilization is therefore possible for you. By using your intelligence as a PHYSICIST, you can be more useful than a thousand sergeants, despite all the respect I have for that honorable rank. . . .

Seriously, though, it seems to me this is your duty right now: to find ways to help us win. All other duties take second place or twenty-fifth place! You're lucky to have your true duty so simply and clearly before you.

Throw yourself into it and neglect everything else.

Marie added a few lines to the letter, seconding Perrin.

Paul Langevin wasn't the only scientist in his forties to be employed in making earthworks while younger men went and got themselves killed. One of them was Marie's favorite co-worker, Jean Danysz, a captain of the artillery.

The scientific aspect of the mobilization, however, really began one day in April 1915, when some battalions of Algerians holding trenches in front of Ypres were enveloped in a green cloud, coughed, choked, and fell to the ground unconscious, their lungs filled with chlorine.

This green cloud was the first attempt anyone had ever made to use poison gas. A great chemist had given the Germans the idea. The Kaiser Wilhelm Institute of Organic Chemistry in Berlin had been transformed into a military installation with a staff of over 2,000, including 150 university professors—a fact which only came out much later.

At that time, several French chemists, including Corporal Debierne, who had been given a military medal, were recalled from the front. Charles Moureu put together a team to develop toxic substances. André Mayer, a physiologist at the Collège de France, transferred to Paris, and there improvised a gas mask.

212

Moureu and Mayer had already experienced the effects of mustard gas, because the Germans had used it at Ypres too, filling the hospitals with half-blind men coughing up their lungs. The French were to make abundant use of it themselves.

When Painlevé became head of the Ministry of Public Education in October 1915, physicists and mathematicians were also recalled to Paris. Langevin oversaw experiments in ballistics and worked on a recoilless cannon. Perrin explored the possibilities of using sound to locate artillery and airplanes, a method that would be operational by 1918.

But disaster threatened at sea, where elusive German submarines were destroying the Allied reserves of men, coal, and food. In 1916, the Allies lost 936 ships; 2,681 would be sunk in 1917. "Very soon," Winston Churchill was to write, "the submarine war will have starved us into an unconditional surrender. Our success has been hanging by a thread, a very slender thread, and one that is in great danger."

This slender thread was in the hands of the scientists. The English, who had also recalled their scientists, including Rutherford, were desperately looking for a way to counter the German underseas maneuvers. How could they be detected?

In France, an engineer named Constantin Chilowski suggested picking up waves, or rather the sound vibrations caused by waves, which the human ear could not hear and which were called ultrasound waves. But how could they be picked up? Langevin, with two of his former students, was put in charge of tackling the problem.

The first attempts he made at detection by ultrasound, carried out in the Seine, showed that he had solved the problem in principle, at least. But the reception of the ultrasonic echo, first by a condenser, then by a carbon microphone, was not very good. Then Langevin had an inspiration—he would use the piezoelectric effect of quartz, the phenomenon that Pierre and Jacques Curie had discovered.

He took the section of quartz that Pierre Curie had had mounted and that one of his students had piously kept, removed it from its mountings, and used it to make a microphone: this was how the ultrasonic microphone was invented. For another few months, the team worked feverishly. By 1917, Langevin had perfected a receiving apparatus that could detect waves whose amplitude was no more than one ten-billionth of a millimeter.

In the Toulon roads, a submerged submarine was detected at a distance of two kilometers in the presence of specialists from the Admiralty. The submarine detection devices developed afterward by Great Britain owed everything to Langevin's apparatus, as do the innumerable applications of ultrasound technique today.

In the midst of all the comings and goings of the scientists between England and France, Rutherford happened to find himself in Paris one day in 1917. Just after noon he saw a taxi driven by a soldier pull up in front of his hotel. In the taxi were Perrin, Langevin, Marie, and Debierne. "They took me to lunch and treated me royally," he was to say later. After lunch, the small group went off to hear Rutherford's lecture, then to the Pavillon Curie, where Marie made tea. Rutherford found her "rather gray, worn out, tired" that day.

She was tired. Over the past twenty years, she had been exposed to more radiation than any other human being and she continued to expose herself to it every day. She traveled around in all sorts of weather in cars that had to be started by cranking the engine and that couldn't go faster than about fifty kilometers an hour at best. She slept wherever she could, ate whatever was at hand. And yet she had acquired something she had often lacked in the past—good humor.

Having to mobilize all one's inner resources to respond to an emergency is undoubtedly the best way to help one forget oneself. Relieved of the morose pleasures of introspection, Marie was at peace with herself.

The winter of 1918 was particularly harsh. There wasn't enough gas and the Seine was full of ice floes. Ration books, thought up by André Citroën, were distributed and bread was rationed. The news of the Treaty of Brest-Litovsk, under which Bolshevik Russia gave Poland and the Ukraine to Germany, reached France on March 3, the same day that fashion designers showed their new collections—short jersey dresses.

In April, the Germans crossed the Aisne River, Soissons was evacuated, and Château-Thierry was abandoned. Near Château-Thierry an obscure American soldier fell, and on him was found a journal in which he had written: "America must win this war. I will therefore work hard, I will economize, I will make sacrifices, I will endure, I will fight cheerfully and do as much as I can, as though the outcome of the war depended on myself alone."

Through some miracle, Marie, who usually came down with a bad case of the flu every autumn, was spared the Spanish flu, which was killing two thousand people a week by October. Two of its victims were Guillaume Apollinaire and Edmond Rostand.

In early November, the 944th wounded man was x-rayed in Car E. He had a splinter of shrapnel in his left shoulder.

On the evening of November 8, 1918, in the Michel Theater, where Raimu was performing in *L'Ecole des Cocottes*, and in the Casino de Paris, where Maurice Chevalier was singing with Mistinguett, and in every theater in Paris (except for the Opéra, where the musicians were striking for higher pay), the show was interrupted by an announcement that Wilhelm II had fled his country.

When the cannon thundered at eleven o'clock in the morning on November 11, the 1,561st day of the war, Marie was in the laboratory with Marthe Klein. The two women ran to the nearest store to look for blue cloth, white cloth, and red cloth, made a flag, and put the flag up across the Pavillon Curie. Then, like everyone else, they went off to the Champs-Elysées.

THE STATUE

eighteen

FRANCE had been victorious; Poland was free—and the pianist Paderewski was president of the Council at Warsaw; Marie's family had emerged unscathed, her dearest friends were safe and sound even though a million and a half Frenchmen had been killed, the Institut du Radium and the radium itself were untouched . . . Marie could not have hoped for more. She was a very lucky woman.

She was not thrown into a panic by the Russian Revolution. When the President of the United States, presenting the fourteen points which he felt had to be the basis for the peace treaty, had cried out: "The voice of the Russian people is more poignant and compelling to my ears than any of the many other voices that are causing the troubled air of the world to vibrate with emotion," Marie had agreed. In the same way, she had been enthusiastic about the plan for the League of Nations.

The dawn that was breaking after four years of night showed a field of dead, but it was still the dawn of a new world. "I have paid a visit to the future, and it works!" said a member of the American delegation sent to Lenin by Wilson in 1919.

Marie was no doubt disappointed, however, as were many others, by some of the other ideas Wilson expressed in the peace treaty, ideas about Russia as well as Germany.

"Either the Germans have to be exterminated down to the last man, which is unthinkable, or else they have to be given a peace they can tolerate," said Marie.

Once summer came, she gave herself a real, long vacation for the first time in a very great while. It was a pure delight,

219

even though, naturally, she took along some work—a book to write about radiology and the war.

Thanks to Marthe Klein, who took her there, she discovered how magnificent Provence was, with its splendid August nights when she could sleep out on the terrace, and the warmth of the Mediterranean, in which she started swimming again. There weren't many tourists, only a few English people on the beach.

"If only the hotel were a little more distinguished," she wrote to Irène, "there wouldn't be a better place to work."

She took such a liking to the area that later she had a house built at Cavalaire, overlooking the sea on three sides, and painstakingly planted a terraced garden next to it. Her passion for stones was the only material passion she was known to have, but it was a strong one: she was to buy another house, in Brittany; and she kept the Brunoy house until the end of her life.

As always when she was separated from her daughters, she wrote them long letters full of precise descriptions. This time, she wrote as a mother—and not as Marie squeezing herself into the role of a mother.

In her letters she talked about "the preserves we made which have begun to get moldy and which we will have to recook." She gave advice about moths, she complained about problems with the maids. She wrote in a tone which was relaxed and tender and which marked a new gentleness in her relations with Irène, her "dear big girl," to whom she confided "the responsibility for order in the laboratory. Do as much as you can to keep people from making a hash of things while I'm gone."

"I often think," she wrote, "of the year of work stretching before us, and I would like something good to come of it. I also think of both of you and of all the sweetness, joy, and worry that you give me. You are truly a great wealth for me and I hope that I still have a few good years left in which to share my life with you. I know you will be happy to be back with your old friend of a mother and that you will do all sorts of nice things for her once again." Marie, who was now over fifty, seemed to have entered what they call a second youth—which is, in fact, just the opposite of youth.

She was less demanding, she was less anguished, she enjoyed the precarious pleasure of being "still" agile, "still" young, "still" capable of riding horseback and going skating with Irène. How much longer could it go on? There would come a last time. Meanwhile, however, life lay before her. And Marie, who had not stopped conceiving of her life and describing her life as a martyrdom, loved life passionately.

She was still small, thin, supple, she walked bare-legged in espadrilles with the motions of a young girl. Depending on the day, she could look ten years older than she was or ten years younger.

For some time now, she had had to wear glasses, but wasn't that natural?

Her fame had been obscured for a time by . . . But what had all that been about, anyway? It seemed very far away, almost unreal, after the cyclone that had swept across an entire continent, an entire epoque, changing society and her own way of life.

When she went back to Paris, the intoxication of victory had died down. Certainly it was true that "Paris was a festival" and would remain so through years of madness, madness that sprang from a passion for life. Certainly France's supremacy would never again appear to be more sure, its culture more radiant, its creative people more fertile, its attraction more powerful than in the twenties. But these pearls and diamonds had been embroidered on the most fragile cloth, as people would see when the cloth ripped.

Yes, Paris was a festival, but not for everyone. Thousands of highly skilled people from the armaments factories were out of work, hungry, and cold. Thousands of others saw their buying power melt away. Salaries had tripled, but prices had quadrupled.

The city was divided between those who were afraid of serious trouble and those who actively wanted it. In his last

221

public speech, Jaurès had made the following prediction: "As the typhus fever finishes the work begun by the artillery shells . . . disillusioned men will turn towards the German, French, Russian, and Italian leaders and ask them what reason they can give for all these dead bodies. And then the growing revolution will say to them: 'Go and ask forgiveness of God and of men!' "

Not as lyrical, but just as convinced—for different reasons—that Europe was being overtaken by a proletarian revolution, Lenin ushered it into Russia, where it was to remain. Aborted in Germany, rejected in Poland, deflected in Italy, the revolution didn't come to France at all.

In France, the Socialists thought they could bring about a revolution by winning elections, using the democratic process, and then, bolstered by popular support, setting up the new program that Léon Blum had worked out and that had been the basis of their campaign.[1]

Instead of the majority they were counting on, they ended up with fewer representatives than before, about 60 deputies out of 350, in a "sky-blue" Chamber. This was in November 1919.

At the beginning of 1920, there were widespread strikes. On the evening of May 1, 1920, 90 percent of all metro employees and 70 percent of all postal workers had stopped work. In order to force the nationalization of the railways, which were then owned by private companies, the Federation of Railway Workers declared an unlimited strike. Employees of transport companies, miners, dockworkers, sailors, and construction workers followed suit in two waves.

On May 29, the strike that had begun a month earlier in a spirit of enthusiasm ended in a complete rout. The secretary-general of one union of railway workers killed himself. The workers' movement had been successfully repressed. Eighteen thousand railway workers were fired. It was over.

---

[1] This program contained most of the same ideas as the program of the National Council of the Resistance in 1945.

Something else was about to begin: the schism of the Left into two parties, completed in December at the famous Congress of Tours. As we know, at this congress the Socialist party joined forces with the Third International, a decision that necessarily involved accepting the twenty-one conditions set by the Bolsheviks. We also know that, whether or not it was adventitious, or, at least, a result of the economic situation in 1920, this split between the Socialists and the Communists, as they would call themselves from now on, was to become a part of the structure of French society.

A brief discussion of this situation is not out of place here, because a good many scientists, and particularly the "Curie clan," were closely involved in the political life of the twenties and thirties. And their positions were not always exactly the same, though this never affected their friendships.

Their positions weren't all that different, either. But then this was a time when the dividing line between communism and socialism wasn't very clear, and it was easy to go back and forth across it. What we can say is that from the end of the war on, there were perceptible nuances of difference among the members of the "clan."

In 1919, Langevin, who was a professor at the Collège de France, signed a "message of sympathy" to the intellectuals of Russia. In this new Russia, he had learned, research institutes were opening where none had existed before, even though the country was in the midst of civil war, and workers' schools were being created to train people who had never received any secondary education before. This inspired hope.

He also signed the *Intellectuals' Manifesto*, along with Anatole France and Maurice Ravel, protesting the blockading of the Russians.

At the time of the strikes in 1920, when he was a professor at the Ecole de Physique et de Chimie Industrielles, he was the only professor to object publicly to the use of student volunteers from the professional training colleges to break the railway strikes.

The director of the Ecole, Albin Haller, the same man who

223

had been Langevin's second along with Painlevé at the time of his duel with Gustave Téry, favored suspending courses to facilitate the volunteer effort. On May 18, Langevin published an "open letter" detailing his reasons for objecting to "the introduction [into the school] of conflicts in which the young people find themselves prematurely forced to take positions. As yet, they know nothing about the world of industrial labor, which they will one day enter and in which their present position may create terrible problems for them later. Our duty should be to ensure that our schools are not deflected from their normal activity."

This was to be one of his first public acts that demonstrated the political position he had been brought to by his fiery temperament, his generosity, his experience of the workers' poverty, and also his conviction, widely shared at that time, that a period of justice, equality, and human dignity was beginning in Bolshevik Russia.

In that same year, 1920, he took part in a campaign demanding amnesty for the "mutineers of the North Sea," the sailors from the French fleet (among them André Marty) condemned for refusing to fire on Odessa.

In none of these cases did the names of Marie Curie, Jean Perrin, or Emile Borel appear next to that of Langevin.

On October 21, Marie wrote to Irène:

"All things considered, I'm happy that Marty was elected. This will give pause to the reactionaries and the capitalists."

But she didn't sign her name to this campaign anymore than the others.

The whole clan, who were entering the second half of their lives, were still full of the passion for reform they had had when they were young. Their ardor hadn't been dampened by the titles, the honors, the positions they had all received. Their conviction that the fate, the future, of society depended on science—and therefore on the place given to science, and on the methods of training scientists and conducting research—was only strengthened by the war.

As they very well knew, the First World War had been a war of technologies as much as of men. But Langevin believed that only a society whose structures were transformed would be able to give science its rightful place and the resources it needed. Borel believed that the structures of society would be transformed by science. Jean Perrin and Marie believed in concrete actions and concrete results. But in concrete terms, French science was in a disastrous situation.

What about human "equipment"? Ten percent of able-bodied men were dead. Half the students in the classes of 1911, 1912, and 1913 at the training colleges had been killed or wounded. Those who had been wounded hadn't gone back to school. And so the young men who should have become France's mathematicians, physicians, chemists—the scientific minds of the twenties—had been literally bled away.

What about the ones who were left? The most brilliant of them were reluctant to commit themselves to university careers, where the salaries had not kept up with the rising prices, and they were drawn to industry.

The status of researcher didn't even exist. All "disinterested" research was still being done by the teaching profession. And, as Jean Perrin put it so well, "Tiresome as it may seem, brains have stomachs too."

As for resources for work, in 1920, the Faculté des Sciences had nothing with which to pay off its debts.

At the Institut du Radium, Marie didn't even have a typewriter. It was only because she had had the idea of buying back war surplus at low prices that she managed to gather a little equipment; by personally harassing the minister of finances, she managed to obtain two vans.

It was true that she had received a nice official letter from him indicating that they would make available to her "all the necessary credits, all the indispensable apparatus and other resources." But only to the extent possible. And what was possible was ridiculous.

There wasn't much philanthropy either. People who had

225

made enormous fortunes from the war knew nothing about the great tradition of patronage, and many of the others had lost a good deal of their wealth.

Financial support for science, when it existed, tended to be given to purely medical research.

In 1920, Henri de Rothschild, who was a medical doctor, created a foundation for developing radiation therapy, started it going with a large private donation, and named it the Fondation Curie. The name was certainly a tribute, but the foundation was, naturally, attached to the section of the Institut du Radium devoted to biological and medical research, the section directed by Dr. Regaud.

This research was not in Marie's domain. The connection between radium and medicine had been a fortuitous element in her career. What she intended to create was a true school of radioactivity, for training researchers in the work methods and experimental techniques that she had developed. The Curie laboratory had to be a place uniquely set aside for the discoveries that radioactivity would surely yield to those who were capable of exploring it with all the necessary means.

Yet when she received her annual allocation from the Caisse de Recherche Scientifique, inflation had eaten away so much of its buying power that this allocation was barely enough to buy two measuring instruments.

The courage, determination, and self-confidence that had twice won her the highest award for her work with radioactivity were powerless before the facts: Paris might have been a constant festival, but French science was anemic. Whom or what could she turn to for help?

The most dynamic of the scientists would try to sound the alarm in writing and in speech everywhere: whether what was involved was prestige, competition of industries, or social progress, a nation that didn't invest in research was a nation on the decline.

Today, everyone is more or less aware of this—though less rather than more. But in the twenties, it was a new idea. Very few French people had associated Germany's strength with its superiority in science during the nineteenth century.

Even fewer had examined the sources of this superiority: the fact that the best minds in Germany and abroad were attracted by the excellence of the organization of the universities, the rational provision of equipment, the abundance of public and private positions, the considerable support of industry.

When Germany's superiority became clear, Great Britain had reacted by creating a series of teaching and research institutes—one of which was the famous Cavendish laboratory in Cambridge where Rutherford worked—and had continued to develop them since the war.

And France? According to the people they were trying to convince, the scientists harped on the idea of "prestige" or of "industrial competition," which was clearly going to resume with Germany, or of "social progress."

Charles Moureu, who was the expert on the subject of poison gases used in war, managed to stir up the nationalist feelings of Maurice Barrès, the author and politician. Barrès, who was at the height of his influence, became emotional in Parliament as he described "the laboratory, the shining star of truth and a model of social discipline" to the flabbergasted deputies from the Bloc National.

Nothing could have seemed stranger to them than the idea of a nation's power being based on its scientific and technical progress. Its power lay in its army. And hadn't the French army just proved that it was the best in the world?

Nevertheless, the campaign of "scientific propaganda" waged by the scientists was not completely futile, especially when a certain event occurred that struck people's imaginations. Once again, Marie Curie found herself in the very middle of it.

nineteen

W E CAN'T be sure exactly where Marie met Henri-Pierre Roché, the art expert and collector, who had had a hand in writing *Jules et Jim* and who was a big success in the segment of Paris society to which artists gravitated. No doubt at the home of one or another of the members of this international society, which the scientists of the time were not too proud to frequent. Or perhaps at Rodin's home.

What we can be sure of is that Roché knew Marie Curie well enough to ask her to have an interview with a representative of the press—a species that Marie especially detested, and with good reason.

Marie was always being asked for interviews and she always gave the same answer: "Mme Curie does not receive representatives of the press except to give technical information; she never talks about personal matters, she never talks about her life or her likes and dislikes."

She was scrupulous about answering requests for autographs, inscribed photographs, lecture appearances, and every other kind of correspondence, especially when it involved a request for her advice about the treatment of cancer. This was the case with the beautiful dancer, Loïe Fuller, who had cancer of the breast and was afraid of having to undergo a mastectomy. Marie referred her to Dr. Regaud.

Despite her dislike of the press, however, one morning in May 1920, in her office at the Pavillon Curie, Marie met with Henri-Pierre Roché and a very small woman named Mrs. Meloney Mattingley, who had graying hair, large black eyes, and a slight limp. Her friends called her Missy, she told Marie right away. Roché, who knew both women, was secretly delighted at the prospect of the fireworks that would result from

228

this meeting, though he was prepared to dampen them by acting as interpreter.

Missy was the editor-in-chief of a respected women's magazine called *The Delineator*. At the age of thirty-nine, she had a fairly important personal position and solid political connections in Washington, and it would have taken more than Mme Curie to disconcert her. Anyway, no one she interviewed ever disconcerted her—and two of the people she was to interview in later years were Hitler and Mussolini.

She had just arrived from Great Britain, where she had interviewed H. G. Wells and Bertrand Russell. She was traveling through Europe to find out what help was actually being given to the disaster victims adopted by her magazine, and she was taking the opportunity to meet a few eminent European figures. At least this was what she said when she asked Marie for an interview. Marie's negative answer evidently didn't discourage her. She found an intermediary who could open the door that was so tightly shut.

Something unexpected happened. The two women liked each other and a friendship sprang up between them which was to have infinitely far-reaching consequences.

For some reason, Marie was charming to the strange little creature. More in keeping with what we know of her character, she was also pleased to prove to Roché that she didn't need an interpreter. About this sort of thing Marie always acted like a ten-year-old. In fact, Missy could speak French quite well, and later the two women would use both languages in their conversations and correspondence. But that day, Missy was perceptive enough to see that Mme Curie prided herself on her English, and so she did not deprive her of the pleasure of using it.

Marie spoke readily. She answered Missy's questions with good grace, perhaps because they were good questions—direct and concise. Missy was a professional. She had prepared for the interview. And she heard some surprising facts.

That there were fifty grams of radium in the United States, in certain specific laboratories—Marie enumerated them—

229

whereas there was only one gram in France, where it had been discovered. That Mme Curie could not go on with her work, for lack of equipment. That she had never earned a penny from the discovery of radium because she had deliberately never taken out a patent on it. No patent, no revenue. Hundreds of men and women with cancer were being treated with radium now, but Mme Curie was. to put it plainly, poor. A poor woman in a poor country.

This was stupefying! It would certainly surprise people on Fifth Avenue. And it would also stir up the Americans Missy tried so hard to reach in her editorials in order to make them fully aware of their duties toward the countries that had been ravaged by the war.

"If you could have one wish, what would you want most in the world?" she asked Marie in conclusion.

The answer came without hesitation: "A gram of radium."

Missy wrote it down, thanked her, and left.

Two days later, she rang Marie's doorbell again, this time at the quai de Béthune apartment. She had had no trouble making this second appointment. By the fifth, she would know more about Marie than many people who had known Marie ten years. What did she intend to do with this knowledge? Missy was good-natured, she liked to admire people, and Marie seemed admirable to her. She liked positive actions, and what could be more positive than working for the benefit of mankind? Along with her excellent disposition, she had a good deal of common sense. Missy, who compared herself to a locomotive, could move mountains.

How much did a gram of radium cost? A million francs, or a hundred thousand dollars. This was in 1920, when one dollar was worth ten francs. A hundred thousand dollars could be found, when the money was for a good cause associated with a famous name. Missy thought she would be able to raise it by appealing to a few of her rich fellow Americans.

Once she succeeded, of course, Marie would have to come in person to get her gram of radium. In the meantime, if it was properly publicized, an autobiography could earn her sub-

230

stantial royalties. How would Missy herself benefit from all this? In a purely moral way. The Butterick Company, publishers of her magazine, would have exclusive rights to the first articles about the venture when Marie arrived in America. Was this proper? Unquestionably.

Marie liked this kind of language, because it was simple and direct. She had only one objection to the arrangement: if she was going to be talked about in the United States, the American press would dig up the Langevin affair.

Her confidence in Missy had grown to the point where she was able to broach this taboo subject. Missy understood perfectly. America in the twenties was much more puritan than France had ever been. When she left Paris, she and Marie agreed on a code that would allow them to communicate by telegram about this delicate subject. Missy's telegram address in New York was IDEALISM. It was, in fact, also a program.

The two women had certain characteristics in common. Both had tremendous energy in a frail body—Missy had had tuberculosis. Both followed "men's careers"—Missy, the daughter of a doctor, had begun doing newspaper work at the age of sixteen, at a time when American journalism was an exclusively male province. Both knew how to handle money, but were disinterested personally. Both had missionary zeal. But their immediate sympathy also suggests that Marie recognized in Missy one of those kindred spirits she was so good at sniffing out among her women friends—the goodhearted, motherly, reliable women, the ones who were always ready to rush to her when she needed them, who might be far way but were always present in spirit. Bronia over and over again, in different guises.

Fifteen years after their first meeting, Marie was to write to Missy to ask her to destroy all the letters she had sent her over the years, because "they are part of me and you know how reserved I am in my feelings."

Missy had the good sense to sort through them before destroying them. What remains of their correspondence—during certain periods they wrote almost daily—attests to the enduring affection that existed between these two warriors, both disabled, both fearless.

Once she was back in New York, Missy accomplished an enormous amount of work in six months. Nothing is simpler, in theory, than raising money for a good cause. In practice, it is always a little more laborious.

As it happened, women with millions of dollars did not rush to help Marie, or at least not enough of them. Seeing this, Missy decided quite simply to start a national subscription. She formed a committee of scientists who would give the project the necessary authenticity. She mobilized the wife of the oil baron, Mrs. John D. Rockefeller; the wife of Vice-President of the United States, Mrs. Calvin Coolidge; the founder of the American Society for the Control of Cancer, Mrs. Robert Mead; and a few other ladies of the same caliber, and she threw herself into the most amazing public relations enterprise ever undertaken.

First, however, she delved into the newspapers of 1911 to find out how much repercussion the Langevin affair had had in the United States. It had made enough noise, particularly in Hearst's newspapers, so that Missy feared the worst. She decided to take the bull by the horns—or, in this case, to take each bull by the horns. She would approach the editor-in-chief of every newspaper in New York and appeal to his finer sentiments. Sentiment was not exactly the strong point of these men. But she was so eloquent that not one of them refused to do what she asked—to bury this aspect of Mme Curie's past.

Not only did they all keep their promises, but Missy left the office of the most hard-nosed of them all, the director of *The New York Evening Journal*, with a check for a hundred dollars for the "Marie Curie Radium Fund."

Starting in early 1921, the correspondence between Missy and Marie became delightful. If anyone knew her own worth,

232

it was Marie. If anyone was prepared to appreciate Marie's worth, it was Missy. But they both felt it was important to be "straight" with each other.

Marie had promised she would come get her gram of radium herself, and she was going to. She had said she would write her autobiography, and she was going to. Four different publishers were making her offers.

In the letters with which she bombarded Marie, Missy sometimes talked about a grain of radium and sometimes a gram. On January 12, Missy received the following cable, signed Pierre Roché: "Mme Curie asks if one grain or one gram. Grain insufficient to justify absence from laboratory because equal to fifteenth of gram."

Missy confirmed that she was talking about a gram, and she added another detail—that the President of the United States himself would give it to Mme Curie during a reception at the White House.

Fine. Marie wrote that she would be able to stay two weeks.

Missy answered that the king and queen of Belgium had stayed six weeks. The queen of radium had to pay a visit that was just as royal. Besides, it would take six weeks for Marie to carry through the ambitious program Missy had arranged. What was involved was nothing less than crossing the United States from east to west, going from universities to laboratories, from colleges to banquets, and receiving honorary degrees, medals, and tributes of all sorts, which would often be accompanied by subsidies.

Marie pointed out that six weeks would be a long time to be away from her daughters. Missy replied that she should bring her daughters.

Missy had caused such an uproar in the American press about Mme Curie's imminent visit that the Colony Club hastened to offer its hospitality to the visitor.

What? The Colony Club? Just a minute! The fact that Marie was going to visit the United States was all Missy's doing. She hadn't embarked on this fantastic undertaking just to advertise the Colony Club. She wrote: "The Colony Club is a very

233

beautiful and luxurious place, but I'm not sure you would be as peaceful there as you would like to be. Naturally, I would feel very honored if you would agree to move in here with me. My husband and I lead a very simple, quiet life, like most of the people here who are involved in the literary world. I would like you to be my guest as long as you are in New York and I don't want this visit to cost you anything."

All right, said Marie, but what about my daughters? Missy's neighbor, "my friend, Mr. John R. Crane, ambassador to China," was away and would be pleased to lend his apartment.

The Paris newspapers announced that the United States was preparing to make a gift of one gram of radium to the Université de Paris. Marie became furious. Missy had always said that the gift would be made to Mme Curie. Missy's answer: "The gram of radium is for you, *for your personal use,* and you will be the one to decide how it is used after your death." And she added this superb sentence: "I would be happy to be of some use to the Université de Paris if it needs help, but for the moment I am devoting all my time and energy to your interests."

If Marie had ever doubted this, she was completely convinced of it now. "I won't accept a single offer without your agreement," was her way of letting Missy know it.

One false note in the symphony of publicity filled Missy with apprehension. A newspaper which had a "Curie dossier" in its archives, consisting of clippings from the Paris newspapers, fished out from the dossier the information that Mme Curie was Jewish. As was pointed out earlier, that piece of information was written in order to keep Mme Curie out of the Académie. Missy made sure the mistake was corrected the next day. There was to be no other cause for alarm about the past being resurrected.

In March, another telegram came from New York: "Cable cost laboratory South of France. Send also new photos you and your daughters."

It was true that Marie had been dreaming about a private

234

laboratory somewhere in the South of France. But she had talked about it without really believing it could ever come to pass, and had certainly never gotten to the point of drawing up an estimate of the expenses involved. She answered by letter that such a laboratory would certainly benefit her health and her peace of mind, and would also be very useful for work requiring the treatment of large quantities of minerals, something that couldn't be done at the institute. She ended by saying: "If I also tell you that my present laboratory needs to be enlarged, and that it is so deficient in credits and staff that I have no help at all in my work and that even now, at this moment, I am typing this letter to you myself—then you will have no trouble understanding that I very badly need some generous assistance."

All that remained now was for her to go accept this assistance where it was being offered to her. They arranged that she would go in May. Marie asked Missy to make an appointment for her with an eminent specialist in New York.

She had just written in a letter to Bronia:

> My eyes are very weak now, and probably not much can be done about it. As for my ears, I am plagued by an almost constant, sometimes very intense, humming. I am very worried about it: it may interfere with my work—or even make it impossible. Radium may have had something to do with these problems, but we can't be certain of that.
>
> So these are my afflictions. Don't talk to anyone about it, I particularly don't want any rumor of it to get around.

Radium might have been to blame? This was the first time she spoke of such a possibility. She would soon find out that she had a double cataract.

When people in Paris learned that the President of the United States was going to give Mme Curie the miraculous result of a nationwide collection, there was some agitation in the news-

paper offices and the office of the minister of public education. How should this thing be handled?

The minister discreetly asked Marie if she would accept the
Legion of Honor. She refused, for the second time. She did it
out of loyalty to Pierre. Editors-in-chief rebuked the younger
reporters, who were saying, "What's Mme Curie up to now?"
and, without consulting one another, all opted for a lyrical
and patriotic tone.

The magazine *Je sais tout* dreamed up the plan of sponsor-
ing a gala to celebrate her departure. Marie was skeptical.
The magazine hastened to assure her that the gala would also
include an appeal for funds for the Institut du Radium. It
would be a large-scale demonstration benefiting French science and its most prominent figure.

The prominent figure agreed. She was still typing her letters herself.

Sacha Guitry was given the responsibility of organizing the
evening. The cream of French science was mobilized and, on
April 27, 1921, gathered in the theater of the Opéra in honor of
Marie, whose entrance was greeted by prolonged applause.
Sarah Bernhardt, with her golden voice and the weight of the
years on her wooden leg, recited an "Ode to Madame Curie,"
fourteen stanzas by Maurice Rostand. Jean Perrin and Dr.
Regaud each recited a speech of congratulation. Guitry performed two acts of a play judiciously entitled *Pasteur*.

At least Missy had already succeeded in doing one thing:
she had indirectly caused her heroine to be publicly rehabili-
tated in France.

A few days later, she shepherded Marie and her daughters
on board the *Olympic*, a steamship of the White Star Line
whose president had been persuaded to come in person to
take Mme Curie to her cabin—the suite usually reserved for
honeymooners.

This was where Marie spent most of her time during the
crossing. She was worried about what lay in store for her.

twenty

MARIE'S FIRST contact with the new world was a disaster. She had never given a press conference before. She was so unprepared for it that, despite Missy's warnings during the crossing, she had naively written a statement that she intended to type and hand out to the reporters, just as she did in Paris to the respectful reporters from *Le Temps.*

When she appeared on the upper deck of the steamship where Missy had arranged for her first encounter with the press, something happened that seems quite normal to us now—the press charged her like an infantry regiment. Horrified, Marie hunched over in her seat and clutched her handbag; her hat was knocked from her head, revealing her white hair. Fired at by photographers, sometimes blinded, harassed by newsreel cameras, plied with question after question about her private life, she remained almost completely silent, her lips pinched together.

From the dock came the murmur of the crowd that had been gathering for several hours to catch a glimpse of the famous discoverer of radium, the "benefactress of the human race." A brass band was alternately playing "La Marseillaise," "The Star-Spangled Banner," and the national anthem of Poland. Battalions of girl scouts were singing songs of welcome, many different welcoming committees were cheering and waving banners, the Polish delegation of three hundred women shouted and waved red and white roses.

Without responding to all this exuberant hospitality, not even by a wave of her hand, Marie walked down the gangplank with her head bowed and plunged into the first of the enormous limousines which Mrs. Andrew Carnegie had made available to her; it was as though she were running away from

237

a fire. Her admirers were disconcerted by this behavior: didn't Mme Curie like America?

In an issue of *The Delineator* largely devoted to Mme Curie, her works, and the honors she had received, Missy had described her as a woman "of rare beauty," a "Greek statue" with a "generous back," a "sweet, round" face. The other reporters saw something different: her frail shoulders, her stooped back, her wrinkled forehead, the fact that her face no longer looked at all young.

The pictures in the papers showed that they were right. The cruel truth was that she had aged a good deal.

And so Mme Curie did not conquer America. But she did better—she touched the hearts of Americans.

In a country where mink coats and orchids were indispensable signs of social status, and where women had the illusion that by talking loudly they could lay down the law, this "poorly dressed scholar," this "shy little woman," this "tired visitor," her steps dogged by journalists who had to report her silences since they couldn't report anything she said, this anti-star of the Curie show had bombed, as they say in the theater.

And what a price she had to pay! She had to work almost as hard to extract the second gram of radium from the gold mine of America's spontaneous generosity as she had had to work to extract her first gram from the stubborn pitchblende.

After less than a week of running from one women's college to the next, from one banquet to the next, from Carnegie Hall to the Waldorf, from West Point to the Museum of Natural History, amid the sound of anthems and speeches, in an atmosphere reminiscent of a country fair (one overly hearty admirer shaking her hand so hard that her wrist was sprained), she was almost dead from exhaustion, with her arm in a sling. And this was only the beginning.

Afraid that she would collapse before the reception at the White House, she delegated her daughters to go to some of the parties being organized in her honor by each of her rich benefactresses, who asked nothing in return for all their frenetic activity but to have her sit in their living rooms for an hour.

Wild as a deer, brusque, badly dressed, clearly bored, Irène was if anything less suited than her mother to these kinds of festivities. Eve, on the other hand, though only sixteen, was a delight. Wearing a pretty hat, excited by her own success, talking to people who had no more interest in physics than she did and just as much in jazz, the girl "with the radium eyes" was at last—at last!—more useful to her mother than Irène, and no doubt she reveled in it. She didn't always have much fun in Paris, this little sister who didn't like mathematics.

The ceremony in Washington was supposed to take place on May 20. On the nineteenth, after one last reception in New York, Missy went to see Marie in her room to show her the document that would be given to her the next day along with the radium.

The two women were both worn out. Marie put on her glasses, examined the document, and said calmly: "We have to add something." By the end of that evening, Missy and Marie understood each other better than ever before.

What did Marie want? A more explicit paragraph about her full power to dispose of the radium. What was she afraid of? She was afraid of dying. She was afraid of what would happen to the radium when she died. Whom would it belong to then? Once she had received the radium, Marie wanted to have the right to pass it on, so that it would become the property of the Curie laboratory.

This problem of inheritance had obsessed her ever since Pierre's death, when she had had trouble because of it. As for her own death, by referring to it as an imminent event, she seemed to be able to ward it off.

Missy agreed. The document would be corrected. But the wording of the added lines would have to be checked by a lawyer.

Find a lawyer, answered Marie.

The donors would also have to agree, said Missy.

239

Find the donors, answered Marie.

Of course, Missy did find a lawyer willing to drop everything to be of service to Mme Curie. She also found two women to represent the donors. One of them was Mrs. Calvin Coolidge. Everything was done the way Marie wanted it done. Afterwards, even though it was very late, Marie brought up the question of how the money that was continuing to pour in would be used—there was already a good deal more than the hundred thousand dollars needed to pay for the radium.

That evening, the American women who had established the Marie Curie Radium Fund had the unpleasant feeling that Mme Curie was definitely not the person who had been described to them and they began to react to her with the same sort of irritation felt by scientists who had to confront her in conferences. She was no weakling, and she held out for a long time. The discussion was cut off before the question was settled, and the money—more than fifty thousand dollars—was frozen in a bank for several years. But in the end, as one would imagine, Marie had her way.

The White House reception was crowded with ambassadors and members of the French and Polish colonies. The guests filed by in front of Marie, whose arm was still in a sling, and her daughters greeted the guests for her, in French, English, and Polish. What Marie wore for the occasion was the same black lace dress she had worn ten years before when she received her second Nobel Prize.

President Harding was a pleasant and inconsistent man. He had landed in the White House because of the internal rivalries tearing apart the last Republican convention: the only man everyone could agree on was the most innocuous one, a man who had been catapulted onto the political scene by the iron hand of his wife, whom he called "the Duchess." He once said that he wasn't made for his job and that he never should have been there. The remark did credit to his good sense, at least.

240

Harding graciously produced a few platitudes about Marie, calling her the "soul of radium" and a "noble woman, a devoted wife, a loving mother who, along with her crushing work, performed all the duties a woman must perform."

He put a ribbon around her neck with a golden key hanging from it, the key to the small mahogany box that was displayed on a table. Lined with lead, the box weighed fifty kilos—fifty kilos and one gram, of course, the gram of radium.

There were more lunches and receptions, lectures and banquets; Marie traveled by train and bus to Philadelphia, Boston, Pittsburgh, Buffalo, and Chicago; she appeared at universities and before scholarly societies; she visited factories and laboratories. Crowds of people waited for hours on end to catch a glimpse of the woman who had found the cure for cancer.

Here and there in the crowds there may have been some young workers from a factory where luminous numbers were painted on the faces of clocks and watches with a paint containing radium and mesothorium. These workers had a habit of licking their brushes to give them a sharper point. Most of them died within a few years of cancer of the jaw.

The cause of the disease, which was dubbed "radium jaw," was discovered in 1924 by a dentist in New York. For his patients, however, it was already too late.

As we know, although the rays of radium and other radioactive metals can effectively destroy cancerous cells, they can also cause cancer, because they attack healthy cells too. But in 1921, no one had any notion of the dangers that determine how we use radiation therapy today.

When Missy's doctor examined Marie, he diagnosed low blood pressure and said it was imperative that she rest. And yet at this stage of the visit, the sickly little Missy, dragging her shorter leg behind her, was the more tired of the two. She was just as good as Marie at flogging the beast when it balked, but she, too, had reached the critical point at which the poor beast simply lay down and gave up. The crazy project she had dreamed up and then organized had caused a recurrence of her tuberculosis.

As for Marie, she would now come close to fainting at the sight of a welcoming committee with bouquets of flowers in their hands and songs on their lips.

One newspaper headline expressed it this way: "Too much hospitality! We nearly killed Marshal Joffre by our excessive enthusiasm. Are we killing Mme Curie?" It must be said, however, that this demonstration of excessive enthusiasm didn't extend to the scientific world.

Although American researchers had not distinquished themselves at the beginning of the century—one of them, the physicist Rowland, remarked at that time that America confused science with mechanical invention—the war had caused questions to be asked, and here, as elsewhere, people had begun to answer them.[1]

But all the relatively recent work in fundamental research was still being financed with private funds. The Carnegie Corporation and the Rockefeller Foundation were contributing the most. Now, what had Mme Curie come to the United State for? To dip into private funds. She had already benefited greatly from Andrew Carnegie's generosity. Whatever she took away with her to France would be so much less for American laboratories. And anyway, why was all this fuss being made over a lady who really hadn't done anything for ten years?

Some of the larger universities, including Yale and Columbia, did receive Marie and gave her honorary degrees as doctor of science, but the oldest and most arrogant, Harvard, which was dedicated "to learning and to the fear of God," was determined to do nothing. The entire physics department had been opposed. Marie's old enemy, Beltram Boltwood, who had

---

[1] The Second World War had a decisive effect on American research. Between 1901 and 1938, twelve Nobel Prizes were given to Americans (in physics, chemistry, medicine, and physiology). Between 1939 and 1976, Americans received eighty-eight.

never hidden the fact that he found her worthless as a scientist and personally unbearable, also had a part in this opposition.

Boltwood, however, came face to face with her when, at the invitation of the American Chemical Society, Marie spent two hours at the Sloane Laboratory. He found her "touching" and "unusually amiable," and seemed to discover only now "her great interest in scientific subjects," which makes all his past judgments suspect, at the very least.

Other researchers grumbled in the newspapers about Marie's forays into American wallets. But they still didn't know everything.

Even though Missy had canceled the "circus" 's tour of the West, where Irène and Eve were standing in for their mother, what Marie had collected in the United States, aside from the $100,000 for the radium, was $22,000 in mesothorium and other precious minerals; $6,900 from various fees; the $52,000 remaining in the subscription, which hadn't been closed yet; and many gifts of all sorts of equipment. This was enough to turn the Curie laboratory into the shrine of physics and radioactivity she had dreamed of, on a par with the most sophisticated laboratories abroad. And for several years Missy managed things so that the money continued to flow in. All in all, it had been a fabulously successful raid.

On top of this, Marie had pocketed a $50,000 advance for an insipid autobiography. Missy had not only kept all her promises, but had done even more.

When the two women said goodbye on a steamship about to leave for Le Havre, watched by a swarm of photographers, Marie was heard to murmur: "Let me look at you one more time, my dear dear friend. . . . This may be the last time I will ever see you."

The crystalline lenses of her beautiful ash-gray eyes were becoming more opaque every day. She was convinced that before long she would be blind.

Crying, Marie and Missy hugged each other.

In spite of their weakened condition, the two women did meet again at the White House seven years later to accept money from another president to buy another gram of radium offered by the American people. The radium was for Poland this time.

Meanwhile, Missy, who was by now the editor-in-chief of a weekly supplement published by *The New York Herald Tribune*, had received her own dose of radiation as an experimental treatment of a tumor that seemed to be malignant.

As for Marie, she had undergone three operations on her cataracts, and yet had continued to make trips to Holland, Brazil, Italy, Denmark, Czechoslovakia, Spain, Scotland, and Poland. Not to mention several visits to Geneva, where she took part in the League of Nations commission for intellectual cooperation, and to Belgium for the Solvay conferences.

Clearly, Missy and Marie shared at least one quality: they would not let themselves be defeated.

On her way back to France, Marie wrote an affectionate letter to Missy, telling her how worried she and her daughters were about their dear friend's health: "We wonder if you have agreed to seek the kind of care you need. I beg you, let us know as soon as possible. We all love you and we want to see you strong and happy."

But in the same letter she also worried about the $52,000 deposited in the Equitable Trust Company: "Of course, it would be difficult for me to argue about decisions you and the committee might arrive at to make life easier for us, for my daughters and me. . . . As far as the general allocation of the funds goes, I'm sure that the women who gave their money for my cause would like this money to be used as I see fit and I think my advice may be useful to you."

When the boat train arrived at the Gare Saint-Lazare from Le Havre on July 2, 1921, there were no bouquets, no photographers to greet Mme Curie. Only three people were waiting for her: Marcel Laporte, a young researcher from the laboratory who was immediately handed the precious box of radium, and two reporters who both asked Mme Curie the same question: "What do you think of the Carpentier-Dempsey fight?" This was also the last question she had been asked in the United States. She answered dryly that she had no opinion.

Undoubtedly she would have had more to say about it a few hours later. There were no taxis waiting in front of the station. Only loudspeakers broadcasting, round by round, the fight that was taking place in New York for the world championship title. And everyone in Paris was out in the streets, watching for the flares in the sky that would announce the victory of the Frenchman by a knockout in the fourth round. Everyone in Paris, including the cabdrivers.

This was why Marie returned to the quai de Béthune on foot on a beautiful summer's night, with ample leisure to reflect, as she walked, on the relative values of different kinds of fame.

A few years later, Marie again found herself in a "notoriety contest" with a boxer on a railway station platform. This time she was in Berlin and the boxer was Jack Dempsey. She wrote to her daughter: "A crowd that had gathered on the station platform ran around cheering the boxer Dempsey, who was on the same train I was on. He seemed pleased. Is there really very much difference between cheering Dempsey and cheering me? It seems that there is something about the very fact of cheering this way that is not very commendable, no matter who the object of the gesture is."

No, it wasn't very commendable. But Marie added: "And yet I don't understand very clearly what one should do or to what extent people should be allowed to confuse the person with the idea that this person represents."

She was to devote the best part of her remaining years to representing an idea. The idea was a simple one, a powerful one, and one that is still opposed today: the idea that science is the only source of progress.

twenty-one

WHILE Marie was scouring America, her friends in Paris traded on the fuss made about her expedition and discovered a simple principle: take money wherever you can get it. They were prepared to apply to the devil himself, but Edmond de Rothschild, already an old man, was more like the Good Lord, at least where artists were concerned. He also had a lively interest in science.

He began by giving ten million francs to create a foundation for awarding grants to young researchers. One of these grants would later allow a student of Langevin's who had no university degree to begin a career as a researcher at the Curie laboratory. His name was Frédéric Joliot.

The old baron wanted to look through a microscope and see the dance they called Brownian movement with his own eyes. Brownian movement was caused by the chaotic agitation of molecules in collision with the invisible atoms whose observation had made Jean Perrin's name. He offered to show it to Rothschild.

Perrin's red curls had turned white by now, but his vitality, his charming enthusiasm, were undiminished.

When the old baron reached the top of the steep flights of stairs that led to the laboratory situated under the rooftop of the Sorbonne, he declared that "clearly, science is poorly housed in France." And he decided to give fifty million francs for the creation of an institute of physical and chemical biology. Its directors were to be Jean Perrin, André Mayer, and Georges Urbain.

Emile Borel brought him together with the representative of the Rockefeller Foundation. Through joint financing, they created the Institut Henri Poincaré for mathematics and mathematical physics. Borel was its director.

This institute was to be built in the twenties, around and in the extension of the Institut du Radium in the rue Pierre Curie.

The appeals the scientists made to Parliament also elicited a response; though more symbolic, it was not negligible. After hearing their colleague Maurice Barrès describe "the damp, dimly lit rooms with crumbling walls where instruments are rusting away," a majority of the deputies, from both the right and the left, recognized a new principle: that there should exist a category of research independent of teaching and supplied with its own credit.

The Curie laboratory was one of the beneficiaries of this resolution. Marie allocated a fifth of what she received from it to pay for the work Irène was doing—for Irène was by now the "crown princess" of the laboratory, to the undisguised irritation of several colleagues.

Borel, who, like Langevin, was scolded by his friends for engaging in so many different activities, but who was amused by too many things ever to be willing to be bored for even five minutes, had the good idea of becoming the deputy for his native department, Aveyron, where his father had been a minister.

He claimed he didn't want to hear any more talk about higher mathematics, and after the war he went off on a tour of China. When he was urged to run against General de Castelnau, he agreed on the condition that the Socialist Paul Ramadier appear on the same list of candidates.

The list won. This was in 1924, and the country was leaning toward the left. Once he was elected, Borel naturally made science his special concern. He was the one who invented what was known as "le sou du laboratoire" (literally, "the laboratory's penny"). Parliament was discussing the imposition of a tax on industry to support professional training (it was called the apprenticeship tax). Borel pointed out that without scientific research, modern industry wouldn't exist.

247

Painlevé was the president of the Chamber, Herriot was the president of the Council, Léon Blum was the head of the Socialist party. The long-standing ties among the former students of the Ecole Normale had something to do with the final vote.

The next year, Borel was made a minister—the minister in charge of the navy, naturally, since he had no expertise at all in this area. But that is another story.

By the end of the twenties, the structures within which scientific research was practiced had not changed in any fundamental way, but the situation seemed to have improved. The Institut Pasteur, the Institut du Radium, and the Fondations Rothschild together constituted a category of research independent of the university system.

At the same time, Langevin had been engaging in one of the hardest internal struggles in the history of science—and there had been many.

Starting in 1909, he had been teaching a course at the Collège de France on the special theory of relativity, and he had invited Einstein to come give a talk on the subject. This plan had had to be postponed because of the war.

When Langevin revived it after the war, the general theory of relativity seemed to have been confirmed. Toward the end of 1919, British newspapers were carrying headlines that read: "Revolution in science: Newton's ideas destroyed." The fact that gravity caused light rays to curve had recently been verified during a total eclipse of the sun.

Nevertheless, for a long time most physicists and mathematicians fiercely resisted opening what Langevin was to call "a new window on eternity." The word relativity was not even mentioned by the jury when it gave Einstein the Nobel Prize in 1921.

As a way of goading French scientists into recognizing what was radically new about Einstein's thought, Langevin took the bold step of inviting Einstein to come give a series of lectures in Paris. This was in 1922. On both sides of the Rhine, nationalism was intense.

Not until 1927 were German scientists invited to take part in the Solvay Congress, the third since the war. Einstein had been invited in 1923 but had refused to attend when the Belgian institute refused to invite other Germans.

Einstein, who had become a Swiss citizen at about the age of eighteen, had not been active during the war except in the area of science. In 1914, in an attempt to justify the violation of Belgian territory, ninety-three German intellectuals (including Max Planck) had signed a *Manifesto to the Civilized World* in support of their country's militarism—according to them, their country was only defending German culture.

A countermanifesto drawn up by Professor Nicolai called for cooperation among university teachers of the warring nations in order to safeguard the future of Europe, and proposed the creation of a League of Europeans. This manifesto was signed by three people, including Einstein. Along with certain other intellectuals, including Bertrand Russell in Great Britain and Marie Curie in France, Einstein was constantly astonished at how people who theoretically believed in the highest values of the mind could so quickly become intoxicated by the idea of spilling blood.

When Einstein received Langevin's proposal, the minister of foreign affairs, Walter Rathenau, an ardent socialist and internationalist, persuaded him that it was his duty to accept, even though he was a perfect target for German nationalists.

He was also a perfect target for French nationalists, who protested vigorously against the presence of a "German Jew" in Paris and announced that they would stop him from speaking. And so the first meeting at which Einstein appeared, at the Collège de France, took place with police protection. Plainclothesmen mingled with the crowd of guests, which included, of course, Marie, Perrin, Borel, and Painlevé, as well as Henri Bergson, Countess Greffulhe—who certainly loved science, or at least a certain scientist—and Mme Ménard-Dorian, who was one of Proust's models for Mme Verdurin; in short, it was a distinguished crowd.

Like everyone else, the Countess de Noailles, whose poetry

seemed very good only to those who were captivated by her charm, wanted to meet the great man. Emile and Marguerite Borel gave a dinner at their home and invited Langevin and Perrin, who performed brilliantly, Marie, who was laconic, as usual, the voluble Anna de Noailles, and Einstein, who was delighted to play a game of cat's cradle with the pretty countess.

But Einstein's visit was more than just a succession of distinguished parties. He gave several talks to scientific audiences, and met a number of politicians at Borel's house, as well as Paul Valéry. He left with the feeling that his visit had helped the cause of international reconciliation.

When he returned to Berlin, he was warned that his name was on the list of people the nationalists intended to assassinate, and he shut himself up in his home. Rathenau was killed in June.

A few months later, it was Einstein's turn to invite Langevin to Berlin, where the two of them attended a meeting in support of democracy and peace. Submitting to the threats of the nationalists, the prefect of Berlin did not allow either one of them to speak.

Einstein had never been political. Langevin, however, became more and more involved in politics as he promoted the cause of modern physics more and more vigorously. The combination of these two interests had something to do with the fact that he twice failed to be admitted to the Académie des Sciences.

On the other hand, he was always welcome in the best houses in Paris, including that of Queen Elizabeth of Belgium. It is true that in these houses he talked less about the accomplishments of the U.S.S.R.—although this probably wouldn't have disturbed his hosts, since at that time all hope for mankind seemed to reside there—than he did about fascism, whose triumph in Italy, whose manifestations in Germany, promised war.

This pacifist, who was so passionately urging different nations to come together to preserve the peace, still looked like nothing so much as a cavalry officer. He was, in fact, a whole-hearted follower of Jaurès, inspired by the same ideals. The man who once used to say, "Oh, how I would have liked to be an actor!" had become an eloquent speaker at meetings—people listened to him.

Build institutes? Find credit for research? Perrin, Borel, Marie, his other friends were right to make a big issue about all this, and he was even helping them, but what would be left, he asked, if there was another war? And who could prevent war if not the people, the people of different nations?

In 1927, Langevin presided over the first large antifascist meeting in Paris, held in the Salle Bullier. Eight thousand attended. Marie apparently did not go. There was no question of how she felt about the subject. What kept her firmly out of the political fray was not that she made no distinction between the adversaries involved in it. She had taken a position long ago. She had opted for democracy over autocracy, justice over injustice, social progress over conservatism, freedom of the mind over obscurantism and dogmatism.

But which forces would bring about social progress? The popular forces, said Langevin. The forces of science, said Marie; and these are the forces that we, as scientists, should try to liberate. Every man and woman we train to develop a scientific mind, every man and woman we give to science, serves the cause of progress. She had never become ecstatic about revolutionary romanticism, a lyrical illusion from which she had already dissociated herself by the time she was twenty. She didn't actually condemn it, unless it brought violence in its wake, but she wouldn't pin her hopes on it either.

When she went to Spain at the invitation of the Republican government, she wrote home to Irène: "The people here are full of delight in their young republic, and it is very moving to see how confident the young people are about the future, and many of their elders too."

But she added: "I very sincerely hope there won't be too many disappointments."

251

"My mother died before she could see the fascist reaction that ravaged Spain," Irène would later write. "She would certainly have considered the fascists to be criminals, but would she have concluded that the Republic of Spain shouldn't have been so kind to them? I have no idea. She had little patience for arguments in favor of expediency when they ran counter to principles she felt to be important."

Impervious to all influences, but believing that "when a thing is right, one must do it, even if one has a thousand reasons for not doing it," Marie would sign only two petitions in her life: one, as we have mentioned, in support of the English suffragettes; the other, in 1927, for Sacco and Vanzetti.[1]

She was an unusually single-minded and independent woman.

What she wouldn't give to Langevin—her name, her signature, her endorsement, her commitment—she gave to Jean Perrin, because he appealed to his old and dear friend on behalf of "the cause," the cause of science.

He said, "One can't fight all the battles. Life is short." He chose to fight the battle of research, not for personal ends—he had reached the summit of the university hierarchy, and in 1926 received the Nobel Prize in physics—but for the coming

---

[1] Nicola Sacco and Bartolomeo Vanzetti were Italian immigrants to the United States who were arrested in 1921 after the murder of a paymaster and sentenced to death even though no proof of their guilt had been produced. Anarchist propaganda material, however, had been found in their car, and the United States was in the grips of a "red scare." A defense committee formed. The affair dragged on for six years and had attracted worldwide attention when French intellectuals became involved. They did not adopt a position on the fundamental issue—the defendants' guilt or innocence—but on the fact of the death sentence being imposed in such circumstances. The execution of Sacco and Vanzetti shocked the American public, driving a number of liberals to sympathize with the Soviet Union, while conservatives viewed it as a triumph of the established order.

generation, and also, quite simply, for his country. Because two facts seemed striking to him.

First of all, France hadn't absorbed the impact of modern physics, and it was now in third place as far as scientific production in Europe went, maybe even in fourth. He saw this as a danger.

Secondly, a significant proportion—Perrin believed it was as much as three-quarters—of the scientific potential of France was being lost because of the fact that young people were rejecting research as a career since they couldn't make a living at it and didn't come from families with money. (Not everyone was as well off as Maurice de Broglie and his brother Louis, who was to discover wave mechanics—each had his own personal laboratory.)

Pestering first the professors at the Sorbonne, then the heads of government and their ministers, whatever party they belonged to, mobilizing Marie—who cut a more and more impressive figure and had "the look and the moral strength of a Tibetan monk"—to work with him, Jean Perrin finally brought to pass what he and his friends had dreamed of, and it took the form of the very famous Centre National de la Recherche Scientifique (the National Center for Scientific Research).

The C.N.R.S. did not take final, concrete form until after Marie's death, during the last weeks of the government of the Popular Front, to which Jean Perrin belonged, and it came into being during a fierce battle waged in the Senate by Perrin against . . . Joseph Caillaux.

In the last period of his stormy career, the cynical seventy-three-year-old, who was president of the Finance Commission, had a passionate contempt for scientists and, more generally, for any sort of technological progress. Today, there would have been people who agreed with him. Caillaux did not succeed in strangling the newborn C.N.R.S.—Perrin wanted to make sure it had a long life.

It would take us too far away from our subject if we were to follow the involved history of the creation of this institution and of its different stages. But because it was the work of the "Curie clan," of that small group bound together for so many years by a consuming passion for progress and the certainty that scientific research was the key to it, it deserved to be mentioned, at least.

No doubt their faith had its utopian aspect, as does any faith. But if there exists another way to reduce the small fraction of human misery that can be reduced—the greater part of it being even more stubborn than the atom itself—no one has yet pointed it out.

twenty-two

WHEN SHE returned from her trip to America, Marie wrote to Bronia:

> I have suffered so much in my life that I have no more suffering left in me. Only a real catastrophe could affect me now. I've learned what it is to be resigned and I try to find a few small joys in the grayness of daily life. . . .
> Tell yourself you can build houses, plant trees, cultivate flowers, watch them grow and not think of anything else. We haven't much life left ahead of us, so why go on tormenting ourselves?

Resignation, wisdom . . . this was Marie playacting again, just as she had when she was a girl of twenty pretending that her only ambition was to find work as a governess.

To judge from this letter, which is dated August 1921, we might imagine that she spent the thirteen remaining years of her life brooding on her past and quietly allowing herself to be buried under her flowers, beyond the reach, at last, of the incorrigible agitation of the human heart.

In fact, not only would she always continue to want to have a hand in shaping the future, she couldn't even tolerate the idea that she wouldn't always be a part of it. "When people talk about the splendid work I've done, it seems to me I am already dead, that I see myself being dead," she said to Eve.

It is not enough to say she did not want to die. If she had, she would have been dead long ago. But as little as six weeks before she died, Marie Curie was busily overseeing the construction of a new house.

Then what kept her on her feet? What sustained this woman, who was so thin, so worn by her exposure to radioactivity, so exhausted by the suffering she had undergone? The answer was . . . her passion and her pride. She had never stopped challenging herself, and she had never stopped trying to meet that challenge.

At Arcouëst, the Breton hamlet of sailors and farmers that had been colonized by a group of *sorbonnards* who had settled there in the wake of the historian Charles Seignobos and the biologist Louis Lapicque, Marie, proud of how neat her figure looked in her black bathing suit, worked methodically on the overarm stroke her daughters had taught her, and declared: "I think I swim better than M. Borel. . . . Jean Perrin did very well, but I went farther than he did, didn't I?"

When they played "letters" in the evening—people didn't call it Scrabble yet—she also liked to win. And she did.

These were innocent challenges. Others that she accepted were less innocent.

When the fog thickened before her damaged eyes, only her daughters and her sisters knew about it, and they swore to keep it secret. No one must suspect that Mme Curie was losing her sight.

At the Sorbonne, she continued to walk up onto the rostrum of the lecture hall by herself and speak before a crowd of students whose faces she could not distinguish, sometimes consulting lecture notes that she had written in enormous letters, and writing numbers on the blackboard that she could not make out.

On the table in the small laboratory next to the office where she worked, she had had the guiding marks of her measuring instruments rewritten in large colored numbers. For reading, she used a magnifying glass.

When the doctors decided to operate for the first time, she entered the hospital under an assumed name, Mme Carré.

After long weeks of complications, of hemorrhaging, she left the hospital at night. Her eyes were no longer opaque. And from Cavalaire, she wrote to Eve, who had nursed her tenderly: "I've gone on two walks along pebbly, uncomfortable mountain paths. I can manage pretty well, and I can walk quickly, without accidents. What bothers me most is my double vision, that's what prevents me from recognizing people when they come up to me. Every day I do exercises in reading and writing. So far, that's harder than walking."

In the following months, two more operations had to be performed. Then there was a respite of six years.

She was so determined to remain in good health, to recover enough use of her eyes to be able to work, move about, travel by herself, that she succeeded. And this particular challenge she set herself was so touching, this determination so touching in such a frail woman, that a conspiracy spontaneously developed to keep the "boss" from realizing that in spite of her ruses she had been found out.

The long brick building with its narrow hallways had been her idea. She had watched over it as it was being built, she had provided it with radium and other minerals, as well as the necessary equipment, she had been entirely responsible for organizing it. Now it was the international center for measuring radium samples for medicine and industry, but this was only one aspect of it.

The Curie laboratory contained the largest known sources of the principal natural radioactive elements (about forty had been identified, all of which were derived from uranium or thorium). Marie had accumulated these riches through her inexhaustible patience, by knocking on doors and making sure they were opened, particularly the doors of the Mining Union of Upper Katanga, the Belgian firm that controlled most of the mining interests in Katanga (present-day Shaba, in Zaire).

Marie had about forty researchers working under her direction, and many were young women, whom she always welcomed. One of them, Marguerite Perey, a chemist who had no university degree, was to achieve international renown for isolating francium.

French researchers often worked in the laboratory during a large part of their careers, as did a few foreigners who had had to leave their countries. Young scientists came here to work from all corners of the world—the U.S.S.R., Brazil, Bulgaria, Japan. After receiving their doctorates in France, they would often return home to create similar institutes specializing in radioactivity, and they would maintain close ties with Paris.

New arrivals at the laboratory who hadn't had any previous experience were attached to a head of research, as Irène had been to her mother. Frédéric Joliot also started as Marie's assistant. Once a researcher had proved himself, he would be given independent work to do. Those who were especially gifted would have their own equipment and were authorized to choose whatever research subject they liked, so long as it was still in the field of radioactivity.

Under Marie, the Institut du Radium became one of the few laboratories in the world where radioactivity was studied. Its great rival was the Cavendish laboratory, now run by Rutherford, who was sometimes reproached in his own country for restricting the laboratory to a domain that seemed too remote from industry.

In 1919, he bombarded the nucleus of an atom of nitrogen with alpha rays and transformed it into an atom of oxygen. He had discovered how to transmute a nucleus at will. And so his discovery marked the birth of nuclear physics. People hoped it would have important practical results, that a new energy might be liberated.

"Compared to this discovery," wrote Perrin, "the discovery of fire doesn't count for much in the history of mankind." Rutherford agreed with him. Even before the war, he had pointed out what fantastic, terrifying possibilities the radioactive elements promised where the development of armaments was concerned.

Frederick Soddy, the chemist who had observed the phenomenon with him, wrote that these elements, which changed into different elements—which transmuted—when they gave off energy would no doubt provide a solution to the problem of the exhaustion of coal reserves.

But at the beginning of the twenties, no one believed in

spectacular applications of atomic energy any longer. The physicists who continued to work on the nucleus of the atom were not in the mainstream of physics, and they conducted their research "as though it were a kind of sport," according to Chadwick, or for the esthetic satisfaction they derived from their observations. Pure science, pure science. The old dream.

Surrounded by her "laboratory children," whom she nurtured and guided with her incredible experience, examining the work of each of them in detail herself, Marie was fulfilling this old dream, and she was at her best doing this.

Throughout her life she had had to cultivate a certain aggressiveness, first in order to make her way into an exclusively male territory, then to be recognized there for what she was worth, and finally to defend her kingdom there. This aggressiveness was quick to resurface and made her seem hard, ruthless, implacable in competition. But she always left it at the door of the laboratory as though it were an overcoat.

She did not have a court of admirers around her. She did not have any subjects. She had "children" who, once they were admitted into the family, were in some sense marked with her seal. The Curie seal. As in all clans, some children were more gifted than others. But all of them had a right to her care. And then there was the favorite, the flesh-and-blood child, the princess by birth, Irène, who did not always have enough talent to be forgiven for this.

Was she really favored by her mother? Whatever the truth was, some people certainly thought so. One day something happened—no one is sure exactly what it was—and fists rained on the locked door of Marie's office. Her head of works, Fernand Holweck, yelled through the door, "Pig! Pig!"

No doubt she could be a pig. She was actually capable of anything.

Perhaps a fight had started because of Irène's brusque and haughty manner, and Marie had arbitrated in favor of her daughter? Or perhaps Irène had been promoted too rapidly. Or perhaps the conflict had been over Marie's attitude—which some still hold against her—toward a researcher named Salomon Rosenblum who discovered the fine structure of alpha rays in 1929 using an intense source of radioactivity that Marie had prepared for him with her own hands.

It is impossible to find out the truth about this story. People say that after Rosenblum made his discovery, which was to be one of the glories of the Curie laboratory, and the first one, Marie gave him fewer facilities and resources than she did to Irène and made very little effort to see that the young man's work was properly honored. Scientists are not saints.

Like any other place in which one group of people is together all the time, the Curie laboratory was certainly the scene of jealousies, antipathies, love affairs, physical fights. But Marie was able to hold it together, to enrich it, and she made everyone privileged enough to work there feel proud to have been one of her collaborators.

But if it is clear that she was happiest in the laboratory, that she was incapable of giving it up, as she wrote to Bonia, it would still be wrong to believe that this happiness came entirely from the enjoyment of the power she had over others. Her greatest pleasure was to concentrate completely on performing an experiment, calculating in Polish, moving her hands with a precision and virtuosity that reduced the coefficient of personal error to zero. At these times she seemed like a diver slipping through deep water into a silent world, protected from the turbulence above, not even conscious of her own noises, infinitely happy, ecstatic.

One of the women who worked with her described her as she was in the last year of her life, when she had stepped down from the management of the laboratory, which Debierne was to take over after her:

> The workday isn't long enough for the separation [of a radioactive element]. Mme Curie stays in the laboratory during the evening, skipping dinner. But the separation of this element is taking a long time: we will therefore spend all night working. . . .
> It's two o'clock in the morning and there is still one more

operation to be done: the centrifuging of the liquid for an hour around a special support. The centrifuge turns with a wearying noise, but Mme Curie stays next to it, not wanting to leave the room. She contemplates the machine as though her ardent desire to succeed in the experiment could cause the actinium X to precipitate by the power of suggestion alone. For Mme Curie, nothing exists right now except this centrifuge—not her life the next day, not her fatigue. This is a total depersonalization, a concentration of her whole soul in the work she is doing.

But every diver has to come back up to the surface now and then. At these times, Marie would restore her image to its former position.

The fact was that since her return from America, she had become a national monument.

She was now willing to put up with the ceremonies that continued to be held in her honor, where people heaped her with tributes. She submitted graciously, the way a queen does. This was a professional obligation. She embodied something. But what? The fame she was enjoying now was rather ambiguous.

The great Frenchwoman who had defeated cancer was venerated, honored, given a pension (forty thousand francs a year, which would go to her daughters after her death); but, for her, radiation therapy was incidental. It was a secondary consequence of her work.

Her public image had become that of the Healing Mother, and as such she inspired a fervent respect. It was the Académie de Médecine, for example—rather than the Académie des Sciences—which unanimously appointed her an independent associate member "in recognition for the part she played in discovering radium and a new form of medical treatment, Curie therapy."

The Fondation Curie, devoted to radiation therapy, celebrated the twenty-fifth anniversary of the discovery of radium with the President of the Republic, ministers, delegations of all kinds, and the usual folderol, in the large lecture hall of the Sorbonne where she was still teaching.

At the same time, hundreds, even thousands of people who were handling radium, radioactive substances, and X rays in factories, laboratories, and hospitals, without using any real protection or taking any real precautions, were destroying their bodies just as she had destroyed her own—but her resistance was extraordinary—and just as Irène was destroying hers. One of them was a charming young woman named Mme Arthaud whom Marie had known: there was sudden news that she had died of "anemia." Her work had been to add radium and mesothorium to certain medicines. Another had been Maurice Demenitroux, a chemist who had worked with Pierre and Marie when he was a young man and who had recently died at the age of forty, also of "anemia." He had worked in a factory in Creil, perfecting a procedure for extracting thorium X. Still another had been Marcel Demalander, Marie's onetime personal assistant. He had died of leukemia.

Because of these deaths and many others which occurred wherever people were handling radioactive substances, several countries had already created committees to study the possible dangers from exposure to radiation.

There were no such committees in France, and the unwritten rule at the Curie laboratory had always been, if not to deny, at least to underestimate that danger. Ever since the experiments Pierre had conducted on guinea pigs in 1904, researchers had protected themselves only from the direct beams of the rays behind wooden or lead screens. There weren't even ventilation systems for removing radioactive gases.

Right up to the end of her life, Marie behaved toward radium like a mother who won't believe that her glorious and beloved son is also a murderer in his spare time. Even as the evidence mounted, she rejected it.

This glorious son which had cost her so much excruciating

262

work remains associated with her name today as a truly inspired discovery, whereas Marie's real work of genius was a hypothesis that she alone had formulated and revealed: that radioactivity is the result of a phenomenon occurring in the interior of the atom. The rest was no more than obstinacy, courage, and hard work.

She was anxious that her brother and sisters be present, the day of the twenty-fifth anniversary ceremony at the Sorbonne. Jozef, Bronia, and Hela came from Poland just for the occasion. For a long time now, it had been clear that the little sister had more than kept the early promise: "The gifts that without any doubt exist in our family must shine through one of us."

But the fact was that they were here to witness the official tribute of France, which had tried to reject her, and of the Sorbonne, which had tried to expel her.

Neither years nor distance had ever uprooted Marie from the land of her family. It was her source. She was to return to Poland several more times. "This river," she wrote of the Vistula, "has a profound attraction for me—I'm not sure why." The only trace of lyricism we find in her writing is inspired by Poland.

Since of course Warsaw should have a radium institute, Bronia began a campaign for it: she inundated the country with leaflets proclaiming, "Buy a brick for the Marie Sklodowska-Curie Institute," with postcards depicting in facsimile a handwritten statement by Marie. The institute would be built. Bronia would run it. But for it to function, Missy would have to become involved once again.

twenty-three

WHEN Missy came through Paris on her way back from Italy, where she had been interviewing Mussolini, Marie went to see her. The two women had not stopped writing to each other. Marie had made sure Missy was awarded the Legion of Honor, and this was the only recompense the little American—who had never asked for any—would receive for what she had done. This and an inscribed photograph of Marie, which she had humbly begged for.

Missy was tired. She had aged. Her husband had died of tuberculosis. Her profession was not a very secure one. And America in 1928 was not what it had been in 1921. Her idealism, which had been so precious to Missy, had deserted her. Her friend Coolidge, who had become president after the sudden death of Harding, and then the elected president in 1924, had declared: "This country is a businessman's country and it wants a businesssman's government."

He had chosen not to run for president again, and the country was in the midst of the presidential campaigns.

Compared to the businessman's America, the intellectual's America was profoundly disillusioned. Joseph Wood Krutch wrote that science had destroyed people's faith in moral values, human dignity, and life itself. H. L. Mencken declared that doing good was in bad taste. Walter Lippmann wondered how humanity would be able to satisfy the human needs that had made necessary the myths that people could no longer believe in.

Now and then someone would write that this intoxication with money is a repugnant thing.

Missy, who knew the world she lived in, had no illusions. There was no question of exciting the American public about

Poland's need for radium. For Marie herself, Marie the Bene-factress, however, if she would be willing to come in person again, they could manage it.

Why was Missy throwing herself into this enterprise? Be-cause, as she so lucidly expressed it, "I don't see much in life anymore that is worth the trouble, but to serve a great cause, even by performing humble tasks, brings me real rewards."

As always—and like Marie—when she undertook some-thing, she intended to succeed.

There was therefore no question of Marie coming to the United States, as she had intimated, in company with Bronia, as a "Polish woman."

I insist on it, said Marie.

No, Missy said gently.

Yes, answered Marie. Besides, I often get sick in the winter. My sister is a doctor, I need her.

No, answered Missy, still gently but firmly. We have to forget Poland as well as France this time. You have to come over as Mme Curie, citizen of Radium, to receive the money from a subscription that was meant for her alone.

Marie gave in.

To make sure the project was successful, Missy said, impor-tant figures in the political world would have to be persuaded to take part. She predicted that the Republican Herbert Hoover, "an admirer of yours," would be elected. And she advised Marie to send him her congratulations.

I never get involved in politics, Marie answered.

Hoover is not a politician, wrote Missy. He is "a scholar inspired by humanitarian ideas."

In fact, Hoover was no "scholar," but an engineer who, at the start of the war, had organized the relief supplies for Belgium so masterfully that he was made chairman of the European Relief and Reconstruction Commission.

Dismayed at the sight of the old continent transformed into "an inferno of hatred," he took part in the discussions at the Paris Peace Conference with the hope that the idealism which had transcended collective selfishness during the war would

265

help regenerate Europe. The first conference of Allied ministers that he attended stripped him of his illusions. From then on, his only concern would be to accomplish his mission: provide relief to the continent. According to a young English diplomat, John Maynard Keynes, who was equally disgusted, so disgusted, in fact, that he resigned from his delegation, Hoover would be "the only one to emerge from the ordeal of Paris greater than he had been before."

He had been completely sickened by the Europeans. Nevertheless, he became a member of the patronage committee of the Marie Curie Radium Fund in 1921. Marie therefore paid her dues, and in return, Hoover invited her to visit the White House.

I don't want any interviews, autograph sessions, picture-taking, or handshaking on my program, she said.

You won't be expected to do anything but visit laboratories, go to scientific conferences, and be present at small official receptions, Missy answered. And what she had said turned out to be true.

The support of the President of the United States had been crucial. He personally handed her the sum of money intended for the purchase of one gram of radium, the gift of the American people. Once again, the subscription had brought in more than was needed. Marie, a more touching figure than ever behind her thick glasses, had once again managed to win over the businessmen Missy had carefully selected.

One of them, Owen D. Young, who was both a member of the Federal Reserve Board and president of the General Electric Corporation, helped her to negotiate the purchase of the radium at the lowest possible price and to invest the remainder of the subscription profitably. She brought back substantially more radium than she had come to get, and also a solid collection of samples of radioactive minerals, new free equipment for the laboratory, and new grants for her researchers.

Because she was given the same reception as a head of state on a private trip, she was spared the fervor of the press.

Telling Irène about an escape into the country, she wrote: "They made me go down the service stairway to avoid the sixty reporters who were waiting in front of the main entrance. Then we had a sensational ride from New York to Long Island. In front of us, a policeman on a motorcycle blasting his siren and energetically waving aside the cars on the road with one hand or the other—so that we sped along like a fire truck going to a fire. It was all very entertaining."

The following year, Missy told Marie that "Mr. Ford would consider it a personal pleasure and honor to make your task easier by offering you an automobile for whatever use you would have for it in your country. Mrs. Henry Moses has said she would be very happy to provide you with a driver."

Marie accepted.

twenty-four

E VER SINCE Missy had taught her the power of public relations—a lesson she never forgot—Marie had become a
conscientious traveling salesman for science, accepting all
trips that seemed in the least useful.

During a visit to Prague, she wrote to Irène: "I am stupefied
at the life I'm leading and I can't say anything intelligent to
you. I ask myself what fundamental defect in the human
organization makes this kind of agitation to a certain extent
necessary: We are *dignifying science*, Mrs. Meloney would say.
And what can't be denied is the sincerity of everyone doing
these things and their conviction that they have to do them."

Irène went to Brazil with her, Eve went to Spain, where
"she is making her usual conquests," and to Geneva, where
"M. Einstein is being very nice to her."

Marie went to Geneva because of the League of Nations. The
International Committee on Intellectual Cooperation, of
which she was a member and would soon be president, was
like all commissions. A lot of speeches were made. As for the
rest: "Its members may be efficient, but this is the most
inefficient enterprise I've ever been associated with," Einstein
was to say of it.

But once Marie had embarked on something, nothing in the
world could discourage her from persevering and hoping.
"However imperfect it may be, Geneva's creation has a great-
ness that deserves to be supported," she was to say to Eve.

She managed to have several provisions adopted that
would put some order into what she called "the anarchy of
scientific work in the world" and, after a long battle, induced
the commission to admit the principle that scientists had
ownership rights over their discoveries.

The discussion got bogged down when it came to defining the conditions under which the principle would be applied. The scientists would own their discoveries in order to do what with them? Make a profit from them? Horrors! Control the ways the discoveries were used? Inconceivable! Science belonged to everyone. That was agreed. But how did one go about making discoveries? One needed money, heavier and heavier machines, more and more spacious facilities, larger and larger teams of assistants. Puttering about in sheds was a thing of the past! And you didn't have to be a genius either.

Einstein could work on his knees, with his pencil and his scraps of paper, and remark that "the ideal job for someone who wants to devote himself to theoretical physics is to be a lighthouse keeper."

But the construction of the large electromagnet at Bellevue in France, for example—one of the first installations in the world for probing atoms, and the accomplishment of Pierre's and Marie's old friend, Aimé Cotton—cost almost two million francs in the twenties (7 to 8 million francs, or one million dollars today).

Marie did not have the satisfaction of seeing the idea she had worked so hard for result in what we now call research contracts.

One of the first was arranged in 1939. Frédéric Joliot and his co-workers, one of whom was Francis Perrin, the son of Jean Perrin, who had also become a physicist, were trying to discover how to unleash nuclear energy. The agreement was that they were to hand over any eventual profits they might receive from their research. They were given the uranium they needed (from the Mining Union of Upper Katanga) in exchange for half of these future, hypothetical profits, and the resources necessary to do the work (from the C.N.R.S.) in exchange for the other half.

According to the terms of the agreement negotiated by Joliot's team, the "discoverers" were guaranteed control of the use of the profits by the C.N.R.S.—the profits were to be automatically reinvested in other research projects.

269

This was the practical realization of what Marie Curie had hoped for: no personal profit for scientists, but the resources to go on with their work, and the use of a part of the profits drawn from their work for the benefit of science.

In the early thirties, a form of discussion that wasn't yet called a colloquium, a seminar, or a symposium, but quite plainly a debate, began to flourish.

In 1933, Paul Valéry asked Marie to preside over a debate being held in Madrid on "The Future of Culture." Most of the participants were writers and artists from different countries, "Don Quixotes of the mind fighting against their windmills," as Valéry called them.

They had gathered in Madrid to say that culture was undergoing a crisis, creativity was being sterilized by standardization and specialization, and threatened by science.

By science! What did that mean!

> I believe [declared Marie] that Science has great beauty. A scientist in his laboratory is not a mere technician: he is also a child confronting natural phenomena that impress him as though they were fairy tales. We mustn't let anyone think that all scientific progress can be reduced to mechanisms, machines, gearboxes . . . though these things, too, have their own beauty. . . . I also don't think that the spirit of adventure is in danger of disappearing from our world. If I see anything vital around me, it is this very spirit of adventure, which seems ineradicable and is very closely related to curiosity.

There was only one thing she liked about traveling to attend these meetings, which were often a burden to her, since very few things amused her and very few people interested her: still passionate about excursions, she would often disappear, wandering away in search of some local treasure. Because for the fifty years of her life she had been very secluded and had seen almost nothing.

From all over the world she wrote to her daughters, describing things to them. Writing was not really her field. She

270

found the Southern Cross "a very beautiful constellation." The Escorial was "very impressive." The Arab palaces of Granada were "very beautiful."

The Danube was lined with hills. The Vistula. . . .Ah! The Vistula "meanders lazily in its broad bed, sea-green close up, and bluish in the distance with the gleams of sunlight. The most adorable sandbanks, etc., etc." But the Vistula was in Poland, and there she was no longer simply an observer, satisfied with noting things down, as she usually was—we are almost surprised, as we read her letters, that she doesn't record the dimensions of the palaces in Granada and the number of rooms in the Escorial.

Except for the "very beautiful" oaks and maples she saw from her car around Washington, on her second trip to the United States she did not write about any "wonders of nature." But of course, she had already admired Niagara Falls on her first trip.

The kind of sightseeing she did on this trip was different, and it left her feeling a little thoughtful: as she went through various American laboratories, she saw how they had changed over the period of a few years.

The physics department at Columbia University, for example, occupied a thirteen-story building and was devoted mainly to studying the atom. The building that housed Marie's own laboratories consisted of only three stories, including the basement.

Modest though the facilities of the Institut du Radium may have been, by comparison, it was here that a crucial discovery was made, one that was to please Marie very much. The discovery was made in 1933 by Irène and her husband, Frédéric Joliot, after they had been cheated out of several earlier important discoveries.

Together, they had developed some very elaborate chemical procedures that allowed them to gather traces of polonium remaining on vials of radon after they had been used in medicine. Marie had collected these vials all over the world.

271

Using their technique, Irène and Joliot were able to obtain the purest and most highly radioactive samples of polonium in the world.

Instead of portioning them out among the different researchers in the laboratory, they concentrated them in one single powerful source, and using this source, they came very close, it is said, to discovering the neutron. But Chadwick discovered it first.

In the course of studying the neutron, they nearly made a second important discovery. But other people were quicker to see the explanation for the enigmatic positional phenomenon they had observed.

In 1933, they set up a new experiment, again using their source of polonium. The results of this experiment were to be presented in October to the Solvay conference, to which they had been invited because of the importance of their previous work. Langevin now presided over the Solvay Scientific Committee. He had also invited Rosenblum and, as always, the foremost scientists in international physics.

In his opening speech, Langevin asked that a message of sympathy be sent to Albert Einstein, who had not been able to accept his invitation. When Hitler had come to power in March, Einstein happened to be abroad. He had immediately announced his decision not to return to Germany and to refuse to serve the cause "of those who seek to undermine the ideas and principles that won the German people an esteemed place in the civilized world."

He had also refused to sign a manifesto against the war because the text implied a "glorification of Soviet Russia."

He said that from all the information he had been able to gather, "it seems that at the top a personal struggle is taking place which has purely selfish motives and uses the most sordid tactics. At the bottom, individual freedom and freedom of expression seem to have been completely suppressed. One wonders if life is worth living in such conditions."

At the time the Solvay conference was beginning, Einstein arrived in the United States, where he eventually decided to stay; Germany under Hitler had just withdrawn from the League of Nations. In Brussels the debate was going to be about "the structures and properties of atomic nuclei."

One other woman besides Marie and her daughter had been invited to the congress, and this was a German of great renown, Lise Meitner. She was attached to the celebrated Kaiser Wilhelm Institute in Berlin, where she worked with the director, Otto Hahn, the eminent radiation chemist and Marie Curie's longtime rival. Also present, of course, were Rutherford, Pauli, Niels Bohr, Heisenberg, Maurice and Louis de Broglie, Chadwick, Cockroft, Enrico Fermi,[1] and others.

Irène and Joliot were no doubt proud to be explaining to such an illustrious group what they believed their experiment demonstrated. But for the most part, their explanation met with skepticism, categorical on the part of Lise Meitner.

Chadwick sided with her, and that may be why Marie snubbed him at lunch when he tried to tell her how much he admired her. She greeted him, turned away, bent over her plate, and did not speak another word to him.

Irène and Joliot returned to Paris at once depressed and stimulated, because Niels Bohr and Pauli had encouraged them to continue.

And so they went on bombarding aluminum with alpha rays from their polonium. By persisting in this, they caused the reaction that physicists had been trying to set off for years—they caused artificial radioactivity. They had produced an artificial radioactive element.

They jumped up and down for joy in the basement room where they worked at the Institut du Radium. Then they sent word to Marie, who was at home.

What did she do? She went to Langevin, and together they

---

[1] Fermi, an Italian, followed Einstein into exile because his wife was Jewish. His team achieved the first controlled chain fission in the United States in 1942. Before her flight to Sweden, Lise Meitner participated in the chemistry experiments which were to lead to Otto Hahn's discovery of fission in 1938.

arrived at the little laboratory, where an ecstatic Joliot explained it all to them.

With her burned fingers, Marie picked up the tube containing the artificial radioelement. She held it in front of the Geiger counter, which had been checked for precision—in those days the machines were not very dependable—by a German specialist named Gentner who was training at the laboratory.

The machine crackled. Marie's face lit up. "I will never forget," Joliot said, "the expression of intense joy that came over her face."

In a futuristic novel entitled *The World Set Free*, which he wrote after becoming inspired by the scientific publications of Frederick Soddy, H. G. Wells had predicted that artificial radioactivity would be discovered in 1933. In the same book, he also predicted that one day "atomic bombs" would destroy cities with fire and radiation, and he described the first explosion: "The world was now no more than a purplish red glare and a noise, a deafening noise that penetrated everything. It gave the impression of a fat ball of purplish red fire, like a living creature gone mad. . . . The atomic bomb had reduced international problems to complete insignificance. . . . It seemed clear that these bombs and the even greater powers of destruction of which they were the precursors could very easily shatter all human relations and all human institutions." The time would necessarily come when "a person could carry in a handbag a quantity of latent energy sufficient to demolish half a city."

But in the same book, which was published in 1913, the prophet Wells announced that this terrifying war would be followed by the creation of a global State which would use atomic energy to transform society and nature for the benefit of the whole planet. All hope should therefore not be abandoned.

274

By the following year, when Irène and Frédéric Joliot received the Nobel Prize in chemistry for their discovery, radioactivity had already killed Marie. She was not there to witness the repeat of the scene in which she had taken part thirty years before.

The day of the award ceremony in Stockholm, Irène was not in the audience listening to her husband, but on the stage. And it was she who stood up first, to give the customary speech.

twenty-five

IF MARIE CURIE had had sons instead of daughters, they would probably have had a hard time of it. It is possible—though difficult—for a son to put up with having a famous father, but a famous mother is something else.

By her own admission, Eve had trouble dealing with the freedom Marie gave her. She dreamed of having an authoritative mother, if only to be able to rebel against her, and she hesitated over her choice of a profession.

Marie was rather disconcerted by the creature she had brought into the world—a very pretty young woman to whom their dear friend Einstein deferred far more readily than he did to the serious Irène, even though Irène obviously understood much better what he was doing.

The talents of this young beauty, with her innate elegance, were foreign to Marie. Marie was pleased when Eve seemed to have found a vocation in the piano, and she bravely put up with the sounds of scales and arpeggios that filled the apartment on the quai de Béthune. But her own ambition had been too amply satisfied for her to be able to transfer it to her daughter. She could not make Eve submit to the confinement, the renunciation, the desperately hard work that the career of a concert pianist requires.

For Irène, on the other hand, the line had been drawn very early. But apparently the two daughters' rivalry, banal as it was, for their mother's affection, led Irène to put herself in a peculiar position in relation to Marie.

In the Curie family during the twenties, Eve was the child of the house, Marie played the same part she had played before, and Irène played the part of the man. This was a

276

happy arrangement for Marie; it gave her the emotional stability she needed.

Marie herself was hardly "masculine" at all. The kind of courage she had, as well as her obstinacy, her laborious work methods, her long familiarity with physical suffering (which she always overcame), the fact that there were two sides to her—gentle and harsh—and her depressions, and her pagan relationship to the earth as the source of life, all expressed her womanliness. She was also an unwavering admirer of Colette, her contemporary.

The only trait that distinguished her sharply from other women of her generation and the generation that came after was the fact that she never doubted herself. She certainly knew what it was to be afraid. And right up to the end of her teaching at the Sorbonne, she was tortured by stage fright. But her unerring and unshakable consciousness of what she was worth in the order of her own values never failed her. This was what made her original, unique.

Other people might have thought she needed male endorsement of her work—Pierre's endorsement. She never had any use for male endorsement.

And yet this self-confidence and independence didn't mean she couldn't enjoy the more traditionally feminine pleasures—making jam, breastfeeding her children, loving men, and needing them. Her epithet for Owen D. Young, the American who was overseeing her financial transactions in the United States, was "my protector." Would a man of sixty, and a famous man to boot, have thought of calling a competent friend "my protector"? On the other hand, she certainly wouldn't ever have accepted a "protector" in a scientific debate.

Irène, taking Pierre's place next to Marie, and no doubt satisfying her own need for stability, at least for a time, in that role, formed a sort of couple with Marie.

The different ways in which the two sisters have reported some scenes from the life they shared with their mother when

277

they were young girls show something of their exchanges within this emotional economy.

Irène wrote:

> It was my habit to rise early, heat up breakfast and bring it to my mother's bedside on a tray; this was a peaceful time for literary or scientific or other kinds of discussions.
>
> When she was young, my mother had read a lot, she loved poetry and knew many poems by heart. . . . When I had discovered some poetry by Victor Hugo, Verlaine, Kipling, that I thought was particularly wonderful, she was always ready to listen to me recite it and to comment on it. Also, when I took a book out of the library that had been there for years and left it on my table, planning to read it, there was a good chance my mother would suddenly feel inspired to reread it and it would disappear from my room and appear in hers.
>
> . . . When I went to see a classical play or an opera in the evening, I had gotten into the habit of going to sit next to her bed when I came home and we would have a late-night discussion of the show.

Eve reports the following: If she was going out to a concert after dinner, Mme Curie would come lie down on the couch in her room. She would watch her dress. Their opinions about women's clothes and what constituted beauty in women were completely contradictory. "Oh, my poor dear, what frightful heels! No, you will never make me believe that women were meant to walk on stilts. . . . And what is this new fashion, dresses with low-cut backs? Low-cut fronts were tolerable, but these kilometers of bare backs! Firstly, it's indecent, secondly, you risk catching pneumonia, and thirdly, it's ugly—the third argument ought to move you if the others don't."

The most painful times were while the makeup was being put on. Marie would examine Eve loyally, scientifically. She was dismayed. "I have no objection in principle to this daubing. I can only say one thing to you: I find it frightful. . . . To console myself, I will come kiss you in your bed tomorrow morning, before you have time to put these horrors on your

278

face. And now, off with you, my little child. Goodnight. Oh! Do you have anything I can read?"

To Irène she would write things like "I'm delighted that you're satisfied with the magnetic deflection. How does the polonium behave on nickel?"

To Eve, on the other hand, she would write, "I think it is unsatisfactory to let all one's interest in life depend on feelings as stormy as the feeling of love."

Irène was twenty-six years old, she had received her degree, and she was handling part of the teaching load that fell to the laboratory when she came to her mother's bedside one morning in 1925, to bring her her breakfast and give her a piece of news as interesting as it was unexpected: she was engaged to be married. Marie asked who the man was.

Frédéric Joliot's entrance into the "royal family" was not easy. And according to his friends, he never completely forgot the unkind interpretations of his marriage that made the rounds of scientific circles.

After leaving the Ecole de Physique et de Chimie, he had gone through a period of training at an industrial laboratory, then had done his military service. As he came to the end of the service, he asked himself what he would do with his future. Would he go into industry? Why not? Or would he embark on a purely scientific career? He liked that idea better, but how would he support himself? He was not a graduate of the Ecole Normale, and therefore had no hopes for the Sorbonne.

A friend in the same situation went to their former teacher, Paul Langevin, and asked his advice. This was in 1922. Langevin urged them to apply for a Rothschild grant, and recommended Frédéric Joliot to Marie.

When the young man presented himself before Marie, still wearing his engineer officer's uniform and very intimidated by her, she told him he would start work the next day. He pointed out that he still had three weeks of military service

279

left to do. No problem. "I'll take care of it," Marie said. "I'll write to your colonel."

And the next day, Joliot became one of the "laboratory children." He was a tall, well-groomed young man, an athlete with a passionate and cheerful nature, who smoked too much and liked to proclaim that he wasn't an intellectual.

Irène, who was far ahead of him scientifically at that time—and would always remain a better chemist—helped him acquire the technical competence he needed, just as she had helped others.

Three years went by, during which Frédéric Joliot also had to teach in a private school and do other jobs on the side to make ends meet. Then he was appointed to one of the first salaried positions created by the C.N.R.S.

> It never entered my head that we would get married [he said later, speaking of Irène]. But I watched her. It started with watching her. She had a cold look on her face, she sometimes forgot to say hello, and because of that, people around her at the lab didn't always like her very much. As I watched her, I saw that inside this girl, whom others looked on as pretty much a rough block of stone, there was an extraordinarily sensitive and poetic creature who in many ways was like a living example of what her father had been. I had read a good deal about Pierre Curie, I had talked to professors who had known him, and I saw in his daughter the same purity, the same good sense, the same calm.

When people in the lab and outside learned that "the boss's daughter," the rough-edged Irène, was going to marry the handsome and fiery Joliot, who was three years younger, tongues began to wag. Irène remained supremely indifferent to the gossip. Unlike her mother, she cared very little about her "image" and had a good sense of humor.

"Some husbands carry pictures of their wives around with them," she would say. "Ask Fred to show you the picture he has in his wallet." The photograph showed a magnificent pike that Joliot, who was an avid fisherman, had harpooned.

280

With the same determination as her father, Irène had chosen the man she thought was best suited to share her life. And she had chosen wisely.

Joliot apparently had more trouble putting up with the suspicious banter of certain people, and ten years went by before he would admit that he really did love his wife, even if he also loved her because she was the daughter of Marie and Pierre Curie.

In any case, Marie was the last one who would have been fooled by the nature of his feelings. Distrustful and sharp-sighted from the age of twenty, almost never mistaken in her judgments, she watched the young man during Irène's engagement, asked only that he not smoke in her presence, and gave the two of them her affectionate blessing, painful though it was. For it was clearly a wrench to lose Irène, who had been such a constant companion, even if the ties remained close when Irène and Joliot left the apartment on the quai de Béthune after living there for several months.

"This boy," Marie said of Joliot to her old friend Jean Perrin, "is full of fireworks." He was to give some brilliant demonstrations of it in the years to come.

Nevertheless, the fact that he was called Joliot-Curie showed clearly enough that since he wasn't a blood prince, he at least had to be given a title.

A curious effect of this can be seen in French dictionaries, where Pierre Curie is listed as the physicist who discovered radium with his wife, Marie Sklodowska, whereas Irène Joliot-Curie is listed with her husband, Frédéric Joliot-Curie, as the author of numerous discoveries which won them etc., etc.

Yet Irène was no more successful than her mother at entering the Académie des Sciences, to which she presented herself as a candidate twice. At least no one would ever suggest that she made a career for herself by riding on the shoulders of her husband.

Marie Curie-Sklodowska was born too early in the history of women.

twenty-six

MARIE turned sixty-five, then sixty-six. She had remained supple, youthful in the way she moved her body; when she was working at home, people most often came upon her in her favorite position—sitting on the floor with papers spread out around her. But her beautiful ash-gray eyes, which had been operated on four times by now, were dull, and her face was emaciated and wrinkled.

She still occupied the chair of general physics at the Sorbonne, where she taught on Mondays and Wednesdays at five o'clock, and she still went to the laboratory every morning, but there she was gradually relaxing her hold. She didn't have many reservations about doing this, since Irène was taking over, but she wasn't very happy about it either.

And then she had to go home every evening. Wearing slippers, with a jacket thrown over her shoulders because she was chilly these days, she would wait for the maid to announce dinner, wandering through the vast rooms of the apartment where the grand piano and a ping-pong table looked so small. Sundays were sometimes sad.

Her daughters always remained attentive, close to her; they came whenever she asked them to, but they were involved in their own lives, as was normal, as was healthy, and she never interfered with that.

Irène gave birth to a daughter, then a son. About their birth, she wrote something worthy of her mother: "I realized that if I hadn't brought children into the world, I would never have gotten over having missed the opportunity to experience something so surprising."

Eve still lived at the quai de Béthune apartment, but with

282

her mother's consent she had rented a small apartment of her own.

Marie's friends did not neglect her, they came to consult with her about various things. Debierne was always there when she needed him.

The Joliots, who regularly had lunch at her apartment, kept her in touch with what was going on in the world, or as much of it as she was still interested in: Hitler's Germany had begun hunting down "Jewish science" . . . more than a million people were on strike in France . . . the Stavisky scandal had come to light . . . right-wing extremists had caused rioting on February 6, 1934, during a demonstration by veterans, and several people had been killed . . . a Vigilance Committee of Intellectuals Against Fascism had been started and was headed by Langevin, the philosopher Alain, and Paul Rivet . . . Joliot was a member of the Socialist party . . . Frédéric Joliot joined the Communist party during the war. Langevin joined after the war, in September 1944.

Marie listened, rubbing her burned fingertips against her thumb. And she talked to them about the laboratory.

She had not been abandoned—far from it—and she had plenty to do. But she was lonely. She wrote to Missy, she wrote to Bronia, who had been hard hit by the deaths of her two children and then her husband.

"Even though you feel lonely, you have one consolation: there are three of you in Warsaw and so you can have some company and some protection." A little company, a little protection. Where could Marie herself find these things now?

"Believe me," she went on, "a united family is the only thing worth having, in the end. I know, because I don't have it. Try to take some comfort from it and don't forget your sister in Paris. Let's see each other as often as possible."

One day she slipped in the laboratory, fell, and broke her right wrist. She didn't take the fracture seriously, and a number of complications followed.

Then she was tormented by a large gallstone. Would she

283

agree to an operation? Her father had died after a similar operation. She refused and instead put herself on a very strict diet. Irène and Fred, worried at seeing her so obviously in pain, persuaded her to join them in the Savoie, where they had gone to ski.

If they thought she was sick, if they thought she was finished, Marie would show them they were wrong. She was still agile, and she skated or went off on snowshoes to explore the mountains. One evening, they began to worry. She hadn't come back. Where was she? She had wanted to watch the sunset on Mont Blanc and she came back after nightfall, not a little proud of her adventure.

She begged and pleaded with her dear Missy to take a vacation with her. But Missy herself was ill with peritonitis. When she recovered, she wrote a reassuring answer to the insistent and agonized question Marie had been asking—whether the radium really would remain in the laboratory after she died and whether people really would respect the legal provisions that made Irène the heir to the radium, that defined the use to which the radium could be put, and that specified the disposition of the remainder of the American subscription.

Missy promised that her wishes would be respected, and as always, the promise was kept. But Missy was far away. Marie thought of going to see her in the United States. She decided not to. Then Marie had wonderful news: Bronia said she was coming for the Easter vacation. The two sisters drove down to Provence, making a thousand detours because Marie wanted to show Bronia some beautiful landscapes and stop by Montpellier to see Jacques Curie.

Before leaving, she had said to Irène:

I have written a provisional resolution on the subject of the gram of Ra which can serve as a will and I have put it with the documents from America in a packet: the contents are indicated in red on the outside.

All this is in the drawer of the chest in the drawing room, below the locked drawers.

She also got rid of some of the material from the forty-seven files containing her archives, obliterating everything that could change the image she intended to leave of herself, and she asked Missy to destroy her letters.

This last expedition into Provence turned out badly.

When she arrived at Cavalaire, exhausted, suffering from a cold, in an icy house, she burst into tears in Bronia's arms. She returned to Paris, cheered by a few days of sun, but feverish.

Once again Bronia would be leaving from the Gare du Nord feeling uneasy. She had so often come here because Marie needed her, so often left again with a heavy heart. But this was the last time she would look out the window of the train as it pulled away from the station and watch Marie's silhouette recede into the distance.

A few days later, on a May afternoon, in 1934, Marie was in the laboratory, where she had wanted to do some work. She murmured: "I have a fever, I'm going home."

Before leaving, she walked around the garden, examined a rosebush that she had planted herself and that didn't seem to be doing very well, and asked someone to look after it right away. Then she left for the last time.

What was wrong with her? Apparently nothing. No essential organ had been damaged, she didn't seem to have any particular disease that the doctors could identify and treat.

She lay in her bed, weak, feverish, suddenly unprotesting as people lavished attention on her, took her to the hospital, brought her home. Nothing did any good.

Her friends came to visit, entering into the game Eve was playing, as she displayed samples of cloth and paint intended for the new, smaller apartment that Marie planned to move into while she was waiting for the new house to be built at Sceaux.

The fever did not go down. The doctors spoke about a sanatorium, pure air. Eve arranged for a consultation among four eminent professors. They approved. Marie's fever, they thought, clearly indicated that old tubercular lesions had become active again. She should go to the mountains immediately. Were they afraid to be left with the responsibility for Mme Curie?

Marie went with Eve and a nurse. The journey was an agonizing one for her, and at the end of it she fainted in the train, in her daughter's arms; it was not only agonizing, but also useless.

Once she was installed in the sanatorium at Sancellemoz, under an assumed name, of course, Marie underwent more tests, more X rays. Her lungs were intact.

But her temperature rose to 40°C. A professor who had been summoned from Geneva compared different analyses of blood specimens and diagnosed fulminating pernicious anemia.

Marie examined the thermometer herself; it was impossible to hide from her what it showed. But she had been so afraid of having to have a gall bladder operation that she was relieved by the diagnosis of anemia. She had reached that state of grace in which even Marie Curie could not recognize the truth. And the truth was that she was dying.

She smiled one last time when, holding the thermometer in her little hand and reading it, she saw that her temperature had gone down suddenly. But Marie, who had always been so careful to record every number, no longer had the strength to make a note of it. This drop in her temperature signaled that the end was coming.

Eve, distraught but under control, as her mother had always taught her to be, did not leave Marie's side again, and she heard Marie murmur, as she looked at the cup of tea she was trying to stir with a spoon:

"Was it made with radium or mesothorium?"

Then there were a few indistinct words.

When the doctor came to give her a shot, she said, "I don't want it. I want to be left in peace."

Another sixteen hours went by before her heart stopped beating at last. She had not wanted to die, no, she had not wanted that. Marie Curie-Sklodowska was sixty-six years old when she reached the end of her life.

One last time, on Thursday, July 5, 1934, Madame Curie made the front pages of newspapers all over the world.

She was buried as she had wanted to be, in the presence of her children, her family, and a few friends. The gates of the cemetery at Sceaux had been closed to keep out the crowd of onlookers.

Bronia and Jozef each threw a handful of earth on the coffin as it lay in the grave. The earth was from Poland.

And this was the end of the story of an honorable woman.

March 1981

All the Letters quoted in the text are taken from the following sources:

Madame Curie by Eve Curie (Gallimard); La Bibliothèque Nationale; *Marie Curie* by Robert Reid; Cambridge University Library; Columbia University Library; *Albert Einstein* by Banesh Hoffmann (Seuil), and *Paul Langevin, mon père,* by André Langevin (Ed. Français réunis).

Picture sources: Institut du Radium and the Palais de la Découverte.

BIBLIOGRAPHY

Eve Curie: *Madame Curie*, Gallimard 1938.
Almost all the letters exchanged between Marie and her Polish family, as well as the extract from her "Journal" and numerous personal details are taken from this work.

Robert Reid: *Marie Curie*, New American Library 1975.
This English author's biography revealed the existence of documents bearing in particular on Marie's relations with Rutherford and Boltwood.

Spencer Weart: *La Grande aventure des atomistes français*, Fayard 1979.
In this work, Dr. Weart, the director of the American Institute of Physics and a historian of science, provides solid documentation for the situation of science and scientists in France between the two world wars, and for nuclear physicists during and after the Second World War.

P. Biquard: *Paul Langevin*, Seghers 1969.

J. D. Bredin: *Joseph Caillaux*, Hachette Littérature 1980.

H. Contamine: *La Victoire de la Marne*, Gallimard 1970.

E. Cotton: *Les Curie et la radioactivité*, Seghers 1963.

H. Cuny: *Louis Pasteur*, Seghers 1963.

M. Curie: *Pierre Curie*, Payot 1923, Denoël 1955.

M. Curie: *La Radiologie et la guerre*, Alcan 1921.

A. S. Eve: *Rutherford*, Cambridge University Press 1939.

J. Galtier Boissière: *La Grande Guerre*, Productions de Paris.

O. Glasser: *Dr. W. C. Röntgen*, Thomas. Springfield, Ill., 1945.

H. Goldberg: *Jean Jaurès*, Fayard 1970.

E. Hausser: *Paris au jour le jour*, Ed. de Minuit 1968.

B. Hoffmann and H. Dukas: *Albert Einstein créateur et rebelle*, Seuil 1975.

J. Hurwic: *Marie Sklodowska-Curie*, Institut d'Histoire de la Science et de la Technique de l'Académie des Sciences polonaise.

A. Langevin: *Paul Langevin mon père*, Ed. Français réunis 1971.

288

F. Lot: *Jean Perrin*, Seghers 1963.

C. Marbo: *Souvenirs et rencontres*, Grasset 1968.

V. Margueritte: *Aristide Briand*, 1932

P. Robrieux: *Histoire intérieure du P.C.F.*, Fayard 1980.

C. P. Snow: *The Two Cultures*, Cambridge University Press 1968.

A. Schlesinger, Jr.: *(The Age of Roosevelt)*, Houghton Mifflin 1971.

Z. Sternhell: *La droite révolutionnaire*, Seuil 1978.

J. Terrat Branly: *Mon père Edouard Branly*, Corréa 1949.

S. P. Thompson: *The Life of Lord Kelvin*, Macmillan 1910.

Le Congrès de Tours, presented by A. Kriegel, Archives Julliard 1964.

La science contemporaine, P.U.F. 1964.

La correspondance Marie–Irène Curie, Ed. Français réunis 1974.

The archives of the following have been consulted:
La Bibliothèque Nationale (Fonds Curie and the French press), Laboratoire Curie, Cambridge University Library, Yale University Library, Columbia University Library, New York Public Library, United Nations Library, and the Library of Congress.

AFTER MARIE'S DEATH

Ernest RUTHERFORD, who was made Lord Rutherford of Nelson, fell from a tree as he was lopping branches and died at the age of sixty-six in 1937.

Jean PERRIN was appointed under secretary of state for scientific research, a position created by the government of the Popular Front. He managed to triple the amount of credit granted to the C.N.R.S., and he founded the Palais de la Découverte in Paris. In 1941, he left occupied France and joined his son Francis in the United States, where he died at the age of seventy-one in April 1942.

Paul LANGEVIN, arrested in 1941 by the Gestapo, was put under house arrest in Troyes. His son-in-law, Jacques Solomon, a physician and one of the founders of the clandestine organ *L'Université Libre*, was shot in 1942, and his daughter was deported. He himself managed to flee to Switzerland. After the liberation, he and Henri Wallon drew up a plan for the reform of education, which is still famous though it was never implemented. He died in 1946 at the age of seventy-four. His ashes and those of Jean Perrin were moved to the Panthéon on the same day in 1948.

Emile BOREL was removed from his position as mayor of Sainte-Afrique by the Vichy government, arrested by the Gestapo, and then released. After the war, he resumed his functions as mayor and his duties on the council of the Legion of Honor, presided over the International Society of Statistics, and happily celebrated the fiftieth anniversary of his marriage. He died in 1956 at the age of eighty-five.

Irène JOLIOT-CURIE became under secretary of state for scientific research in the government of the Popular Front, a position she occupied only briefly, at her request, before ceding to Jean Perrin. She was a lecturer at the Sorbonne in 1937. She came close to discovering fission, but failed because she did not know how to interpret the results of her research—results which later enabled Otto Hahn to find the true solution to the enigma of the explosion of the uranium nucleus. After the war, she was director of the Institut du Radium, and later one of the three members of the Commission for Atomic Energy, alone with Francis Perrin and Pierre Auger. She died of leukemia in 1956 at the age of fifty-nine. She was given a state funeral.

Frédéric JOLIOT became a professor at the Collège de France in 1937. At the beginning of 1939, he produced physical proof of fission at the same time as Otto Hahn (a nephew of Lise Meitner), who was working in Copenhagen. That same year, he and the two other members of his team, Hans Halban and Lew Kowarski, demonstrated the theoretical possibility of the chain reaction at the same time as Enrico Fermi's group in the United States succeeded in producing one. In June 1940, his laboratory at the Collège de France was taken over and used by the Germans, among whose number was a former researcher from the Curie laboratory, Wolfgang Gentner, who was to do as much as he could to protect French scientists. Joliot was an active member of the Resistance. When de Gaulle created the Commission for Atomic Energy in October 1945, he was named high commissioner. He oversaw the construction of the first nuclear reactor. He was the star scientist of the Communist party, and he declared publicly that "If they ask us tomorrow to do war work, to make the atomic bomb, we will say no." He was removed from office in 1950. He died at the age of fifty-eight in 1958. He was given a state funeral.
The first Soviet thermonuclear explosion took place in 1953, thanks to the work of André Sakharov. The first French explosion took place in 1960.

Eve CURIE joined the Free French forces during the war. She was a war correspondent for a number of American newspapers and co-director of *Paris-Presse*. She married Henri Labouisse, who was first the United States ambassador to Greece, then director general of the United Nations Children's Fund (UNICEF). In this capacity, Labouisse went to Stockholm in 1965 to accept the Nobel Peace Prize from the king of Sweden on behalf of UNICEF. And so once again a member of the Curie family was present at the Nobel Prize ceremony.
Eve Curie-Labouisse, who is still beautiful at more than seventy-five years of age, lives in the United States.

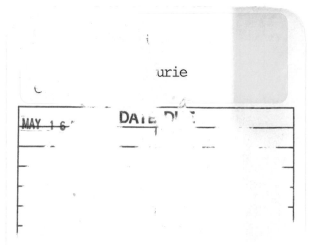

urie